Ships and Shipwrecks
of the
Late Tudor Dynasty

Ships and Shipwrecks
of the
Late Tudor Dynasty

by James D. Taylor Jr.

Algora Publishing
New York

Library of Congress Cataloging–in–Publication Data —

Names: Taylor, James D., 1958- author.
Title: Ships and shipwrecks of the late Tudor era : a collection of logs,
    records and first-hand accounts of missing ships and lost treasures /
    James D. Taylor Jr.
Description: New York : Algora Publishing, [2022] | Includes
    bibliographical references and index. | Summary: "In the 1500s, British
    ships plied the seas laden with precious spices, Spanish silver, war
    matériel, and adventurous souls. Many went to the bottom, leaving only
    tantalizing hints, sparse records and a few legends. This unique
    collection of logs, data and narratives from 1547–1603 brings them to
    life"— Provided by publisher.
Identifiers: LCCN 2022046070 (print) | LCCN 2022046071 (ebook) | ISBN
    9781628944945 (Trade Paperback) | ISBN 9781628944952 (Hardcover) | ISBN
    9781628944969 (pdf)
Subjects: LCSH: Shipwrecks--Great Britain. | Great Britain—History,
    Naval—Tudors, 1485-1603. | Underwater archaeology—Great
    Britain—Archival resources.
Classification: LCC G525 .T328 2022 (print) | LCC G525 (ebook) | DDC
    910.4/52094205—dc23/eng20221123
LC record available at https://lccn.loc.gov/2022046070
LC ebook record available at https://lccn.loc.gov/2022046071

Printed in the United States

Dedicated to Lili.

Two islands joined by an ocean.

"The fisherman knows that the sea is dangerous and the storm terrible, but they have never found the sea dangers sufficient reason for remaining ashore."
Vincent Van Gogh.

Preface   1

Part 1. The Ships   9

Types of Ships   10
1-1. Ship Complements.   13
1-2. Event Records of English Ships.   29
1-3. Event Records of French Ships.   104
1-4. Event Records of Miscellaneous Ships.   114
    Cargoes; About Pepper   133
1-5. Recorded Storms that affected ships in shipping lanes.   138

Part 2. Captains' Logs   141

2-1. A Victorious English Sea Battle, 1593.   141
2-2. Spanish Quicksilver, 1592.   146
2-3. The capture of the *Madre de Dios*, a Spanish Ship.   147
2-4. Sea Fight of Flores, 1591.   151
2-5. Lost Treasure, 1596.   157
2-6. The Wrecking of the Delight, 1583.   160

Part 3. Shipwrecks   163

3–1. Four English Wrecks at Flamborough Head   163
3–2. Four French Wrecks Off Amsterdam   170
3–3. Castle de Mino Voyage, 1559/60.   173
3–4. Three Goodwin Sands Wrecks. 1593.   176
3–5. Three French Wrecks, 1560.   177
3–6. Zealand Wreck, 1560.   178
3–7. Dover Wreck, 1558.   178
3–8. Three French ships, 1560.   180
3–9. Seven or Eight French Galleys Lost, 1555   180
3–10. Four Italian Galleys Lost, 1555   181
3–11. Lost Cargo of 1.4 Million Spanish Reals   181
3–12. The *Clement* Wreck, 1547.   182
3–13. Irish Ship Sunk, 1552.   183
3–14. The *Anne Galland*, 1556.   184
3–15. A Hoy of Newcastle.   184
3–16. The *Black Raven*, 1573.   185
3–17. The *Popingay* Wreck, 1574.   186
3–18. Goodwin Wreck, 1577.   187
3–19. Five Sussex Wrecks, 1576.   187
3–20. Sandwich Wreck, 1576.   188
3–21. The *Angel Gabriel*, 1575.   189
3–22. The *St. Catherine*, French, 1577.   190
3–23. The *Peter* of Bristol, 1576.   190
3–24. The *Eagle* of Bremen, 1577.   192
3–25. The *Tobie*, 1593.   192
3–26. The *Dragon* and *Hunter*, 1582.   197
3–27. The Bark *Allen*, 1576.   198
3–28. Hurst Castle Incident, 1579.   198
3–29. Wrecked barque, 1579.   199
3–30. Bristol Wreck, 1579.   199
3–31. The *George*, 1580.   199
3–32. The *Fortune*, 1577.   200
3–33. Newhaven Wreck, 1578.   201
3–34. Thames Wreck, 1577.   201
3–35. The *Hospital*, 1588.   202
3–36. The *Esperance*, French, 1589   203

3–37. *St. Petero Maior*, 1589.   203
3–38. The *Revenge*, 1591.   204
3–39. The *Treasurer*, 1589.   206
3–40. The *Rose*, 1589.   207
3–41. The *Dudley*, 1590.   207
3–42. The *Elephant*, 1590.   208
3–43. Scottish Ships, 1559.   209
3–44. The *Katherine* of Calais, 1601.   210
3–45. The *Exchange*, 1592.   210
3–46. The *Symond*, 1579.   211
3–47. The *Nightingale* wreck, 1593.   211
3–48. The *Fortune*, 1595.   212
3–49. Goodwin Sands, 1568.   212
3–50. The *Grey Fawlcon*, 1596.   212
3–51. Barbary wreck, 1597.   213
3–52. Goodwin Sands, 1567.   214
3–53. Goodwin wreck, 1598.   214
3–54. The *Reindeer*.   215
3–55. The *Sea Cock*.   215

Bibliography   217
    Primary   217
    Manuscript collection consulted   219
    Picture Sources   219

Index   221

PREFACE

Only those who have been to sea and witnessed some of the rare and spectacular sights for themselves can truly appreciate the tales mariners have shared for centuries about their experience. In the following pages, I pass on several stories of incidents and accidents not published before; and somewhat less entertaining, yet perhaps even more important, I present a unique collection of factual data illustrating the sizes and the cargoes, the destinations, and the fates of sailing ships originating in or sailing in English waters in the time from 1547 to 1603. There was no single source gathering information regarding English Tudor era ships and shipwrecks prior to this book.

Searching for relics of the past requires more than knowing how to use various hand tools, then picking an arbitrary place on the surface of the planet to push a shovel into, hoping to come up with something; it requires knowing where to dig and having the training to be able to identify something if found. Nowadays, many relic and treasure hunters utilize tools such as SONAR or magnetometers to map a section of an area under water to search for relics and facts. LiDAR is a fairly recent technology that is revealing many new places for archaeologists to explore on land. Those are a couple of examples of how the constantly evolving tools help researchers and treasure hunters to uncover new discoveries. They are wonderful tools and have produced fabulous results, but it is still like searching for the proverbial needle in an extremely large haystack that is hundreds of square miles wide. Even using a 'magnet' to locate the needle is very time and cost consuming.

These high-tech tools can be augmented by plain old-fashioned, time consuming, tedious archival research seeking information of maritime historical significance in rare, dusty, dark and cool archives. We live in an age of instant gratification and unfortunately not enough people are willing to put the time in for research.

The scope of this book is two-fold. My aim is to provide several bodies of information in one single volume: data helpful to explorers whose motivations may range from the historical to actual artifact recovery; all the recorded information available regarding the lives of many ships from their birth and service in the defense or livelihood of their countries to their sometimes violent deaths; and records of the men who served and sometimes died with them. This information has not been accumulated in this quantity, until now, and is in itself a treasure. The information comes from original documents first recorded in 1547–1603, then stored in archival volumes. Not all the original documents survived, and we are often left with just a synopsis (sometimes poorly written) or a snippet at best. Nevertheless, they provide a rare opportunity to view the life of sailors and their ships.

One particular record that my research turned up helped to fuel the desire to produce a book such as this. While in Seville, Spain, Thomas Gresham wrote the following to the Privy Council (official advisers to the kings and queens of England) on 30 November 1554.

> These had been twice told over by the tenant and other officers, were all packed, sealed, matted and corded, and the mules hired for their conveyance, when a difficulty was started as to whether, notwithstanding his passport and letters, he was the Queen's factor and possessed the especial power. At last, on his finding two natives born and two Englishmen to testify to her Majesty's hand and seal,

the officials came on the 28th and 29th, and after opening one case, counting over its contents again, and seeing it repacked, gave him his dispatch at 5 o'clock of the latter day. The cases have been sent off today, he with two of his servants besides the scryvano [escribino] and his servant seeing them shipped. There are 50 of them, each marked with the broad arrow and numbered from 1 to 50, and each contains 22,000 silver Spanish rials, (Reals) amounting to 2,000 ducats at 11 rials the ducat. These shall be shipped at Puerto Real in such good merchants' vessels as shall be present with the advice of Mr. Wood. The rest, which he will have in readiness, and which will not exceed 110, 000 ducats, he intends to put on board two of her Majesty's ships which will be a venture in each of 16,000l, and therewithal to come himself. There is no small exclamation among the commons of this town that so much money should go out of the realm, the scarcity thereof being so great; and for his own part he cannot with his pen set forth the great scarcity now throughout all Spain.

[*Calendar of State Papers, Foreign Series, of the Reign of Mary*, 1553–1558. Page 141. London, 1861].

That shipment of Spanish silver had an approximate current market value (2021) of $55,000,000, but there is no further correspondence to be found — nothing indicating that it had been received, lost, or plundered.

Another example this book will share is a dispute over the very precious cargo of a Venetian ship and the many English Privy Council sessions to settle it. Gold, silver you may think? No, pepper. Pepper was the most important spice of this era and was followed in popularity by cinnamon, ginger, and cloves. Certainly, a prize cargo worthy of debate, and certainly worth fighting over. Harrison, in his *Description of Britain* printed in 1577 quotes Queen Elizabeth: "I add, to the end all men should understand somewhat of the great masses of treasure daily employed upon our navy."

In 1576, Martin Frobisher departed England with three small ships to explore the northern seas for a passage near the North Pole to the coast of China and the East Indies. Queen Elizabeth rewarded him with a ceremony and gold chain in addition to promoting him to eminent positions. Some of his ship's activities will be read in the events in part 1.

In 1578, a grant was issued to Sir Humphrey Gilbert "for peopling and planting our colonies in North America."

Furthermore, the voyages of Sir Francis Drake are well known to many, but the ship he sailed on is not the same one mentioned in recent accounts as documents from the period indicate, and not surprisingly recent sources of "mis-information" fail to cite their sources. John Barrow in *The Naval History of Great Britain*, 1761, shares this information as I share it with the reader. The *Elizabeth* of 100 tons and the ship Francis Drake was on; the *Marigold* of 30 tons; the *Swan* of 30 tons and the *Christopher* a pinnace of 15 tons departed 13 December 1578 from Plymouth England. These are among the rewards I was given for many hours of reviewing archives of old books and manuscripts. Unfortunately, some documents were lost and damaged by fire in the British Museum.

Sir Walter Raleigh obtained a commission in 1584 to explore parts of America not yet possessed by a European country. He sailed from Plymouth with two barques on 25 March 1584 and arrived on the coast of Florida on 2 July. The account he shared with the queen when he returned had pleased her very much. In honor of the Queen Elizabeth I, the location was called Virginia.

The Spanish invasion attempt in 1588 and the subsequent wrecks, primarily along the coast of Ireland, are very well known and written about, this book will primarily cover the ships and events around England and not the Spanish armada. The voyages of Drake, Raleigh, Frobisher, and the other great English mariners are known through numerous publications; this book will embark on a voyage of discovery to fill the undiscovered voids.

A Note About the Author

The author is a well-decorated veteran of the Unites States navy who served honorably from 1977 to 1983. His duty station was the U.S.S. Wichita AOR–1, homeport at Naval Air Station in Alameda California. In 1980, the ship was assigned to a WESTPAC (Western Pacific) cruise that included ports of call in Hawaii, Subic Bay Philippines, Shanghai, Hong Kong, Japan, Australia, Taiwan, Singapore, Diego Garcia, Misera, Oman and Pattaya Beach Thailand, traversing the North Pacific, Sea of Japan, East China Sea.

In the Philippine Sea, the crew encountered a persistent typhoon. The ship rocked so much that the following day the author had to clean his footprints off the bulkhead (wall) of a hallway outside the fireroom (boiler room). He had to use the seatbelt in my rack that night so he could sleep in a bunk 6 feet under the flight deck. On a different occasion, the team lost a CH–46 helicopter in a side flare. The helicopter crew chose to ditch in the ocean rather than attempt a landing in a damaged and unreliable helicopter, making them true heroes. The burial at sea was only for 3 flight helmets. Mr. Taylor will always remember the shark-tooth-outlined chunks missing from one helmet. There were no bodies recovered.

This voyage continued through the Gulf of Thailand, the Bay of Bengal and last, but certainly not least, with a considerable amount of time in the Indian Ocean supporting the operation into Iran to rescue United States hostages which began with the loss of the U.S. Embassy in Tehran. Military and civilian lives were lost in the failed first attempt by US forces to rescue the hostages.

On the return trip to Naval Air Station Alameda, one of the propeller shafts spun a stern tube bearing and the shaft had to be locked down. The last port call was to Pattaya Beach Thailand and while transiting the Gulf of Thailand, the ship encountered a boat full of Vietnamese refugees being robbed by Thai pirates. The crew rescued the refugees and took them to Pattaya Beach where they were taken to a refugee camp.

During his time at sea, the author participated in what is called the Line Crossing Ceremony as a "pollywog," a ritual that marks one's first crossing of the Equator. After completing a grueling two-day ceremony, Mr. Taylor was admitted to the honored ranks of King Neptune himself. The origins of the Line Crossing Ceremony, "Order of Neptune," are lost in time. The ritual dates back at least 400 years in Western seafaring. In the 19th century and earlier, the line-crossing ceremony was quite a brutal event, often involving beating pollywogs with boards and wet ropes and sometimes throwing the victims over the side of the ship, dragging the pollywog in its wake. In more than one instance, sailors were reported to have been killed while participating in a line-crossing ceremony. The ceremony is sometimes explained as being an initiation into the court of King Neptune.

This is a copy of the author's Shellback certificate from his first line crossing on 17 July 1980.

The navy has toned down the ceremony since the author's time in service (and imagine what forms such "hazing" could have taken centuries ago!) At the time of this writing, we have a much kinder and gentler navy.

The Ceremony of ducking under the tropic.

[A New Universal Collection of Authentic and Entertaining Voyages and Travels. London, 1768].

The sources for this book date from the late 1590s to late 1700s and include accounts as history recorded them, from a short log by an admiral of five English ships of war wrecked off the coast of Northern England to a series of 32 books with a total of 14,400 pages.

It was years ago, while conducting research for a biography about a figure in Elizabethan England, that the author uncovered two pieces of valuable information that helped inspire him to produce this volume. The first was a record of four ships that were blown onto the coast of Holland during a violent tempest that swept through the English Channel 13 January 1560. There is enough information to place the ships within about a 20-square-mile area off the coast. This is one of two events that motivated the desire to prepare this book, which will fill in some gaps in maritime history. This data will certainly enable us to rewrite earlier, erroneous accounts long thought to be accurate; and it enables us to announce the final resting place of ships that gave their lives in protection of their crews and country, even if some were plundered.

Following this edition will be *Ships and Shipwrecks of the Early Stuart Dynasty*. As a result of excellent records kept by the East India Company, additional information is known including records of the loss of valuable treasures.

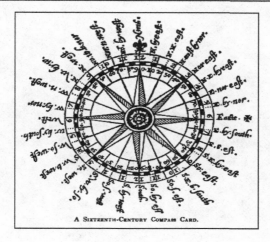

A SIXTEENTH-CENTURY COMPASS CARD.

Prepare your ships to sail. Set your rigging to explore the locations of lost and unknown shipwrecks and the events that led up to their loss during the late Tudor period of English history. Your chart is the information contained in this book. Calibrate your compass and we will locate shipments of gold and silver in various forms, sheets of copper, brass and iron cannons by the hundreds, hand tools, gun powder and ammunition, wheat, wine, and of course spices. All these goods are among the cargoes carried by ships ranging in size from 50 to 1000 tons, some of them war ships.

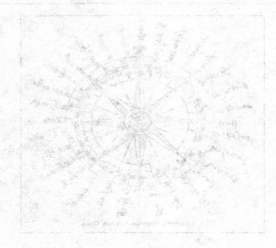

Part 1. The Ships.

For those readers lacking an extensive maritime engineering background, here are a few brief descriptions of the ship types generally found during the time of this book (1547–1603), written for landlubbers (!).

The two categories of ships that are our focus are merchant ships and those that served the Crown (ships of war); bearing in mind that sometimes merchant ships were asked to defend the Crown as well.

The common bond between the two was seamanship. A full knowledge of their ship and all its components and how they relate to each other is what makes a wooden object, sometimes up to 1000 ton, into a life form of its own. The skills taught, acquired and refined by mariners were taught dearly, as these men had to work among often-times unbathed, underfed, thirsty, cold, sick, injured shipmates, sometimes on long, hot and windless voyages or sometimes fighting to survive not only the violent tempests that can flare up in the English Channel, but illnesses or injuries, on call 24 hours a day, 7 days a week, while seeking to evade the threat of having their cargo stolen, loss of ship or life, and striving to make proper decisions and work as a cohesive team. And just imagine, the enemy is bearing down on you in a 1500 ton vessel carrying 250 armed soldiers, 140 mariners, officers, 25 to 50 gunners with two or three decks of iron and brass cannons, sometimes up to 40 to 60 guns per deck, and you only weigh 50 tons; but you are carrying Spanish reals or gold (stolen from someone who had stolen the treasure before). It all makes for a hazardous journey.

Soon after her ascension to the throne, Elizabeth addressed the increasing threats of piracy in the waters surrounding her kingdom by granting permission to captains to prevent their cargo from being plundered (by anyone, foreign or domestic) by any means necessary. Of course, some took that as a license to steal with the Crown's blessing. Needless to say, the Crown received a percentage of 'prizes' taken at sea.

From late 1559, the narratives describe the increase in piracy, intermingled with the recorded events and accounts of the ships' activities from actual documents recorded in history that have resided in a dark archive and have never been read or shared in 350 years. The majority of the sources reviewed are from about 1740 to about 1850 and are becoming too fragile to handle and too fragile for conversion to digitalization. In the archives I noticed a change to longer descriptions in letter synopsis beginning about mid-1590, better enabling me to share more of a story than from the snippets often encountered. Many documents from about 1575 to 1580 were destroyed or mutilated by fire in the British Museum.

These accounts not only offer a window into a life not shared in this information age, but they are also a reflection of a time of war, or defense of the kingdom from outside invaders like the attempted invasion by King Philip II of Spain in 1588 and his armada of ships. In a letter from 25 October 1590, 40 French ships feared they were insufficiently capable of defending themselves from the Spanish ships that lay between themselves and the passage.

Personal accounts from mariners, captains, or an admiral are very rarely recorded for history but when they are, they help to share life 'of the sea' during the late English Tudor Dynasty.

These accounts include records of the transport of replacement ship parts like masts, copper plates, horses, soldiers, ordnance of iron and brass, ammunition, powder, money for financing operations, and food and supplies for sometimes months at sea. For example, like the operations north into Scotland transporting soldiers, ordnance, gun powder, shot and everything required to rid Scotland of French occupation, with the assistance of England both in men and finances, the latter carried by many of these ships in the form of gold and silver in various forms of that era. Sometimes gold was traded in time of peace, and stolen during war. Spanish reals became popular in quantity after the attempted invasion by King Philip II failed and had turned up in markets along the coast and in London.

Types of Ships

The following is a brief description of the ship types generally referred to in the accounts and events. Please understand, these are not intended to be all inclusive descriptions. Ships of recent times fell into classifications of rate. Several modern individuals indicate this is a recent endeavor. So, allow me to share *Steel's Original and Correct List of the Royal Navy* description of classifications from 1782, a not-so-modern description.

1st rate: 100 guns and upward. 750 to 850 men.
2nd rate: 90 to 98 guns. 700 to 750 men.
3rd rate: 64 to 80 guns. 580 to 650 men.
4th rate: 50 to 60 guns. 350 to 450 men.
5th rate: 30 to 44 guns. 220 to 250 men.
6th rate: 20 to 28 guns. 160 to 200 men.

All ships were sheathed with copper plate. Sloops, bombs, fire-ships, armed ships, and store-ships are commanded by masters and commanders. Cutters, schooners, brigs, armed vessels, armed transport, armed store ships and surveying sloops are commanded by lieutenants.

Many ships in this volume are described by weight.

Barque or sometimes Bark.
General term for a small ship prior to the 1700s. It was later modified to be slightly more specific for a ship with three masts with squared rigged sails on the first two masts. Described as a fast ship with shallow draft.

Caravel.
This ship's design is often attributed to the Portuguese and is seen during the time of this book. It was constructed using the carvel method and was reliable for oceanic exploration voyages of long duration.

Carrack.
This ship is often attributed to being developed in Portugal in the 1400s and is slightly larger than the caravel. One example is the *Santa Maria* used by Columbus, which was a carrack. Sometimes with six sails that constituted the typical design. Carracks were the largest type of ship prior to the galleon, sometimes with a weight of 1000 tons. 3 masts with square sails and very high fore and aft-castles. These often carried multiple decks of brass and iron ordnance. These were often used as ships of war and long deep-sea voyages.

Crayer.
Often described as a vessel of 30 to 50 tons and was used mainly in the English Channel.

Galiot.

Sometimes referred to as a half galley in the 1500s, it was a small, long, sleek ship, 2 masts, and about 2 rows of 8 oars, and a flush main deck. It acquired sails into the 1600s and continued to use oars if there was no wind. Sometimes carried smaller ordnance. This ship is perhaps best known and seen in the Mediterranean.

Galleon.

These ships often transported cargo but were well defended with one or two decks of heavy iron ordnance. King Phillip of Spain used these ships in his famous attack on England.

Galley.

Galleys have a long history for use in trade and warfare. It afforded oars as a second means of propulsion in the event of no winds and was sometimes used in the seas of Northern Europe, but its low freeboard and lack of stability in rough seas meant it was used mainly in somewhat sheltered waters, not the open sea. This ship is seen more around Italy.

Hoy.

This ship's origins are 1400s Flanders with a single mast and usually of about 30 to 80 tons. This lighter vessel was primarily used along coasts or shallower water short voyages. Evolutions of this ship occurred later, and it disappeared in the 1800s.

Hulk.

This vessel has an early history. They were flat bottomed boats distinguished by not having a stem or stern posts or deep keel. They varied in size also and included several English ships such as the *Jesus* and the *Mary Rose*.

Picard.

This ship has its origins into the early 1300s as a single-masted ship of about 25 to 40 tons. This ship often saw service as support for large fishing fleets or transporting cargo from large, anchored ships into port. This ship was widely used around England, Ireland, and Scotland.

Pink.

Two different types of small cargo ships were called Pinks. Both had narrow or "pinched" sterns ("pincke" in Dutch). In the Mediterranean, pinks were flat-bottomed as well as narrow at the stern.

Pinnace.

These were often used as merchant transport and even small war ships. Primarily built by the Dutch, they had a hull that resembled a small 'race built', that were generally square rigged on three masts.

Ship of the Line Man-of-War.

Often regarded as the 'heavy guns' from the 1500–1700s, when they began resembling galleons but were able to carry more ordnance of about 40 to 100 iron and brass cannons. These were large enough to be effective in battle-line tactics and maneuvers, ergo, the name. These ships belonged to the three main sea powers; England, France, and Spain.

1-1. Ship Complements

The following list of ships and complements will be of more use in the subsequent parts when I share the birth, life, service, and death of the some of the ships in this part. This list only represents the ships that warranted mention in documents, logs, or accounts.

Mr. Derrick explained how the tonnage of ships was calculated during the time these ships were in service. He based his information on several 'ancient' descriptions.

Various methods for determining the length of the keel for tonnage are used, as some of the data and different rules for calculating the tonnage have been adopted at different periods. The following is an account of some of the said rules and methods.

The old mode of calculating the tonnage of Men of War was by multiplying the length of the keel by the extreme breadth, and the product by the depth in hold, and dividing by 96.

On a straight line with the lower part of the rabbit of the keel, erect a perpendicular or square line to the upper edge of the wing transom, at the after part of the plank, and at the stern to the fore part of the plank at 5/6 parts of the height of the wing transom; the length between the said perpendiculars added to 1/24 of the extreme breadth (allowing for the stem and stern post without rabbets), from which subtract 6/25 of the height of the wing transom for the rake abaft, and also 3/5 of the main breadth for the rake afore, leaves the length of the keel for tonnage: which multiply by the breadth, and the product by half the breadth, and divide by 94, gives the tonnage. [*Memoirs of the Rise and Progress of the Royal Navy.* London, 1806. Pg. 310]

Ship statistics in 1546

Ship Name	Tons	Soldiers	Mariners	Gunners
Henry Grace a Dieu	1000	349	301	50
Mary Rose	700	185	200	30
Peter	600	185	185	30
Mathew	600	138	138	24
Great Bark	500	136	138	26
Jesus	700	118	158	24
Pawncy	450	136	140	24
Murryan	500	138	142	20
Struce	450	140	96	14
Mary Hamborow	400	119	111	16
Christopher of Bream	400	119	111	16
Trinity Harry	250	100	100	20
Small Bark	400	105	122	23
Sweepstake	300	100	109	21
Minion	300	100	100	20
Larticque	100	80	52	8
Mary Thomas	90	25	47	8
Hope Bark	80	28	28	4
George	60	18	18	4
Mary James	60	18	18	4
Galleys				
Graunde Masterys	450	Soldiers + Mariners 220		30
Anne Gallante	450	Soldiers + Mariners 220		30
Hart	300	Soldiers + Mariners 170		30
Antelope	300	Soldiers + Mariners 170		30
Tiger	200		100	20
Bull	200		100	20
Salamander	300		200	20
Unicorn	240		130	16
Swallow	240		130	30
Galie Subtile	200		242	8

New Bark	200		124	16
Greyhound	200		124	16
Jennet	180		106	14
Lion	140		88	12
Dragon	140		98	12
Pinnaces				
Phawcon	80		54	6
Sacar	80		54	6
Hind	80		54	6
Roo	80		46	4
Phoenix	40		46	4
Marlyon	40		46	4
Less Pinnas	40		40	4
Brigadoon	40		40	4
Hare	15		28	2
Trego-Ronnyger	20		24	1
Row Barges				
Double Rose	20		39	4
Flower de Luce	20		39	4
Portquillice	20		34	4
Harp	20		36	4
Cloud in the Sun	20		36	4
Rose in the Sun	20		36	4
Hawthorn	20		34	4
Three Ostridge Feathers	20		33	4
Fawcon in the Fetterlock	20		41	4
Maidenhead	20		33	4
Rose Slipe	20		33	4
Jolly Flower	20		34	4
Sun	20		36	4

Ship inventory and statistics on 5 January 1548.

Ship Name	Tons	Soldiers / Mariners	Brass ordnance	Iron Ordnance
Henry Grace de Dieu	1000	700	19	103
Peter	600	400	12	78
Matthew	600	300	10	121
Jesus	700	300	8	66
Pauncy	450	300	13	69
Great Bark	500	300	12	85
Less Bark	400	250	11	98
Murryan	500	300	10	53
Shruce of Dawske	450	250		39
Christopher	400	246	2	51
Trinity Henry	250	220	1	63
Sweepstake	300	230	6	78
Mary Willoughby	140	160		23
Anne Gallant	450	250	16	46
Salamander	300	220	9	40
Hart	300	220	4	52
Antelope	300	200	4	40
Swallow	240	100	8	45
Unicorn	240	140	6	30
Jennet	180	120	6	35
New Bark	200	140	5	48
Greyhound	200	140	8	37
Tiger	200	120	4	39
Bull	200	120	5	42
Lion	140	140	2	48
George	60	40	2	26
Dragon	140	120	3	42
Falcon	83	55	4	22
Black Pinnace	80	44	2	15
Hind	80	55	2	26
Spanish Shallop	20	26		70
Hare	15	30		10

Sun	20	40	2	6
Cloud in the Sun	20	40	2	7
Harp	20	40	1	6
Maidenhead	20	37	1	6
Gillyflower	20	38		
Ostridge Feather	20	37	1	6
Rose Slip	20	37	2	6
Flower de Luce	20	43	2	7
Rose in the Sun	20	40	3	7
Portcullis	20	38	1	6
Falcon in Featherlock	20	45	3	8
Grand Mrs.	450	250	1	22
Marlyon	40	50	4	8
Row Galley	200	250	3	28
Brigantine	40	44	3	19
Hoy Bark	80	60		5
Hawthorn	20	37		
Mary Hamburg	400	246	5	67
Phoenix	40	50	4	33
Saker	40	50	2	18
Double Rose	20	43	3	6

Ship inventory and statistics of 22 January 1549.

Ship Name	Tons	Soldiers	Mariners	Gunners
Great Bark	500	136	138	26
Less Bark	105	112	23	240
Sweepstake	300	100	109	21
Hart	300		180	20
Antelope	300		180	20
Swallow	240		142	18
New Bark	200		124	16
Greyhound	200		124	16
Flower de Luce	50		56	4
Double Rose	50		56	4

Inventory of ships described as a "Winter Guard" of 1549.

Ship Name	Tons	Soldiers	Mariners	Gunners
Paunsey	450	136	140	24
Murrian	500	138	142	20
Mary Hambor	400	108	120	18
Jennet	180		104	16
Dragon	140		104	16
Lion	140		104	16
Faulcon	80		62	8
Hinde	80		54	6
Phoenix	40		44	6
Mary Willoughby	140	36	80	14

Ship inventory and statistics of 29 May 1557 under the reign of Mary I.

Ship Names	Burthen Tons	Hack-butters	Soldiers	Mariners	Gunners
Great Bark	500	50	80	190	30
Jesus	700	50	80	190	30
Trinity	300	20	40	140	20
Swallow	240	20	40	140	20
Salamander	300	20	40	140	20
Hart	300	20	40	140	20
Antelope	300	20	40	140	20
Ann Gallant	300	20	40	140	20
New Bark	200	10	20	84	16
Mary Willoughby	160	10	20	84	16
Bull	180	10	20	84	16
Tiger	180	10	20	84	16
Greyhound	180	10	20	84	16
Jer Falcon	120	8	20	66	14
Falcon	80	6	16	54	10
George	100	6	16	54	10
Bark of Bullen	60	4	8	44	8
Saker	60	4	8	44	8
Soone -Sun	50	4		26	4
Flower de Luce	30			26	4

From *The Naval History of Great Britain from the Earliest Times*, published in 1761 in 5 volumes, we learn that for the year 1575, 24 ships were registered with the largest being *Triumph* at 1000 tons to the smallest the *George* at 60 tons. Furthermore, there were 182,929 able bodied fighting men, 2,562 on light horse and the royal navy consisted of 24 ships. This inventory is the same as the following of 1578.

Ship inventory and statistics of 1578 under Elizabeth I

Ship Names	Tons	Mariners	Gunners	Soldiers
Triumph	1000	450	50	200
Elizabeth Jonas	900	300	50	200
White Bear	900	300	50	200
Victory	803	330	40	100
Primrose	803	330	40	100
Mary Rose	600	200	50	100
Hope	600	200	50	100
Bonadventure	600	160	30	110
Philip and Mary	600	160	30	110
Lion or Golden Lion	600	150	30	110
Dreadnought	400	140	20	80
Swiftsure	400	140	20	80
Sallow	350	120	20	60
Antelope	350	120	20	60
Jennet	350	120	20	60
Foresight	300	120	20	60
Aid	240	90	20	50
Bull	160	70	10	40
Tiger	160	70	10	40
Falcon		60	10	20
Achates	80	30	10	10
Handmaid	80	30	10	10
Bark of Bullen	60	30	10	
George	Under 60	40	10	

Next is probably the most complete list of ships I have found. This is a list of the English fleet including names of the ships and captains that served under Charles Lord Howard of Effingham, Lord-Admiral against the Spaniards in 1588.

English fleet that served against the Spaniards in 1588.

Ship Name	Tons	Captain	Mariners	Notes
Art, Raleigh	800	Charles Howard,	425	Lord high
Elizabeth Bonaventure	600	Earl of Cumberland	250	admiral
Rainbow	500	Henry Seymour	250	
Golden Lion	500	Thomas Howard	250	
White Bear	1000	Edmund Sheffield	500	
Vanguard	500	William Winter	250	
Revenge	500	Sir Francis Drake	250	Vice admiral
Elizabeth-Jonas	500	Robert Southwell	500	
Victory	800	John Hawkins	400	Rear-admiral
Antelope	400	Henry Palmer	160	
Triumph	1100	Martin Forgisher	500	
Dreadnought	400	George Beston	200	
Mary-Rose	600	Edward Fenton	250	
Nonpariel	500	Thomas Fenner	250	
Hope	600	Robert Cross	250	
Galley Bonavolia		William Boroughs	250	
Swiftsure	400	Edward Fennar	200	
Foresight	300	Christopher Baker	160	
Aid	250	William Fennar	120	
Bull	200	Jeremy Turner	100	
Tiger	200	John Bostock	100	
Framontana	150	Luke Ward	70	
Scout	120	Henry Ashley	73	
Achates	100	Henry Rigges	60	
Charles	70	John Roberts	40	
Moon	600	Alexander Clifford	40	
Advice	50	John Harris	40	
Spy	50	Ambrose Ward	40	
Martin	50	Walter Gower	35	
Peppin	20		8	
Nightingale	160	John Doate	16	

Ships serving with Sir Francis Drake.

Ship Name	Tons	Captain	Mariners	Notes
Galleon Leicester	400	George Fenner	160	
Merchant Royal	400	Robert Flyke	160	
Edward Bonaventure	300	James Lancaster	120	
Roebuck	300	Jacob Whitton	120	
Golden Nobel	250	Adam Seigar	110	
Griffin	200	William Hawkins	100	
Minion	200	William Winter	80	
Bark Talbot	200	Henry White	90	
Thomas Drake	200	Henry Sparke	90	
Spark	200	William Spark	90	
Hopewell	200	John Marchaunt	100	
Galleon Dudley	250	James Erizey	100	
Virgin	200	John Greenfield	80	
Hope	200	John Rivers	70	Of Plymouth
Bark, Bond	150	William Pool	70	
Bark, Bonner	150	Charles Caeser	70	
Bark, Hawkins	150	Pridexe	70	
Unity	80	Humphrey Sidman	70	
Elizabeth-Drake	60	Thomas Seely	30	
Bark, Buggins	80	John Lanford	50	
Elizabeth Fonnes	80	Roger Grant	50	Frigate
Bark, Sellinger	160	John Sellinger	80	
Bark, Mannington	160	Ambrose Mannington		
Golden Hand	50	Thomas Flemming	30	
Makeshift	60	Peerce Leman	40	
Diamond	60	Robert Holland	40	Of Dartmouth
Speedwell	60	Hugh Harding	14	
Bear-Young	140	John Young	70	
Chance	60	James Foues	40	
Delight	50	William Cox	30	
Nightingale	40	John Gristing	30	
Carvel	30		24	

London ships fitted out by the city.

Ship Name	Tons	Captain	Mariners	Notes
Hercules	300	George Barnes	120	
Toby	250	Robert Barret	100	
May-Flower	200	Edward Banks	90	
Minion	200	John Dales	90	
Royal Defense	160	John Chester	80	
Ascension	200	John Chester	80	
Gift of God	180	Thomas Luntlowe	80	
Primrose	200	Robert Bingborn	90	
Margaret and John	200	John Fisher	90	
Golden Lion	140	Robert Wilcox	70	
Diana	80			
Bark, Burre	160	John Caracole	70	
Tiger	200	William Caeser	90	
Bresabe	160	William Furthoe	70	
Red Lion	200	Jarvis Wild	90	
Centurion	250	Samuel Foxcraft	100	
Passport	80	Christopher Colthirst	40	
Moonshine	60	John Brough	30	
Thomas Bonaventure	140	William Adridge	70	
Relief	60	John King	30	
Susan Ann Parnell	220	Nicholas Gorge	80	
Violet	220	Martin Hakes	60	
Soloman	170	Edmund Musgrave	80	
Anne Francis	180	Christopher Lister	70	
George Bonaventure	200	Eleazar Hikeman	80	
Jane Bonaventure	100	Thomas Hallwood	50	
Vinyard	160	Benjamin Cook	60	
Samuel	140	John Vassell	50	
George Nobel	150	Henry Bellinger	80	
Anthony	110	George Harper	60	
Toby	140	Christopher Pigot	70	
Salamander	120	Samford	60	
Rose Lion	110	Barnaby Acton	50	

Antelope	120	Dennison	60	
Jewel	120	Rowel	60	
Paunce	160	William Butler	70	
Providence	130	Richard Chester	60	
Dolphin	160	William Hares	70	

Coasters with the lord-admiral.

Ship Name	Tons	Captain	Mariners	Notes
Bark, Web	80		50	
John Trelawny	150	Thomas Meek	70	
Hart	60	James Houghton	30	Of Dartmouth
Bark Potts	180	Anthony Potts	80	
Little John	40	Laurence Cleyton	20	
Bartholomew	130	Nicholas Wright	70	Of Aspen
Rose of Aspham	110	Tomas Sanny	50	
Gift of Apsham	25		20	
Jacob	90		50	Of Lime
Revenge	60	Richard Bedford	30	Of Lime
William	70	John Smith	30	Of Bridgewater
Cresent	140		75	Of Dartmouth
Galleon	100	Richard Miller	50	Of Weymouth
Katherine	60		30	Of Weymouth
John	70	John Young	50	Of Chichester
Hearty Anne	60	John Winnol	30	
Minion	230	John Satchfield	110	Of Bristol
Unicorn	130	James Laughton	66	Of Bristol
Handmaid	85	Christopher Pitt	56	Of Bristol
Aid	60	William Megar	25	Of Bristol
Daniel	160	Robert Johnson	70	
Galleon, Hutchins	150	Thomas Tucker	60	
Bark, Lamb	150	Leonard Harvel	60	
Fancy	60	Richard Fern	30	
Griffin	75	John Dobson	35	
Little Hare	50	Matthew Railston	25	

Handmaid	75	John Gatenbury	35	
Marygold	150	Francis Johnson	70	
Matthew	35	Richard Mitchel	16	
Susan	40	John Musgrave	20	
William	140	Barnaby Lowe	30	Of Ipswich
Katherine	125	Thomas Grimble	50	Of Ipswich
Primrose	120	John Cardinal	40	Of Harwich
Anne Bonaventure	60	John Conny	50	
William	80	William Coxon	60	Of Rye
Grace of God	50	William Fordred	30	
Ellnathan	120	John Lidgier	70	Of Dover
Reuben	110	William Cripp	68	Of Sandwich
Hazard	38	Nicholas Turner	34	Of Feversham
Grace	150	William Musgrave	70	Of Yarmouth
May-flower	150	Alex Musgrave	70	
John Young	100	Reynold Veyzey	30	

Volunteers with the lord admiral.

Samson	300	John Wingfield	108	

During the period when Spain was providing for her "Invincible fleet," Queen Elizabeth was relishing the commerce and naval power that England possessed. When the Spanish fleet arrived in the English Channel in July 1588, it appears from several historical accounts that the English fleet was 34 ships strong. The following is a list of those ships in service at that time.

Ship Names	Tonnage	Men
Ark Royal	800	425
Elizabeth Bonadventure	600	250
Rainbow	500	250
Golden Lion	500	250
White Bear	1000	500
Vanguard	500	250

Revenge	500	250
Elizabeth Jonas	900	500
Victory	800	400
Antelope	400	160
Triumph	1100	500
Dreadnought	400	200
Mary Rose	600	250
Nonpareil	500	250
Hope	600	250
Galley Bonavolia	250	250
Swiftsure	400	200
Swallow	360	160
Foresight	300	160
Aid	250	120
Bull	200	100
Tiger	200	100
Tramontana	150	70
Scout	120	70
Achates	100	60
Charles	70	40
Moon	60	40
Advice	50	40
Spy	50	40
Marline	50	35
Sun	40	30
Cygnet	30	20
Brigantine	90	35
George	120	24

Queen Elizabeth I died in March 1603. The following is a roster of the royal navy at the time of her death.

The royal navy in March 1603.

Ship Names	Burthen Tons	Mariners	Gunners	Soldiers	Total Men
Elizabeth Jonas	900	340	40	120	500
Triumph	1000	340	40	120	500
White Bear	900	340	40	120	500
Victory	800	268	32	100	400
Mary Honora	800	268	32	100	400
Ark Royal	800	268	32	100	400
St. Mathew	1000	340	40	120	500
St. Andrew	900	268	32	100	400
Due Repulse	700	230	30	90	350
Garland	700	190	30	80	300
Warspight	600	190	30	80	300
Mary Rose	600	150	30	70	250
Hope	600	150	30	70	250
Bonaventure	600	150	30	70	250
Lion	500	150	30	70	250
Nonpareil	500	150	30	70	250
Defiance	500	250	30	70	250
Rainbow	500	150	30	70	250
Dreadnought	400	130	20	50	200
Antelope	350	114	16	30	160
Swiftsure	400	130	20	50	200
Swallow	330	114	16	30	160
Foresight	300	114	16	30	160
Tide	250	88	12	20	120
Crane	200	70	10	20	100
Adventure	250	88	12	20	120
Quittance	200	70	10	20	100
Answer	200	70	10	20	100
Advantage	200	70	10	20	100
Tiger	200	70	10	20	100
Tramontana	140	52	8	10	70
Scout	120	48	8	10	66
Catis	100	42	8	10	60
Charles	70	32	6	7	45
Moon	60	30	5	5	40

Advice	50	30	5	5	40
Spy	50	30	5	5	40
Merlin	45	26	5	4	35
Sun	40	24	4	2	30
Synnet	20				
George, hoy.	100				
Penny-Rose-hoy	80				

Details of the ordnance that individual ships carried during this era are very rare. One very early account from about 1550 describes the *cannon* of the period as an 8 inch 60 pr. gun (8-inch ball or shot, for a cannon 8 ft 6 in. in length); the *demi-cannon* was a 6.4 inch 32 pr., 11 feet in length; the *culverin* was a 5.2 inch 16 pr., the *demi-culverin* was a 4 inch 9 1/2 pr., the *saker* was a 3.6 inch 6 pr., 6 ft 11 in. in length; the *cannon-perer* is unknown; the *falcon* was a 2.5 inch 2 pr., 8 ft. 6 in. in length. The iron guns were all small caliber.

Ordnance carried by specific ships

Ship Names	Cannons	Demi Cannons	Culverins	Demi Culverins	Sakers	Minions	Falcons	Falconets	Port-Piece Halls	Port-Piece Chambers	Fowler Halls	Fowler Chambers	Curtails
Achatis				6		2	5						
Adventure			4	11	5						2	4	
Advantage				6	8	4							
Amity of Harwich				4	2								
St. Andrew			8	21	7	2					3	7	2
Antelope			4	13	8		1						
Advice					4	2	3						
Ark	4	4	12	12	6				4	7	2	4	
Answer				5	8	2					2	4	
Aid				8	2	4	4						
Bear					2								
White Bear	3	11	7	10					2		7		

Ship Names	Cannons	Demi Cannons	Culverins	Demi Culverins	Sakers	Minions	Falcons	Falconets	Port-Piece Halls	Port-Piece Chambers	Fowler Halls	Fowler Chambers	Curtails
Charles					8		2				2	4	
Crane				6	7	6					2	3	
Cygnet							1	2					
Due Repulse	2	3	13	14	6				2	4	2	4	
Dreadnought	2		4	11	10		2				4	8	
Defiance			14	14	6				2	4	2	4	
Daysey					4								
Elizabeth-Jonas	3	6	8	9	9	1	2		1	2	5	10	
Eliza Bonaventure	2	2	11	14	4	2			2	4	2	4	
Foresight			14	8	3	2				3	6		
Guardland			16	14	4				2	4	2	3	
Hope	2	4	9	11	4				4	8	2	4	
Lion		4	8	14	9		1				8	16	
Mary Rose		4	11	10	4				3	7			
Mere Honora		4	15	16	4						2		
St. Mathew	4	4	16	14	4	4	2						
Mercury			1		1							4	
Marlin							7						
Moon					4	4	1						
Nonpareil	2	3	7	8	12				4	8	4	8	
Quittance			2	6	7	4					2	4	
Rainbow		6	12	7	1								
Scout					4		6						
Swiftsure	2		5	12	8		2				4	8	
Spy					4	2	3						
Swallow						2	1			2		3	
Sun			1				4						
Triumph	4	3	17	8	6				1	4	5	20	
Tremontana					12	7	2						
Tiger				6	14		2						
Vauntguard		4	14	11	2								
Victory			12	18	9						7	13	
Warspight	2	2	13	10	2								

1–2. Event Records of English Ships.

Contained within this section are the recorded events during the life span and service of the ships that were active during the time span of 1547–1603. This part not only shares the rare account of a birth of a ship dedicated to Queen Elizabeth, but the life of service of this ship in defending her realm from foreign invasions. These accounts also share the sometimes-violent end of a ship's life.

Recorded events of ships activities from this era are very rare, obscure, and often overlooked and certainly difficult to locate. As I will share, there are several entries discovered that were not included in the index of the numerous volumes reviewed. Some enterprising researchers will only scan the index looking for information. Many resources were used to accumulate the information presented to maritime historians.

It is interesting to note that at about 1575–1576, the level of pirate activity dramatically increased.

For the sources referenced in this section, see page 103.

Achates.

1) 30 July 1576. Orders to Captain John Thomas to prepare for a voyage to the Narrow Seas and escort 2 English ships from Spain. *APC-V.9, 178.*

2) 19 February 1580. Having returned from Ireland, a request to the lord treasurer to pay the mariners for their service. *APC-V.12, 337.*

3) 7 December 1587. Orders to remain at sea in a 'warlike manner' for six weeks beginning 14 December and to end on 23 January. *APC-V.15, 293.*

Advantage. Of Suffolk.

1) 19 September 1592. Orders to prepare to sail to the Narrow Seas and assemble a crew had been canceled. Orders included to discharge any of the crew that had arrived. *APC-V.23, 204.*

Adventure. Of Bristol.

This ship was mentioned in the inventory at the time of Elizabeth's death in 1603 at 250 tons and with 88 mariners, 12 gunners and 20 soldiers. *MRP.*

1) 25 September 1596. A French ship of war (blank in manuscript) la *Rose* of Lanyon had plundered from this ship while sailing from Brest to Bristol. Items stolen were linen cloth, canvas, wax, and other merchandise to a value of 5000 Sterling. Seeking the arrest of the French ships involved and for restitution. *APC-V.26, 203–204.*

2) 20 September 1597. Sir George Carew was driven back to port from the rest of the fleet. Unsure if this is related to the above incident. Carew was given the *St. Mathew* and to dispose of the *Adventure* "may be disposed of there in safe harbor" after removing what could be fit on the *St. Mathew*. *APC-V.28, 5–6*.

3) 9 July 1602. Instructions to Sir William Monson, vice-admiral of the fleet for the coast of Spain.

> "You shall govern your enterprise principally to prevent the preparations and gathering together of the King of Spain's sea forces, and shall not divide your fleet, nor undertake any exploit that may hinder this business, which concerns the safety and honor of your prince and country. You shall direct your course towards Cape Finisterre and the Groyne, and carefully view the state of that coast, and the ports adjoining. If you find any preparations there, or rendezvous appointed for ships, you shall do your best to destroy or disperse those gathered, and to stop, take, or overthrow all that attempt to consort with them.
>
> If you find those ports clear, you shall ply up along the coast of Galicia and Portugal, as near the shore as you can, till you come to the height of the Rock, look into their ports, and informing yourself of their preparations, try to prevent them. If no important occasion prevents, you shall ply off and on the height of the Rock, till your admiral with the residue of his fleet come up. In such case of your necessary departure, you shall leave some small ship with direction where you may be found.
>
> You shall give advice to the *Quittance* and to the Hollanders of your coming, as soon as you can, and direct them where to find you and what course to hold, and shall assure them of the present return of your admiral and the residue of our fleet, and what care her Majesty has taken for their speedy supply with victuals, and shall encourage them to continue resolute in this service which so much imports the common cause of religion and of both countries.
>
> Above all things you shall refrain from offering violence or interruption to any of her majesty's allies, and shall suffer no man to go aboard them for whose honest carriage yourself will not answer, nor shall, without plain and manifest proofs of goods prohibited or belonging directly to the King of Spain's subjects, seize or stay any vessel or anything therein contained.
>
> If you meet any ship of her Majesty's allies laden with Spanish iron or anchors, you shall buy the same and take order for their transporting to Deptford Strond, giving bill for payment at such reasonable price as may not rebound to the owner's loss. You shall advertise the lords of your proceedings, and all things meet for their knowledge.

So soon as you have sight or notice of your admiral coming, you shall repair to him, and follow his directions.

CSP-D, (1601–1603), 220–221.

Advice.

This ship is mentioned in the inventory at the time of Elizabeth's death in 1603 as 50 tons with 30 mariners, 5 gunners and 5 soldiers. *MRP.*

1) 24 April 1597. Orders to store victuals for 40 men and be ready to sail. *APC-V.27, 65.*

Aid.

This ship is first mentioned in the ship inventory of 1578 at 240 tons with 90 mariners, 20 gunners and 50 soldiers. *NHGB.* As of 1588 this ship had 120 men. *MRP.*

1) 11 October 1565. Orders to patrol the seas of Bedford to apprehend pirates. *APC-V.7, 267.*

2) September (?) 1577.This ship and the *Gabriel* arrived from their first voyage to the northwest parts at Bristol and the council suggested Martin Frobisher to unload the ore there and store it safely in the castle. The *Michael* arrived in the Thames and the ore was to be unloaded and kept safe under guard. The council expressed a strong desire "on the speedy melting of the ore." *CSP-C, 1513–1616, 20–21.*

3) 17 October 1577. Letter concerning the payment of wages of soldiers and mariners of this ship and of the victuals that will not keep and to be moored and tack undisturbed. *APC-V10, 56.*

4) 25 November 1577. 124 tons of ore was unloaded from this ship and 16 tons from the *Gabriel* into the safety of Bristol Castle. *CSP-C, 1513–1616, 24.*

5) 6 March 1578. Request for payment for repairs, but there is no company or corporation by the name mentioned in the letter. Determined to pay certain individuals. *APC-V.11, 65.*

6) 15 March 1578. Orders to receive this ship into the custody of her majesty's navy recently returned from the North. *APC-V.11, 76.*

7) 25 March 1578. Instructions to Martin Frobisher to begin preparations for another voyage her majesty called *meta incognita* (unknown destination) to the Northwest parts and Cathey (North China). He was to acquire 90 mariners for this ship, the *Gabriel*, *Michael* and *Judith*. Furthermore, to hire 130 pioneers and 50 soldiers for 6 additional vessels. Victuals for 90 persons for 7 months to be loaded and to prepare to sail before 1 May and return with 800 tons of ore. *CSP-C, 1513–1616, 35–36.*

8) 1 June 1578. Orders and articles to be observed by the fleet from Captain Frobisher and delivered to every ship under his command.

> "To banish swearing, dice, cards, playing and all filthy talk, and to serve God twice a day and to clear the glass every night according to the old order of England. Signals in case of fogs, trumpets, drums, etc. to be sounded, or contrary winds. Watch words 'Before the world was God' the answer 'After God came Christ his Son.'" *CSP-C, 1513–1516, 37.*

9) 19 February 1579. Orders to remain in port. *APC-V.11, 52.*

10) 11 October 1579. Loaded victuals while at Waterford. *APC-V.11, 283.*

11) 24 March 1580. Stored victuals and to prepared for a voyage to the North Sea and to transport French commissioners. *APC-V.12, 362.*

12) 30 December 1580. Request for payment for wages for mariners, gunners and soldiers that served while off the coast of Ireland. *APC-V.12, 297.*

13) 18 September 1588. Proposed expedition into Ireland and the provision of victuals. *APC-V.16, 280.*

Allen.

1) 14 June 1581. In April 1576, this ship was carrying wool and encountered a tempest and forced to run aground in Dunkirk to save the lives of the crew and the cargo. The record further indicates that the ship was "cut up and spoiled". The cargo was saved and returned to the merchants. *APC-V.13, 83–84.*

Amity.

Records indicate the ship was a pinnace.

1) 30 April 1592. This ship with the *Prudence* had pirated 20 tons of syrup in divers casks, 9 tons in several casks and 17 bags of almonds, 50 packs of buck skins, 77 hogsheads of ale, 30 chests of sugar, 99 hogsheads and six barrels of sugar, 17 half chests of sugar, 685 skins full of anneal, one barrel of dates and other like goods. *APC-V.22, 417.*

2) 20 July 1600. This ship was to transport presents to the king of Barbary.

A wind instrument, eight pair of latten candlesticks, three perfuming pans of satin, seventy-five course sables, eight guilt murrions, one armor parcel guilt, fifty bastard muskets stocked and inlaid with mother of pearl, two cases of enameled pistols and ten buff jerkins plain. *APC-V.30, 521-522.*

3) 17 September 1600. This ship was employed to transport items to Ireland for support of English troops. The ship received further orders to serve for an additional 3 months. *APC-V.30, 617.*

4) 15 March 1601. Orders to prepare this ship with victuals and 134 men to serve patrolling the coast of England for 4 months. *APC-V.31, 225–226.*

Amy Francis.

1) 25 July 1579. Letter of restitution to the French king for plundering this ship by ships in his service. *APC-V.11, 198–199.*

Andrew.

1) 20 March 1558. Orders to prepare to sail to the Low Countries. *APC-V.7, 69.*

Angel, of Wismar.

1) 28 July 1554. Letter mentions that Southampton merchants lost all their goods and had "obtained a favorable decree." *CSP-F, 1553–1558, 123.*

2) 23 October 1555. The French King assigned his treasurer to pay 21,600 Sterling to pay for the lost goods. Based on this, it would be safe to assume the French plundered the ship. *CSP-F, 1553–1558, 190.*

3) 20 March 1558. Orders to prepare to sail to the Low Countries. *APC-V.7, 69.*

Angel. Of Southampton.

Records suggest this was a small bark.

1) 25 March 1579. Orders to release this ship and proceed on her voyage. *APC-V.11, 430.*

2) 8 May 1580. Orders to release the ship for a voyage to Elbing, Poland. *APC-V.12, 6.*

Anne Dowell.

Records suggest this was 70 tons.

1) 8 May 1580. Orders to release the ship for a voyage to Elbing, Poland. *APC-V.12, 6.*

Anne Gallant.

This ship is in a 1546 inventory as 450 tons with 220 soldiers and mariners and 30 gunners. At the time of Mary's ascension, the crew compliment was: 20 hackbutters, 40 soldiers, 140 mariners and 20 gunners. *MRP.*

1) 10 July 1556. Record indicates that this ship belonged to Anthony Lincoln. The ship was lost while carrying ordnance and munitions for the queen to Ireland. But additional records preceding this letter indicate that the ship continued in service. *APC-V.5, 306–307.*

2) 20 March 1558. Orders to prepare to sail to the Low Countries. *APC-V.7, 69.*

3) 20 April 1559. Embargo removed and prepared to sail. *APC-V.7, 90.*

4) 10 November 1577. Letter to the officers of the port of London to release this ship and allow it to travel to Spain. *APC-V.10, 81.*

5) 21 January 1581. This ship was plundered and merchants of Ireland seeking restitution. *APC-V.13, 307.*

Ann Frances. Of London.
1) March 1603. A cargo with a value of £3000 was plundered by a man-of-war of Brittany on May-day last. *APC-D, (1601–1603), 304.*

Answer.
This ship is mentioned in the inventory of 1603 at the death of Elizabeth as 200 tons with 70 mariners, 10 gunners and 20 soldiers. *MRP.*

1) 25 January 1592. Letter to Sir Henry Palmer admiral of the Narrow Seas. Reports that 1500 Spaniards are about St. Mallows. The admiral was on the *Rainbow* accompanied by the *Answer* and assigned to determine the purpose of the Spaniards between Newhaven and Hage for a period of 14–15 days. The admiral had permission to take in any merchant or war ship if he felt it necessary. *APC-V.22, 206–207*

2) 9 July 1602. This ship was under the command of Sir William Monson, vice-admiral of the fleet for the coast of Spain and received the same instructions as the *Adventure. CSP-D, (1601–1603), 220–221.*

Antelope.
This ship is mentioned in a 1546 inventory as 300 tons, with 170 soldiers and mariners and 30 gunners. At the time of Mary's ascension, the crew complement was: 20 hackbutters, 40 soldiers, 140 mariners and 20 gunners. At the time of Elizabeth's ascension, the crew compliment was: 120 mariners, 20 gunners and 60 soldiers. *MRP.*

As of 1588, records indicate this was 400 tons with 160 men. *APC.*

1) 11 March 1551. Orders to prepare ship for sea.

2) 14 August 1580. Mariners, gunners, and soldiers assigned to this ship were supplied with hose (stockings), shoes, shirts, caps, canvas for breeches and doublets, cotton, and other provisions in preparation for a voyage to Ireland. *APC-V.12, 154.*

3) 5 May 1587. Orders to remain at sea from 23 March until 15 June. *APC-V.15, 108.*

4) 21 September 1597. Basically, this ship received orders to stop any ship carrying corn from the East Countries or Low Countries to Spain. The queen is quoted as "that you shall with all diligence lie in wait for them." *APC-V.28, 8.*

5) 6 January 1598. Sir John Gilbert was responsible for capturing two ships: the *Poppingay* of Lubeck and the *Swan* of Rotterdam. The cargos were deemed as legal prize and to be sold. *APC-V.28, 224.*

6) 6 January 1598. This ship and Sir John Gilbert were responsible for capturing the *Swan* of Rotterdam. Some of the cargo was deemed prize goods. *APC-V.28, 224.*

7) 21 September 1601. Reported seeing 40 ships believed to be Spanish while returned from Newfoundland on 14 September. Two additional English ships confirmed they were Spanish ships. *CSP-D, (1601–1603), 100.*

Anthony.
1) 27 March 1559. Orders to prepare to sail. *APC-V.7, 73.*

Ark Royal.
The first mention of this ship was in the English inventory of 1588 against the Spanish armada; it is listed as 800 ton with 425 men. MRP.
1) 25 March 1579. Orders to release this ship and proceed on her voyage. *APC-V.11, 430.*

The Ark Royal.

[*Chatterton, Edward. Sailing Ships. The Story of Their Development from Earliest Times.* London, 1915. Pg. 193]

Ascension. Of London.
This ship was mentioned in the inventory of 1588 against the Spanish armada as 200 tons with John Chester as captain of 80 mariners. *MRP.*

Austen Piers.
1) 27 March 1559. Orders to prepare to sail. *APC-V.7, 73.*

Ballsar.

1) 24 April 1597. Orders to transport wheat and corn to Chester Ireland for supplying soldiers. *APC-V.27, 68.*

Barbara.

1) 22 October. 1552. Reported in port at Dartmouth.

2) 26 January 1554. Mention in a letter.

3) 20 March 1558. Orders to prepare to sail to the Low Countries. *APC-V.7, 69.*

Bark Aucher.

Records suggest that this was a Third-Rate ship of 300 tons.

1) 25 May 1551. Letter describing Sir Anthony Aucher (Marshal of Calais) was seeking legal advice regarding this purchase, (possibly of the ship).

2) 23 May 1552. The Privy Council summoned him regarding a robbery that his ship was accused of on a ship owned by the King of Denmark.

3) 11 January 1553. This ship was ordered to be ready to sail to Spain.

4) 28 May 1553. This ship was reported to have been plundered by a French ship the *Faulcon.*

5) 30 December 1555. Orders for the arrest of all responsible for robbing a vessel. *APC-V.5, 215.*

Bark Burr.

Records suggest this was 90 tons.

1) 2 March 1579. Released to carry wheat to Portugal. *APC-V.11, 424.*

2) 6 November 1586. Duke of Mercury, governor of Brittany, France, filed a claim against this ship for plundering a cargo of wine and other commodities from a French ship. *APC-V.14, 247.*

Bark. Of Boullen.

Records indicate that this was a 60 ton. At the time of Mary's ascension, the crew complement was: 4 hackbutters, 8 soldiers, 44 mariners and 8 gunners. At the time of Elizabeth's ascension, the crew complement was: 30 mariners and 10 gunners. *ARP.*

1) 8 March 1569. Noted all things that were to be provided for the fitting out of this ship for sail. No additional information is shared. *CSP-D–1547–1580.*

2) 7 October 1578. William Nutshaw had provided 4 tons of ordnance for this ship. (Perhaps this ship was recently rebuilt.) This ship was to prepare to sail. *APC-V.10, 338.*

3) 10 April 1579. This ship was made ready to sell. *APC-V.11, 99.*

4) 7 September 1579. William Nutshaw was ordered to deliver his ship to the French for compensation for a ship he took of theirs. *APC-V.11, 259.*

5) 12 May 1588. Orders to prepare this ship to serve the queen against the possible invasion of the king of Spain. *APC-V.16, 61.*

Barkager.
1) 18 June 1548. The lord protector was notified of the arrival of the king's (Edward VI) ship. *CSP-D-Addenda. 383.*

Bear. Of Leicester.
1) 11 March 1579. Captain Richard Farewether was given permission to depart southward with 18 men and 2 boys. *APC-V.11, 416.*

2) 16 July 1596. This ship is one of three under the command of Captain Wood that was funded by Sir Robert Dudley that had sailed from England to China with a letter from Queen Elizabeth to the emperor of China, "...but none of the company ever returned to give account of the fate of the rest," and are believed to have perished. *CSP-C, 1513–1616, 98.*

Bear. Of Warwick.
1) 19 December 1575. A letter requesting assistance regarding the recent piracy committed against it by "men of St. Mallows." *APC-V.9, 62.*

2) 24 April 1597. Orders to store victuals and prepare to be at sea for 28 days or 3 months. *APC-V.27, 65.*

Bear's Whelp.
1) 16 July 1596. This ship is one of three under the command of Captain Wood that was funded by Sir Robert Dudley that had sailed from England to China with a letter from Queen Elizabeth to the emperor of China, "but none of the company ever returned to give account of the fate of the rest" and are believed to have perished. *CSP-C, 1513–1616, 98.*

Benjamin.
1) 16 July 1596. This ship is one of three under the command of Captain Wood that was funded by Sir Robert Dudley that had sailed from England to China with a letter from Queen Elizabeth to the emperor of China, "but none of the company ever returned to give account of the fate of the rest" and are believed to have perished. *CSP-C, 1513–1616, 98.*

Bevis. Southampton.

1) 29 July 1593. Captain Walles had captured a ship *Mary* of Olonne (Les Sables-d'*Olonne* is a seaside town in Western France) and took it to Southampton. APC-V.24, 427.

Biscayne.

1) 13 August 1592. Request sent to Sir Walter Raleigh for payment of wages for mariners of this ship. *APC-V.23, 117–118.*

Black Lion.

Record indicates this was 100 ton.

1) 7 March 1597. At this time, the ship had 20 mariners, a master, and a boy. The ship was blown into Plymouth by "contrary' winds. Permission was granted to allow the ship to continue its voyage to Spain and Portugal. *APC-V.27, 284.*

The Black Pinnace.

[Chatterton, Edward. Sailing Ships. The Story of Their Development from Earliest Times. London, 1915. Pg. 208]

Black Pinnace.

1) 1 July 1593. The council received a letter informing them that this ship and the *Desire* where to pass the Straits of Magellan into the South Sea, "where prizes of great value and riches are often times taken". If the ship was to return with valuable items, Thomas Cavendishe was ordered "to board her and see her hatches nailed down and a just inventory taken." *APC-V.24, 346.*

Black Raven.

1) 19 December 1575. A letter regarding this ship for seeking immediate restitution because the merchandise this ship was transporting was captured by the Portuguese. APC-V.9, 63.

2) 3 February 1576. Additional information regarding the capture of this ship by the *Flying Ghost* of Portugal laden with salt. APC-V.9, 279.

Blue Bear.

1) 19 September 1576. Orders to release the ship from general arrest. At that time, it was owned by Mr. Bates. APC-V.9, 205.

Bolloigne (Boulogne)

1) 27 August 1554. Transportation for Sir Anthony St. Leger and the queen's treasure.

Bonadventure.

This ship is mentioned in a 1578 inventory as 600 tons with 160 mariners, 30 gunners and 110 soldiers. *NHGB.*

1) 6 January 1598. Complaint filed that her cargo of fish, grain and furs was taken "by force and violence" as she was returning from Newfoundland. Seeking restitution. APC-V.28, 227–228.

Boneham. Pool.

1) 20 March 1596. Complaint filed by London merchants after this ship had been driven into Dartmouth "by contrary winds". They encountered two ships from Dieppe that plundered all their cargo and merchandise "in most treacherous and barbarous sort and left them in great peril and danger". APC-V.26, 561-562.

Boyer.

1) 7 March 1579. Hans Bruteman sought restitution for plundering cargo by Richard Scarborough of pitch and stockfish. APC-V.11, 65.

Brigandine.

1) 10 September 1588. Orders to the captain to discharge his men and to see that the ship is looked after and laid up. APC-V.16, 275.

Bull.

This ship is mentioned in a 1546 inventory as 200 tons with 100 mariners and 20 gunners. At the time of Mary's ascension, the crew complement was: 10 hackbutters, 20 soldiers, 84 mariners and 16 gunners. At the time of Elizabeth's ascension, the crew complement was: 70 mariners, 10 gunners and 40 soldiers. *MRP.*

1) 4 December 1556. Report that the ship was unfit for service and recommended it be brought into Harborough for repairs. *APC-V-6, 28.*

2) 8 January 1557. Orders to temporarily accommodate 200 men. *APC-V.6, 235.*

3) 22 October 1587. Orders to remain at sea in a 'warlike manner' for six weeks, beginning 13 October to 2 November. *APC-V.15, 267.*

4) 7 December 1587. Orders to remain at sea in a 'warlike manner' for six weeks, beginning 14 December to 23 January. *APC-V.15, 293.*

5) 18 December 1597. This ship was captured on the seas by Lord Thomas Howard. The council requested "that there are divers English priests and some Jesuits in the army we would have you discover if any of them be disguised amongst those Spaniards." The cargo would be sold to defray costs. *APC-V.28, 192–193.*

Buona Voglia.

This is referred to as the great black galley. The name is "good wish" in Italian. It is possible this was a captured ship.

1) 10 November 1596. Orders to make this ship ready for sail. "You may with boards and the help of carpenters speedily make her able for service, as she sits in the Medway River in Southeast England." *APC-V.26, 312*

Carvel.

This ship is mentioned in the inventory of 1588 against the Spanish as 30 tons with 24 mariners serving under the command of Sir Francis Drake. *MRP.*

1) 16 March 1602. This ship with three other English ships had chased 4 Portuguese ships. One ship surrendered and was left to drift without a crew. The fight with the other three ships lasted two to three hours then all were captured. *CSP-D, (1601–1603), 163.*

Castle. Of Comfort.

1) 23 October 1575. Captain Anthony Carew was ordered to assist the *Thistle* of Wight and Portsmouth. *APC-V.9, 32.*

2) 11 December 1575. The Merchants of the Society of the Stillard complained of the spoils by Anthony Carew on Mr. Thyson. *APC-V.9, 60.*

3) 20 January 1576. William Leffer merchant of St. Mallows in London complained about the spoil of a ship of his by this ship and requests restitution. *APC-V.9, 76.*

4) 1 June 1576. Le Feir, a merchant, had complained of the spoilage of his ship by this ship and to seek punishment by the law. *APC-V.9, 132.*

Centurion. Of London.

This ship is mentioned in the inventory of 1588 against the Spanish armada as 250 tons with Samuel Foxcraft as captain of 100 mariners. *MRP.*

1) 25 March 1579. Orders to release this ship and proceed on her voyage. *APC-V.11, 430.*

2) 18 October 1580. License granted to travel to Spain. Must offload any cargo not destined for that voyage. *APC-V.12, 235.*

3) 9 December 1580. Richard Wiseman and John Hawes, owners, were released to travel to Spain under the conditions that should any negative action be reported against them, they would be placed in prison. *APC-V.12, 274.*

4) 13 April 1589. Charges brought against this ship by the Dutch that their cargo was plundered and seeking restitution. *APC-V.17, 126.*

Ceraphin. (Seraphin or Zeraphin).

Deciphering the letters leads me to believe this was not originally an English ship but was pressed into service in her majesty's navy against the Spanish invasion of 1588. This ship was en route to Newfoundland. It was 200 tons.

1) 1 July 1558. This ship was to replace 2 ships (1 ship and a pinnace) that could not serve against the Spanish fleet. *APC-V.16, 148.*

2) 28 July 1558. Taxes were collected as were other contributions to help pay for this ship's service against the Spanish fleet. *APC-V.16, 201.*

3) 8 September 1558. Additional funds were collected to pay for this ship's service against the Spanish fleet. *APC-V.16, 272.*

Chancewell.

1) 25 March 1597. This ship was "to adventure a voyage of fishing and discovery into the Bay of Canada" (Newfoundland) at the island of Ramea, an island off the southern coast. *APC-V.27, 5–6.*

Charity.

1) 27 March 1559. Orders to prepare to sail. *APC-V.7, 73.*

Charles.

This ship is mentioned in the inventory of 1588 against the Spanish armada under the command of Charles Effingham, lord admiral as 70 tons with John Roberts as captain of 40 mariners. *MRP.*

1) 7 December 1587. Orders to remain at sea in a 'warlike manner' for six weeks, beginning 14 December to 23 January. *APC-V.15, 293.*

Christ.

1) 20 April 1559. Embargo removed and to prepared to sail. *APC-V.7, 90.*

Christopher.

This ship is mentioned in a 1548 inventory as 400 tons with 246 mariners and soldiers with 2 pieces of brass and 51 iron ordnance. *MRP.*

1) 28 May 1550. The Privy Council ordered this ship be released. *APC-V.3, 38.*

2) 19 October 1575. Captain Garbran Dominich, while transporting English merchant goods, complained that he was chased by pirates, and they defended themselves. *APC-V.9, 29–30.*

3) 13 December 1578. This ship was used by Sir Francis Drake in his important expedition into the South Seas. *NHGB–11.*

4) 31 March 1601. This ship had captured cargo while at sea. The council determined that they should give up their prize as it was not lawful. *APC–31, 260–261.*

Christopher Bennet.

1) 22 January 1557. Orders to remain at Plymouth until the queen needed it. *APC-V.6, 247.*

2) 15 January 1581. While at Bristol, there appears to be a release from her majesty's duty and could be employed if a merchant needs it. *APC-V.12, 312.*

Clement. London.

1) 5 April 1547. Humphrey Wilson was master, carrying 8 casks of superfine powder and other munitions of the king for Newcastle. He had confused a church steeple with one five miles from Tynemouth and ran on ground, "But the weather being fair, by the diligence of the country, the greater of the munitions has been saved, only some powder is wet, and half is lost. If you will send some sulphur and saltpeter and a man that understands it, it can be made to serve." *CSP-D-Addenda. 321–322.*

Clement. Unsure if the same.

1) 26 April 1567. Orders to John Cockmaster to transport provisions to Ireland. *APC-V.7, 345.*

Clock.

1) 23 November 1573. John Lane was held for payment and the ship was not allowed to leave. *APC-V.8, 143.*

2) 28 November 1573. The ship pretended to sail for Ireland, but was to be held. *APC-V.8, 149.*

3) 17 February 1574. John Lane of London claimed to a part as the ship was in Portsmouth. *APC-V.8, 196.*

Cock. Of Middleborough.

1) 9 June 1576. Captain Nicholas Reister was taken and detained by his own company on a charge of a misdemeanor. He was charged in piracy and held. *APC-V.9, 138.*

Conquer. Of Plymouth.

1) 20 September 1601. On August 20, Captain Cooper took a Spanish fishing boat that reported 50,000 Spanish and Italian soldiers at Lisbon and Cadiz besides many ships. *CSP-D, (1601–1603), 99.*

Content.

1) 24 June 1601. Master was Peter Motham. This ship was loaded and ready to transport merchandise to Hamburg. *APC-V.31, 451.*

Constantine.

1) 24 March 1599. This ship was to be in service in Ireland for 176 days. Requested payment for that service. *APC-V.30, 191–192.*

Costly. Of Ipswich.

1) 6 November 1597. The council addressed a petition for claims for the Cales (Calais?) voyage from this ship and the *James* also of Ipswich. Some of the crew "Being driven to great misery have been forced to take far less sums." *APC-V.28, 103–104.*

Crab. Of Queenbourgh.

1) 19 September 1576. Complains of "Flusshingers" who spoiled the ship of their merchandise when they left Spain. *APC-V.9, 204.*

Crane.

This ship is mentioned in the 1603 inventory at the time of Elizabeth's death as 200 tons with 70 mariners, 10 gunners and 20 soldiers. *MRP.*

1) 13 October 1601. Orders to transport 100 men and winter apparel to English troops in Ireland. The apparel list as follows: A cassock of broad

cloth, a pair of venetians, a doublet of canvas, a hat cap, 2 shirts of linen cloth, 2 bands of Holland cloth, 3 pairs of Carlisle socks and 3 pair of boots. *APC-V.32, 274–275.*

2) 6 December 1602. It was reported that three "Dunkirkers" had captured this ship and killed the captain and some of the crew. *APC-D, (1601–1603), 268.*

Crescent.

1) 2 June 1588. Within a letter is a description of the high cost of supplying this ship with necessary supplies including munitions, yet this was inadequate for the service it was called into. *APC-V.16, 103–104.*

Dainty.

1) 19 June 1601. Record indicated that Henry Rawlin was master. *APC-V.31, 442.*

Daisy. Of London.

1) 22 March 1597. Orders to transport 360 quarters of wheat and 60 quarters of rye to Carlingford, Ireland for her majesty's army there. *APC-V.28, 369–370.*

David. Of London.

1) 5 April 1598. Merchants of Tuscany, Italy, complained of the plundering of cargo removed from their ship by the *David*. The cargo consisted of Spanish reals and silk. The council reviewed proof that 30,378 pieces of eight and 46 pieces of silk constituted the cargo on the ship. 22,929 pieces of eight and all but 25 yards of silk remained. The Italian merchants wanted restitution. *APC-V.28, 382–384.*

2) 13 April 1598. Orders to the *David* for full restitution to the Italian merchants.

3) 7 June 1598. Several individuals were committed to prison for their part in the plundering of silk and money. They were ordered to compensate the Italian merchants. One man refused and chose to remain in prison.

Defense.

This ship is listed as Royal Defense in the 1588 inventory as ships fitted out in London against the Spanish armada as 160 tons with John Chester as captain of 80 mariners. *MRP.*

1) 19 June 1601. Record indicated that Richard Harris the elder was master. *APC-V.31, 442.*

Defiance.

This ship is mentioned in the 1603 inventory when Elizabeth died as 500 tons with 250 mariners, 30 gunners and 70 soldiers. MRP.

1) 13 October 1601. Orders to transport 300 men and winter apparel to English troops in Ireland. The apparel list as follows: A cassock of broad cloth, a pair of venetians, a doublet of canvas, a hat cap, 2 shirts of linen cloth, 2 bands of Holland cloth, 3 pairs of Carlisle socks and 3 pair of boots. *APC-V.32, 274–275.*

2) 23 September 1601. Instructions from the queen that Sir Richard Leveson would command a fleet of ships in a response to the continual possible threats from the king of Spain. This ship and others would patrol the coast and prevent or defeat any forces against England. *CSP-D, (1601–1603), 101.*

3) 9 July 1602. This ship was under the command of Sir William Monson, vice-admiral of the fleet for the coast of Spain and received the same instructions as the *Adventure*. *CSP-D, (1601–1603), 220–221.*

Depiction of the Defiance in 1588.

Baring-Gould, S. *The Western Antiquary. Plymouth, 1889.*

Desire.

1) 1 July 1593. The council received a letter informing them that this ship and the *Black pinnace* were to pass the Straits of Magellan into the South Sea, "where prizes of great value and riches are often times taken". If the ship was to return with valuable items, Thomas Cavendishe was ordered "to board her and see her hatches nailed down and a just inventory taken." *APC-V.24, 346.* *[See image, next page]*

The Desire. *One of Cavendish's ships.*

[A New and Complete Collection of Voyages and Travels. London, 1778]

Diamond. Of Dartmouth.

This ship is mentioned in the 1588 inventory against the Spanish armada as 60 tons with Robert Holland as captain of 40 mariners. *MRP.*

1) 17 March 1579. Orders to release this ship and prepare to sail. *APC-V.11, 419.*

2) 16 March 1602. This ship with three other English ships has chased 4 Portuguese ships. One ship surrendered and was left to drift without a crew. The fight with the other three ships lasted two to three hours then all captured. *CSP-D, (1601–1603), 163.*

Diamond. Of Lynn.

Records suggest this was a bark.

1) 9 January 1579. Orders to release this ship loaded in the Isle of Garnesy with wheat and prepared for sail. *APC-V.11, 357.*

Diana.

This ship is mentioned in the 1588 inventory against the Spanish armada as 80 tons. *MRP.*

1) 5 September 1589. Inventory of a cargo received in Middleborough of 58 sacks of wheat and 130 sacks of rye. *APC-V.18, 82.*

2) 25 April 1601. Dispute over the ownership of this ship after it returned with a cargo of fish. Request that the council settle the matter. No further mention in archives if this was resolved. *APC-V.31, 297.*

Discharge.

1) 16 June 1591. Henry Sackford requested allowances for lending certain things such as victuals, cordage, wood, and sails to the Venetian ship the *Aragusy* brought into Plymouth. Furthermore, sought pay for the crew's time. *APC-V.21, 207.*

Discovery.

1) 10 April 1602. Court minutes of the East India Company mentions "the company being moved with great hope that there is a possibility of discovery of a nearer passage into the East Indies by seas by the way of the north-west, if the same were undertaken by a man of knowledge in navigation and of a resolution to put in execution all possibility of industry and valor of the attaining of so inestimable benefit to his native country and his own perpetual honor". George Weymouth was, in their opinion, the best man for the job and he was given two ships, this one and the *Godspeed*, and victualled for 16 months. He was to sail to Greenland then through to Northern China. *CSP-C, 1513–1616, 132–133.*

2) 30 October 1602. Examination of the master of this ship regarding the return of captain Waymouth "without any discovery performed". The boatswain, gunner, carpenter, and others revealed that the minister Cartwright was the reason the ship retuned. *CSP-C, 1513–1616, 136.*

Dolphin.

This ship is mentioned in the 1588 inventory against the Spanish armada as 160 tons with William Hares as captain of 70 mariners. *MRP.*

1) 30 March 1592. A matter between merchants of Holland and Zealand and this ship was settled with the merchants to be paid a small amount of money. This ship was free to depart. *APC-V.22, 381–3812.*

2) 11 August 1596. Complaint from Patrick Strange, an Irish merchant, that he was robbed at sea by this ship and cargo of seeds, salt, hides and *aqua vitae* were sold. Seeking restitution. *APC-V.26, 112,148.*

3) 9 September 1596. The council determined that no fault was found of William Harvey, master of this ship. *APC-V.26, 160.*

4) 16 May 1597. A complaint filed against this ship for an act of piracy on the *John* of Waterford. Arrest warrant issued for all that participated. *APC-V.27, 116.*

5) 26 January 1598. An Irish merchant was seeking restitution for the stolen goods of the 16 May 1597 complaint. Many of the plundered goods turned up in several towns in Ireland. *APC-V.28, 282.*

Dominic.

1) 16 June 1578. As soon as this ship returned to port, the cargo would be inspected by merchants to determine that no illegal cargo to Ireland would be found. *APC-V.10, 257.*

2) 15 January 1581. While at Bristol, there appears to be a release from her majesty's duty and could be employed if a merchant needs it. *APC-V.12, 312.*

Dragon.

This ship is mentioned in a 1546 inventory as 140 tons with 98 mariners and 12 gunners.

1) 16 June 1578. As soon as this ship returned to port, the cargo would be inspected by merchants to determine that no illegal cargo to Ireland would be found. *APC-V.10, 257.*

2) 7 March 1580. Loaded for Cades (Cadiz), Spain, certain legalities arose holding the ship in port until settled. *APC-V.11, 413.*

3) 15 May 1582. The record indicates that the ship was carrying Spanish and Dutch merchandise and "cast away by tempest". This could be interpreted as the ship was lost. But, future records exist. The merchants sought restitution for their lost goods stolen by people from a nearby town. *APC-V.13, 418–419.*

4) 5 June 1582. The courts settled the matter and restitution was paid. *APC-V.13, 437–438.*

Dreadnaught.

Records indicate that this was 400 tons. At the time of Elizabeth's ascension, the crew complement was: 140 mariners, 20 gunners and 80 soldiers. *MPR.*

1) 22 August 1576. Orders to Captain Biston to proceed to guard the passage of the Narrow Seas. *APC-V.9, 193.*

2) 30 July 1576. Orders that Mr. Biston was appointed captain and to prepare himself to take charge of the ship by 10 August. Furthermore, he was to report to the new admiral Mr. William Holstock. *APC-V.9, 175*.

3) 26 August 1576. Orders to George Biston, currently at sea, to pick up and transport her majesty's ambassador to France as soon as possible. *APC-V.9, 194*.

4) 20 September 1576. Instruction to Captain Biston 'for the wasting of the merchants adventurers to Hamburg. Furthermore, to assign a replacement captain to the *Handmaiden*. *APC-V.9, 207*.

5) 14 August 1580. Mariners, gunners, and soldiers assigned to this ship were supplied with hose (stockings), shoes, shirts, caps, canvas for breeches and doublets, cotton, and other provisions in preparation for a voyage to Ireland. *APC-V.12, 154*.

6) 23 September 1601. Instructions from the queen that Sir Richard Leveson will command a fleet of ships in a response to the continual possible threats from the king of Spain. This ship and with others would patrol the coast and prevent or defeat any forces against England. *CSP-D, (1601–1603), 101*.

7) 9 July 1602. This ship was under the command of Sir William Monson, vice-admiral of the fleet for the coast of Spain and received the same instructions as the *Adventure*. *CSP-D, (1601–1603), 220–221*.

Dudley.

This ship is mentioned as the *Galleon Dudley* in the 1588 inventory against the Spanish armada as 250 tons with James Erizey as captain of 100 mariners under the command of Sir Francis Drake. *MRP*.

1) 24 December 1590. Formal charges filed by William and Martin Bond and 'one widow Smith' against John Clark who plundered the cargo of the *White Horse* laden with salt and money. They crew thought that it had sailed from Spain, and "very dangerously shot and hurt the said ship and men, took away and rifled the said money and victuals" including cables, anchors, and other furniture belonging to the ship then sank it off the coast. An additional comment that a complaint about the insolence of the clerk was mentioned. *APC-V.20, 158–159*.

2) 6 September 1592. Captain Middleton returned from Brazil with a cargo of sugar and other merchandise into Portsmouth. A challenge was made to some part of the prize by the Earl of Southampton. The items were held under lock until disposition was arrived at. It is possible this was another ship of the same name, or it was not wrecked as of 24 December 1590. *APC-V.23, 176–177*.

Due Repulse.

This ship is mentioned in the 1603 inventory when Elizabeth died as 700 tons with 230 mariners, 30 gunners and 90 soldiers. *MRP.*

1) 23 September 1601. Instructions from the queen that Sir Richard Leveson would command a fleet of ships in a response to the continual possible threats from the king of Spain. This ship with others would patrol the coast and prevent or defeat any forces against England. *CSP-D, (1601–1603), 101.*

2) 8 March 1602. This ship was reported at anchor in Plymouth Sound and ready for sea. *CSP-D, (1601–1603), 161.*

3) 29 July 1602. Curiously, this document reads very similar to 30 October 1592 entry of the *Garland.* Three ships had received the cargo of a great carrack and the remainder was in three merchant ships. The ballast from the carrack was also unloaded and inspected for hidden treasures. The carrack and these three ships were in Plymouth. The carrack was to be held until her majesty determined how to dispose of it. *CSP-D, (1601–1603), 226–227.*

4) 14 December 1602. A warrant was issued to the treasurer of the navy for the estimated repairs of this ship. *CSP-D, (1601–1603), 269.*

Eagle.

1) 10 March 1599. Orders to John Hawkins to appear before the council on charges of transporting deserters from Ireland without permission. *APC-V.30, 163.*

Edward. Of Bristol.

Records suggest that this was a merchant ship at 160 ton.

1) 23 November 1552. This ship apparently captured a French ship and the Privy Council requested that the crew be set at liberty.

Edward. Of Southampton.

1) 23 December 1564. Warrant to Captain Edward Cook, master Thomas West to appear before her majesty's council. *APC-V.7, 180.*

Edward. South Shields.

1) 26 November 1565. Description of the inhabitants of the town and three ships, this being one that was used as a fishing vessel. Was owned by William Lawson. *CSP-D-Addenda. 573.*

Edward Bonaventure.

This ship is mentioned in the 1588 inventory against the Spanish armada as 300 tons and James Lancaster as captain of 120 mariners. *MRP.*

1) September (?) 1555. Merchant's attorneys could only prove that only 7000 Sterling was received for this ship, which was worth £20,000. *CSP-D-Addenda, 440.*

2) 8 March 1569. Note of all things to be provided for the fitting out of this ship. No additional information is shared. *CSP-D-1547–1580.*

3) 10 November 1577. Letter to the officers of the port of London to release this ship and allow it to travel to Spain. *APC-V.10, 81.*

4) 29 August 1580. The crew was charged with piracy while in Spain. Fines paid by members of the crew had caused their wives to be unable to pay rent and feared being thrown in the street. Suggested that their rents be paid until their husbands return. *APC-V.12, 183–184.*

5) 6 November 1580. To be loaded for Levant France should a merchant desire their ship to serve them. *APC-V.12, 258–259.*

6) 1 October 1581. Martin Frobisher wrote to the Earl of Leicester to inform him of certain matters including the sale of this ship to Lord of Oxford for 1500 Sterling, but he wanted 1800. *CSP-C, 1513–1616, 67.*

7) 2 June 1582–8 February 1583. A journal was recorded for this ship's voyage to China and the East Indies, but a fire in the British Museum destroyed or damaged much of the log. Pieces do exist and some better accounts have survived such as that in *The Third and Last Volume of the Voyages, Navigation, Traffics, Discoveries, of the English Nation.* London, 1600, Richard Hakluyt. *CSP-C, 1513–1616.*

8) 10 August 1589. A letter describing divers goods of 'good value' that were stolen by John Bridgeway, John Hall and James Morries after the ship arrived from Portugal in the Thames River. A request was made to imprison anyone determined responsible for the thefts. *APC-V.18, 28–29.*

9) 2 May 1591. Complaints by a London upholsterer for the recovery of goods plundered in the sea near Warmouth while on this ship. *APC-V.21, 81.*

10) 29 May 1597. Request for payment for re-victualing for 129 men taken on her return voyage. The editor indicates this was Sir Frances Drake's last voyage. *APC-V.27, 157.*

Edward Constance.

1) 6 September 1592. Warrant was issued for the apprehension of Captain Edward Glemham for plundering a Venetian ship the gallian *Maniceli* and for bringing the plundered cargo into England. Peter Houghton had made an offer to purchase the *Edward Constance* and should he do so, was required to pay the Venetian restitution. *APC-V.23, 180.*

Eleanor. Of Weymouth.

1) March of 1603 mentions that this ship was plundered and many crew members beaten by 7 French fishing ships returning from Newfoundland. *CSP-D, (1601–1603), 305.*

Elephant.

1) 8 December 1588. Petition originally filed on 12 November to be awarded the sale of this ship to French merchants John Villaunce and Peter Blewell. The sale would include all ordnance, munitions, tackle, and furniture. *APC-V.16, 384–385.*

Ellen.

Records suggest this was 120 tons.

1) 29 September 1588. Within the letter is a description of the high cost of supplying this ship with necessary supplies including munitions yet were inadequate for the service it was called into for several months against the Spanish. *APC-V.16, 294.*

Elizabeth.

Records suggest this was 120 tons.

1) 3 July 1559. Queen Elizabeth was reported to have watched this ship, in her own name, launch. *MRP, 21.*

2) 27 March 1560. Orders to prepare to sail. *APC-V.7, 73.*

3) 20 April 1560. Embargo removed and prepared to sail. *APC-V.7, 90.*

4) 29 November 1573. Released from arrest. *APC-V.8, 151.*

5) 29 October 1577. Lancelott Greenwell, pirate, was apprehended while in command of this ship and the cargo was distributed to those affected. *APC-V.10, 71.*

6) 13 December 1578. This ship was used by Sir Francis Drake in his important expedition into the South Seas. *NHGB-11.*

7) 27 February 1580. License to depart from the Thames River to Newcastle. *APC-V.11, 401.*

8) 8 May 1580. Released to the sea.

9) 5 September 1589. Inventory of the received cargo of 62 quarters of wheat. *APC-V.18, 82.*

10) 13 June 1591. William Hall claimed rights to the goods taken while they were in the Gibraltar Straits. Hall filed a bond for 10,000 Sterling while they were in Exeter. *APC-V.21, 189–190.*

11) 1 April 1593. A complaint was filed against the Captain John Petite, master, and mariners of this ship for plundering a cargo from an Italian ship.

Taken were 700 barrels of red herrings, 315 pigs of lead, 30 barrels of tin, one hogshead of sundry wares and a barrel of starch. *APC-V24, 156.*

12) 5 April 1593. This letter is related to 1 April 1593. But I will admit it is a confusing letter. Basically, it states that 6 ships of Newcastle attacked the *Elizabeth* of London. A mention of a French pirate that took the items to Newhaven was possible. A single note indicates 'Cruisers from Havre de Grace' which is near Normandy. *APC-V.24, 164–165.*

13) 24 April 1597. Orders to store victuals and prepare to be at sea for 28 days or 3 months for 500 men. *APC-V.27, 65.*

14) 22 May 1597. Merchant complaints about Oliver Heard, master of this ship, who "took upon himself to voyage into dangerous and tempestuous weather from Barnstable to Bristol with sugar," and lost much of the cargo. Merchants seeking restitution. *APC-V.27, 140.*

15) 4 August 1599. Members of this crew took parcels of armor sent from Ireland. Orders to apprehend the ship when it arrived in Southampton. *APC-V.29, 742.*

16) 15 July 1600. Orders to transport 2000 men and 130 horses to Ireland.

17) 29 November 1601. Request for payment of ship's services on the coast of Ireland for 6 weeks and 3 days. *APC-V.32, 388.*

Elizabeth. Of Lowestoft.
1) 16 August 1556. Transaction regarding a cargo of 19 casks of herrings to be delivered at Poole. *CSP-D-Addenda. 442.*

Elizabeth Constance.
1) 19 June 1601. Record indicated that Jonas Bonner was master. *APC-V.31, 442.*

Elizabeth Jonas.
This ship is mentioned in a 1575 inventory as 900 tons with 300 mariners, 50 gunners and 200 soldiers. *NHGB.*

1) 15 November 1597. Orders for timber "for the repairing and new building" of this ship that was in drydock at Woolwich, Kent. Her majesty's master ship builder Joseph Pett expressed an urgent need for timber only to be transported over land to make repairs as quickly as possible. *APC-V.28, 120–121.*

Emanuel.
1) 25 March 1579. Letter to Captain Richard Newton regarding a load of ore brought from a northwest voyage. *APC-V.11, 89.*

2) 18 October 1580. License granted to travel to Spain, but first, must offload any cargo not destined for that voyage. *APC-V.12, 235.*

Endeavor.

1) 28 February 1595. Problems obtaining funds for this ship in the town of Exeter. *APC-V.25, 252–253.*

2) 21 March 1595. Continued appeal for funds. Requested seeking funds from wealthier residents. *APC-V.25, 298–299.*

3) 6 September 1596. This ship had returned to Portsmouth with several pieces of ordnance seized at Calais. The council wanted to ensure they were to be used in her majesty's service. *APC-V.26, 142.*

4) 12 July 1597. Request for unpaid wages for the crew for their service. *APC-V.27, 287–288.*

5) 24 November 1598. Complaint that accounts remain unpaid. The letter also expressed the numerous times wages were requested for 5 months of service. *APC-V.29, 304.*

Evan.

1) 26 September 1576. Orders from England to the master Peter Grissel regarding a load of fish from Newfoundland pirated by John Callis about Belisle and carried to the port of Cardiff in Wales. *APC-V.9, 209.*

Exchange.

1) 21May 1601. Service on the Cadis voyage continues to remain unpaid. Requesting payment. *APC-V.31, 367.*

2) 21 June 1601. Additional letters requesting payment for services. *APC-V.31, 449–450.*

3) 8 July 1601. Additional letters requesting payment for services. *APC-V.32, 31.*

Expedition. Of Dartmouth.
Records suggest this was a bark of 30 tons.
1) 17 March 1579. Orders to release this ship and prepare to sail. *APC-V.11, 419.*

Falcon.

This ship is mentioned in a 1548 inventory as 83 tons with 55 soldiers and mariners, 4 brass ordnance and 22 iron ordnance. At the time of Mary's ascension, the crew complement was: 6 hackbutters, 16 soldiers, 54 mariners and 10 gunners. At the time of Elizabeth's ascension, the crew complement was: 60 mariners, 10 gunners and 20 soldiers. *MRP.*

1) 6 August 1554. John Malvin was captain and off the coast of Norfolk and Suffolk apprehending a pirate Lightmaker. *APC-V.5, 55.*

2) 17 November 1554. Serving the king and queen in the narrow seas for 2 months and three weeks. *APC-V.5, 82.*

3) 22 January 1557. Orders to remain at Plymouth until the queen needed it. *APC-V.6, 247.*

4) 11 April 1558. Departed London but should not have. It appears his orders were incorrect. *APC-V.6, 310.*

5) 29 July 1563. Excerpt from a letter by Captain Basing of the *Swallow* that he heard from a passing crayer that 2 or 3 men had been shot as this ship was leaving Portsmouth and the 1200 men and victuals in that convoy before Newhaven. *CSP-D-Addenda, 539.*

6) 19 June 1601. Record indicated that John Oliver was master. *APC-V.31, 442.*

Flower of Comfort. Of London.
1) 26 May 1597. License for William Tehan to transport 600 quarters of grain whereof 60 quarters is wheat; the rest is rye, into Dublin. *APC-V.27, 141.*

2) 24 June 1601. Master Peter Oliver. This ship was loaded and ready to transport merchandise to Hamburg. *APC-V.31, 451.*

Flying Dragon. Of Bristol.
1) 5 June 1598. Complaint and warrant issued for all individuals responsible on this ship for piracy committed on the *Unicorn* of Denmark that was employed for transporting Spanish and Portuguese prisoners to Lisbon for an exchange of English prisoners, but encountered this ship and was plundered. No mention of the fate of the prisoners. *APC-V.28, 485–486.*

Flying Hart. Of Ostend.
1) 13 October 1554. The French captured this ship in Camber. It would appear the French ships were out of Dieppe.

2) 18 October 1574. It would appear this ship was captured by Richard Fitzgarret. *APC-V.8, 301.*

3) 19 October 1575. While transporting English merchant goods, a complaint was filed with the council that he was chased by pirates, and they defended themselves. *APC-V.9, 29–30.*

4) 16 August 1590. Captain Henry Bellingham ordered the release of this ship, and it was brought into Dover where 7 bags of Spanish reals and other merchandise were discovered and that the captain claimed he 'received no direction in that behalf.' Seeking restitution. *APC-V.19, 390.*

Foresight.

This ship is mentioned in a 1578 inventory as 300 tons with 120 mariners, 20 gunners and 60 soldiers. *NHGB.* At the time of Elizabeth's ascension, the crew complement was: 120 mariners, 20 gunners and 60 soldiers. As of 1588 this had 160 men. *MRP.*

1) 28 October 1575. Henry Palmer was to assume captain and to prepare himself to serve her majesty as soon as possible. *APC-V.9, 38.*

2) 30 July 1576. Orders that Mr. John Cobham was appointed captain and to prepare himself to take charge of the ship by 10 August. Furthermore, he was to report to the new admiral Mr. William Holstock and this ship was to prepare to escort 2 English ships from Spain. *APC-V.9, 175.*

3) 30 September 1577. Orders to receive victuals for 6 weeks and to return to sea as soon as possible. *APC-V.10, 42.*

4) 18 October 1577. Orders to Captain Ellice to set sail to apprehend certain pirates. *APC-V.10, 59.*

5) 11 October 1579. Orders to load victuals while at Waterford. *APC-V.11,283.*

6) 26 April 1579. Orders to set sail for the apprehension of pirates. *APC-V.11, 109.*

7) 10 October 1579. Captain Pierce had returned from Ireland and was in Portsmouth waiting for victuals. Allowed 21 days for victuals. *APC-V.11, 302–303.*

8) 7 December 1587. Orders to remain at sea in a 'warlike manner' for six weeks, beginning 14 December to 23 January. *APC-V.15, 293.*

9) 5 May 1587. Orders to remain at sea from 23 March until 15 June. *APC-V.15, 108.*

10) 18 September 1588. Proposed expedition into Ireland and the provision of victuals. *APC-V.16, 280.*

11) 17 September 1592. Complaint filed by Master John Castillon of the French ship the *Salamander* of piracy by Captain Francis Parker of this ship and removed the cargo of salt, sugar, wine, oil, and other merchandise. *APC-V.23, 200–201.*

12) 19 September 1592. Notice that the payment of mariner's wages came from the sales of iron and sugar taken from recent prizes. *APC-V.23, 204.*

13) 23 October 1592. Notice that lieutenant John Scose died 2 days after the ship returned to port. Two stones found in his possessions are mentioned among other items from the great Carrack. *APC-V.23, 265.*

Fortune. Dover.

Records suggest this was 50 tons.

1) 4 March 1579. Captain was ordered to depart for Lisbon. *APC-V.11,408.*

2) 8 May 1580. Orders to release the ship for a voyage to Elbing Poland. *APC-V.12, 6.*

3) 16 August 1590. Report that Captain Bodley had plundered a French ship the *Moon* of wine, brass, pans, honey, soap, and other merchandise while on a voyage to Ireland. Seeking restitution. *APC-V.19, 392.*

4) 22 March 1597. Orders to transport 700 quarters of wheat to Carlingford Ireland for her majesty's army there. *APC-V.28, 369–370.*

Fox.
Records suggest this was 20 tons.

1) 20 March 1558. Orders to prepare to sail to the Low Countries. *APC-V.7, 69.*

2) 20 March 1579. To depart to Flushing with beer pretending to have fish for a cargo. *APC-V.11, 424.*

Frances. Of Calm.

1) 23 December 1575. A letter mentioning the theft of merchandise by French pirates. *APC-V.9, 63.*

Gabriel.

1) September (?) 1577. This ship and the *Aid* arrived from their first voyage to the northwest parts at Bristol and the council suggested Martin Frobisher to unload the ore there and keep it safe in the castle. The *Michael* arrived in the Thames and the ore was to be unloaded and kept safe under guard. The council expressed a strong desire "on the speedy melting of the ore." *CSP-C, 1513–1616. 20–21.*

2) 17 October 1577. Letter concerning the payment of wages to soldiers and mariners of this ship and of the victuals that would not keep and the ship to be moored and tack undisturbed. *APC-V10, 56.*

3) 25 November 1577. 16 tons of ore were unloaded from this ship and 124 tons from the *Aid* into the safety of Bristol Castle. *CSP-C, 1513–1616, 24.*

4) 25 March 1578. Instructions to Martin Frobisher to begin preparations for another voyage her majesty called *meta incognita* (unknown destination) to the Northwest parts and Cathey (North China). He was to acquire 90 mariners for this ship, the *Aid, Michael,* and *Judith.* Furthermore, to hire 130 pioneers and 50 soldiers for 6 additional vessels. Victuals for 90 persons for 7 months to be loaded and to prepare to sail before 1 May and return with 800 tons of ore. Additional note indicated this crew was to include 40 mariners, gunners, shipwrights, carpenters, 30 soldiers, 30 pioneers with victuals for 18 months. *CSP-C, 1513–1616. 35–36.*

5) 1 June 1578. Orders and articles to be observed by the fleet from Captain Frobisher and delivered to every ship under his command. "To banish swearing, dice, cards, playing and all filthy talk, and to serve God twice a day and to clear the glass every night according to the old order of England. Signals in case of fogs, trumpets, drums, etc. to be sounded, or contrary winds. Watch words 'Before the world was God' the answer 'After God came Christ his son.'" *CSP-C, 1513–1516, 37.*

Galeasse. Of Southampton.
Records suggest this was 500 tons.
1) 8 May 1580. Released to the sea.
2) 6 September 1591. This ship was charged with piracy of the capturing two French barques and taking their cargos, one with 35 tons of salt and the other with corn. Seeking restitution. *APC-V.21, 427.*

Galley.
This ship is mentioned as the Galley *Bonavolia* in the 1588 inventory against the Spanish armada with William Boroughs as captain of 250 mariners. *MRP.*
1) 10 September 1588. Orders to the captain for the discharge of his men and to see that the ship is looked after and laid up. *APC-V.16, 275.*

Garland.
This ship is mentioned in a 1603 inventory at the death of Elizabeth as 700 tons with 190 mariners, 30 gunners and 80 soldiers. *MRP.*
1) 30 October 1592. This ship was one of three that received the cargo from the 'great Carrack'. Notice was given to this ship to take care while transporting the cargo along the Thames River. There is mention that some items went missing from the Carrack before being transferred. *APC-V.23, 275.*
2) 17 September 1600. This ship was employed to transport items to Ireland to support English troops. The ship received additional orders to serve for an additional 3 months. *APC-V.30, 617.*
3) 15 March 1601. Orders to prepare this ship with victuals and 134 men to serve on the coast of England for 4 months. *APC-V.31, 225–226.*
4) 13 October 1601. Orders to transport 200 men and winter apparel to English troops in Ireland. The apparel list as follows: A cassock of broad cloth, a pair of venetians, a doublet of canvas, a hat cap, 2 shirts of linen cloth, 2 bands of Holland cloth, 3 pair of Carlisle socks, 3 pair of boots. *APC-V.32, 274–275.*
5) 29 July 1602. Curiously, this document reads very similar to 30 October 1592 entry of the *Garland*. Three ships had received the cargo of a

great carrack and the remainder is in three merchant ships. The ballast from the carrack is also being unloaded and inspected for hidden treasures. The carrack and these three ships were in Plymouth. The carrack was to be held until her majesty determined how to dispose of it. *CSP-D, 1601–1603, 226–227.*

6) 14 December 1602. A warrant was issued to the treasurer of the navy for the estimated repairs of this ship. *CSP-D, 1601–1603, 269.*

George Anderson.
Records suggest that this was a Sixth-Rate 50-ton Bark.
1) 28 May 1550. The Privy Council ordered this ship be released. *APC-V.3, 38.*

2) 20 March 1558. Orders to prepare to sail to the Low Countries. *APC-V.7, 69.*

George Bewicke.
1) 20 March 1558. Orders to prepare to sail to the Low Countries. *APC-V.7, 69.*

George Bonaventure.
1) 15 January 1586. An unfinished letter regarding a cargo of sugar from the Barbery. *APC-V.14, 287.*

George Noble. Of London.
1) 31 August 1591. This ship attempted to assist the *Revenge* even though she had received several shots through her hull. *SFLB, 30.*

Gertrude. London.
1) 19 September 1591. A request to cast 8 demi-culverins and 9 sacres for the furnishing of the recently built ship in the east parts of London. *APC-V.21, 460.*

Gift of God.
This ship is mentioned in the 1588 inventory against the Spanish armada as 180 tons with Thomas Luntlowe as captain of 80 mariners and fitted in London. *MRP.*

1) 4 March 1587. The Privy Council received a complaint of plundering by a ship called the *Merchant Royal* seeking restitution of the merchandise sold to local inhabitants. *APC-V.15, 413.*

2) 14 July 1588. Conflicting directions for this ship after returning from Civitavecchia Rome with a cargo of alum and other merchandise. Because the cargo was hazardous, it was determined to bring the ship into London. *APC-V.16, 158.*

3) 22 September 1589. Complaint filed from the merchants of London that the cargo aboard this ship was appropriated by the Duke of Mercury while in Brittany for his own use and wanted restitution. *APC-V.18, 140–141*.

4) 1595. Sometime during this year, Henry Carpenter purchased this ship from Dennis Rowse. *APC-V.28, 201*.

5) 1 May 1596. An appeal was filed against the French decision regarding the plundering of this ship's cargo by a French ship while voyaging from Newfoundland to St. Mallows laden with fish. The French indicated this was a Spanish prize. *APC-V.27, 82*.

6) 9 November 1600. This ship was transporting winter apparel for English soldiers in Ireland when the ship developed a leak and was repaired, but then lost wind which caused a delay. The council indicated that they had not heard if the ship arrived in Ireland. *APC-V.30, 765–766*.

7) 15 November 1600. The council indicated that no information is known if the ship arrived. *APC-V.30, 769*.

Godspeed.

1) 10 April 1602. Court minutes of the East India Company mentions "the company being moved with great hope that there is a possibility of discovery of a nearer passage into the East Indies by seas by the way of the north-west, if the same were undertaken by a man of knowledge in navigation and of a resolution to put in execution all possibility of industry and valor of the attaining of so inestimable benefit to his native country and his own perpetual honor." George Weymouth was in their opinion the best man for the job and given two ships, this one and the *Discovery* and victualled for 16 months. He was to sail to Greenland then through to Northern China. *CSP-C, 1513–1616, 132–133*.

2) 30 October 1602. Examination of the master of this ship regarding the return of Captain Waymouth "without any discovery performed". It was confessed that the minister Cartwright was the reason the ship returned. *CSP-C, 1513–1616, 136*.

Golden Hand.

This ship is mentioned in the 1588 inventory against the Spanish armada as 50 tons with Thomas Flemming as captain of 30 men serving under Sir Francis Drake. *MRP*.

1) 17 August 1570. Orders to release this ship. *APC-V.7, 383*.

2) 22 October 1591. This ship captured the French ship the *Catalina de St. Vincent*. Restitution was requested by the French for the return or compensation for the munitions, furniture and cargo taken. *APC-V.22, 35*.

Golden Lion. Middleborough.

This ship is mentioned in the 1588 inventory against the Spanish armada as 500 tons with Thomas Howard as captain of 250 mariners under the command of Charles Lord Howard of Effingham. *MRP.*

1) 12 August 1593. The council addressed an issue this ship from November and December 1592, regarding when it hit the Goodwin Sands. Loaded with packs of wax, linen cloth, sails, grogram's and other merchandise, and its cargo was plundered by local inhabitants. Seeking restitution. *APC-V.24, 456–457.*

Golden Noble.

Records suggest this was 100 tons.

1) 10 November 1577. Letter to the officers of the port of London to release this ship and allow it to travel to Spain. *APC-V.10, 81.*

2) 2 March 1579. Released to carry wheat to Portugal. *APC-V.11, 424.*

Golden Royal.

1) 30 March 1589. The letter described that Amias Preston had an agreement with Sir Barnard Drake to sail on an adventure to New Foundland. But Sir Drake died and Amias hoped to begin the voyage with his son John Drake. *APC-V.17, 119.*

Good Savior.

1) 26 May 1601. Request for payment for supplying victuals for voyages to Ireland. *APC-V.31, 380.*

Grace Elliot.

1) 18 October 1570. The council addressed a grievance regarding spoiled wine this ship held. *APC-V.7, 392.*

Grace of God. Of Southampton.

This ship is mentioned in the 1588 inventory against the Spanish armada as 50 tons with William Fordred as captain of 30 mariners. This ship was classified under the 'coasters'. *MRP.*

1) 27 March 1559. Orders to prepare to sail. *APC-V.7, 73.*

2) 22 April 1574. It would appear this ship was captured by a Captain Calles and brought to Wales to have all the merchandise sold in Bristol. *APC-V.8, 230.*

3) 22 December 1577. This ship was ordered to depart London to Rye, East Sussex. *APC-V.10, 123.*

4. 20 March 1579. At that time was at Falmouth. *APC-V.11, 424.*

5) 6 October 1588. A request for money to pay for this ship's service and furnishing, victualing and the employment of mariners for 5 months against the Spanish. *APC-V.16, 304.*

6) 14 March 1596. Captain George Watson had spent time in a Spanish prison perhaps for plundering of a Spanish cargo. He filed a complaint with the council upon his release and was seeking a claim to the prize of goods, money, bullion, and jewels. *APC-V.25, 290.*

Grand Anglais.

1) 27 March 1558. Ordered recall to Bristol. *APC-V.6, 294.*

Great Harry.

1) 23 May 1560. Very short account that this ship and three others were preparing for sail. *CSP-D-Addenda, 502.*

Great Susan.

1) 8 February 1593. Mr. Paul Bayning of London requested payment for his employment by Sir Walter Raleigh. *APC-V.24, 51.*

Green Dragon.

1) 12 August 1579. At Feversham. Claimed to have been plundered and would require further review of the cargo. *APC-V.11, 233–234.*

Greyhound.

This ship is mentioned in a 1546 inventory as 200 tons with 124 mariners and 15 gunners. At the time of Mary's ascension, the crew complement was: 10 hackbutters, 20 soldiers, 84 mariners and 16 gunners. *MRP.*

1) 11 March 1551. Orders to prepare ship for sea. *APC-V.3, 503.*

2) 17 July 1553. The captain was reported as Gilbert Grise. He was to carry many pieces of ordnance, shot and powder. *APC-V.4, 295.*

3) 11 January 1553. This ship was ordered to be ready to sail to Spain. Mention of 26 January 1554. *APC-V.4, 383.*

4) 25 July 1553. Ordered to prepare to sail to the narrow seas before Dover. *APC-V.4, 417.*

5) 17 November 1554. Received 'five demi barrels of serpentine powder.' *APC-V.5, 86*.

6) 3 July 1558. It would appear this ship took another ship called the *Johnson*, and all her goods. *APC-V.6, 338*.

7) 10 August 1589. A letter describing the theft of 'good quality of goods' by a man Atkinson and Hews after the ship arrived from Portugal in the Thames River. A request had been made to imprison anyone determined responsible for the thefts. *APC-V.18, 28–29*.

8) 5 September 1589. Attempt to recover 3 pieces of brass ordnance and other merchandise taken during the Portuguese voyage.

Griffin.
This ship is mentioned in the 1588 inventory against the Spanish armada as 200 tons with William Hawkins as captain of 100 mariners. This ship served under Sir Francis Drake. *MRP*.

1) 16 February 1580. This ship had plundered a French ship belonging to John Baptista de Sambitores and Alonso de Basurto. *PAC-V.12, 332*.

Guyana.
1) 18 June 1600. Complaint filed by the French of pirating their vessel the *Marie*. The council addressed a question regarding the legitimacy of the cargo taken as lawful prize. *APC-V.30, 388–389*.

Hampton.
Records indicate this was a barque.
1) 17 November 1591. The owner of the French ship *Nicholas* had sought restitution for the loss of a cargo of Newfoundland fish by Captain William Tokins. *APC-V.22, 66*.

Handmaid.
The name of this ship turns up twice in the 1588 inventory against the Spanish armada. The first entry is 85 tons with Christopher Pitt as captain of 56 mariners. The second entry is of 75 tons with John Gatenbury as captain of 35 mariners. *MRP*.

1) 30 July 1576. Orders to captain William Biston to proceed to guard the passage of the Narrow Seas. *APC-V.9, 178*.

2) 20 September 1576. Instruction to Captain George Biston to assign the replacement captain young William Biston because the captain of this ship was sick. *APC-V.9, 207*.

3) 30 July 1576. This ship was to prepare to travel to the Narrow Seas and escort 2 English ships from Spain. *APC-V.9, 178.*

4) 4 November 1576. Orders to proceed to Ireland and to add 30 mariners to the crew. *APC-V.9, 226.*

5) 1 March 1579. While at Plymouth, Captain Alderman Pullison requested permission to continue to Bordeaux, France. *APC-V.11, 403.*

6) 29 March 1579. Captain George Thornton was ordered to Ireland and to be loaded with provisions for such. *APC-V.11, 90.*

7) 28 January 1581. The following is a rare account of a refit requested by Captain Thornton for this ship because of a long service on the coast of Ireland.

> Main mast, mizzen mast, bowsprit and two top masts with yards
> for them all.
> Canvas for foresail, spritsail, mizzen and two top sails.
> 'Martin' and twine to make the sails.
> 'Ratlin to ratle all the shrowdes'.
> One cable of five inches compass (diameter) and 100 fathoms long
> for buoy ropes.
> One cable for the boat rope and for main tacks of 7 inches
> compass (diameter) and 100 fathoms long.
> Two warping hawsers and five inches compass (diameter) and 70
> fathoms log a piece.
> Cable of all sorts for new rig the said ship one weight.
> Three cables, whereof two of 9 inches compass, and one of 9
> inches and a half.
> Pitch, six barrels.
> Tar, six barrels.
> One hundred deal bourdes.
> Owners fower dozen.
> Compasses, six.
> Running glasses, twelve.
> A new flag.
> A new ancient of boulter. *APC-V.13, 314–315.*

8) 28 May 1597. This ship plundered cargo from a French ship from St. Malo, France, while at sea. The French seeking the arrest of all involved including John Sheares who was captain. *APC-V.27, 150.*

Hare.
This ship is mentioned in a 1546 inventory as 15 tons with 28 mariners and 2 gunners. *MRP.*

1) Reported as a pinnace. Orders to deliver her to Sir Hugh Pawlet on 31 March 1551. *APC-V.3, 247.*

2) 24 June 1589. Requested permission to be released from port and begin her voyage perhaps to the Low Countries. *APC-V.17, 308.*

3) 30 March 1592. A matter between merchants of Holland and Zealand and this ship had been settled with the merchants to be paid a small amount of money. This ship was free to depart. *APC-V.22, 381–382.*

4) 30 January 1596. Orders to prepare to sail with grain for Dublin, Ireland or other port if weather was bad. *APC-V.26, 452.*

Hart, of Bristol.

This ship is mentioned in a 1546 inventory as 300 tons with 170 mariners and soldiers and 30 gunners. The crew at the time of Mary's ascension was 20 hackbutters, 40 soldiers, 140 mariners and 20 gunners. *MRP.*

1) Orders on 11 March 1551 to prepare ship for sea.

2) Mention of 26 January 1554.

3) 14 January 1555. Orders for the arrest of boatswain Brown and John Hurloge and to bring them to court. Accused of robbing a "Flemings hoy in Tilbery Hope." They were placed in prison. *APC-V.5, 222.*

4) 19 January 1555. Order for the arrest of Edward Foster, Master Gunner. *APC-V.5, 228.*

5) 20 April 1559. Embargo removed and to prepare to sail. *APC-V.7, 90.*

Heathen.

1) 20 November 1588. Requests for additional funds for Captain Millard to cover expenditures this ship incurred during its service. *APC-V.16, 354.*

Henri Grace a Dieu — The Great Harry

1) 27 August 1553. This ship was accidently burned while at Woolrich.

Hercules. Of Rye.

1) 22 March 1597. Orders to master John Davis to transport 700 quarters of wheat to Carlingford, Ireland for her majesty's army there. *APC-V.28, 369–370.*

Holyghost.

1) 20 April 1559. Embargo removed and to prepare to sail. *APC-V.7, 90.*

Hope.

This ship is mentioned in a 1578 inventory as 600 tons with 200 mariners, 50 gunners and 100 soldiers. *MRP.* As of 1588 Robert Cross was captain of 250 mariners. *MRP.*

1) 10 August 1563. Orders to return to the harbor of Gillingham, Kent, as soon as possible and to land men on the coast of Norfolk and Suffolk. *APC-V.7, 138.*

2) 20 March 1597. This ship with two other ships were pirated by French of cargo, tackle, and furniture. *APC-V.26, 552.*

3) 24 April 1597. Orders to store victuals for 250 men and be ready to sail. *APC-V.27, 65.*

4) 14 December 1602. A warrant was issued to the treasurer of the navy for the estimated "new building" of this ship. Considering this ship had been in service for several decades, this must be a refitting and or repair. *CSP-D, 1601–1603, 269.*

Hopewell. Dunwich.

This ship is mentioned in the 1588 inventory against the Spanish armada as 200 tons with John Marchaunt as captain of 100 mariners. *MRP.*

1) 8 February 1595. Complaint filed by a merchant in London loaded by him with corn and other merchandise in the East Countries to be unloaded in London at a value of 1600 pounds Sterling. The ship had apparently been driven on the coast of Scotland by "Contrary winds" near Orkney then plundered by an English pirate. The council did not find enough evidence to pursue the matter. *APC-V.25, 204.*

2) 25 March 1597. This ship was "to adventure a voyage of fishing and discovery into the Bay of Canada" (Newfoundland) at the island of Ramea, an island off the southern coast. *APC-V.27, 5–6.*

3) 1 November 1601. Request for payment for services of maintaining victuals for English troops in Ireland. *APC-V.32, 330.*

4) 13 May 1602. Mention of an examination of William Caverly, sailor that served on this ship. Extracted from the snippet of the original letter, it would appear he was cast on shore after being captured by Spanish galleys, taken to Cadiz, then to Maryport where he was held prisoner for 10 months, then released on 26 April. He received passage on a Lubec ship and then cast on shore in England. *CSP-D, 1601–1603, 189.*

5) March 1603. Request for money due John Mowter and eight others for their service on this ship. *CSP-D, 1601–1603, 308.*

Hound.

1) 25 April 1579. Requesting restitution for being plundered by an English pirate, Edward Roan, while transporting cargo of wood and sugar from the Isle of Canary to Civil Spain *APC-V.11, 106.*

Humphrey. Of Lee.

1) 22 March 1597. Orders to master John Flower to transport 500 quarters of wheat to Carlingford Ireland for her majesty's army there. *APC-V.28, 369–370.*

Hunter.

1) 15 May 1582. The record indicates that the ship was carrying Spanish and Dutch merchandise "cast away by tempest". This could be interpreted that the ship was lost. But future records exist. The merchants sought restitution for their lost goods stolen by people from a nearby town. *APC-V. 13, 418–419.*

2) 5 June 1582. The courts settled the matter and restitution was paid. *APC-V.13, 437–438.*

Isle of Garnesy.

1) 14 May 1587. A report was made by the French that their ship the *Greyhound*, was plundered by Sir Thomas Leighton, master of the *Isle of Garnesey*, of a cargo from Spain. *APC-V.15, 77.*

James. Of Brook.

Records suggest that this was a bark.

1) 19 September 1576. Was at Harwich under general arrest and was laden and freighted from Spain by Alderman Osborn and Mr. Richard Stapler, with salt. Order to release the ship. *APC-V.9, 205.*

2) 14 December 1579. This ship was overtaken by a Frenchman, Monsieur De la Moth, governor of Graveling, and taken into Calais where the crew was imprisoned and the cargo taken. Seeking restitution. *APC-V.11, 343.*

James. Of Ipswich.

1) 6 November 1597. The council addressed a petition for claims for the Cales voyage from this ship and the *James* also of Ipswich. Some of the crew "Being driven to great misery have been forced to take far less sums." *APC-V.28, 103–104.*

James Ellison.

1) 20 March 1558. Orders to prepare to sail to the Low Countries. *APC-V.7, 69.*

Jennet.

This ship is mentioned in a 1546 inventory as 180 tons with 106 mariners and 14 gunners. At the time of Elizabeth's ascension, the crew complement was: 120 mariners, 20 gunners and 60 soldiers. *MRP.*

1) 11 January 1553 this ship was ordered to be ready to sail to Spain.

2) 25 July 1553. Ordered to prepare to sail to the narrow seas before Dover.

3) 17 November 1554 received 'five demi barrels of serpentine powder.' *APC-V.5, 86.*

4) 8 March 1569. Note of all materials to be provided for the fitting out of this ship. No additional information is shared. *CSP-D–1547–1580.*

Jeremy. Of Bristol.

1) 12 March 1592. This ship plundered the cargo of a French hulk of a cargo of fish. The original complaint filed by the French had not been addressed. "We are informed that you have been very remiss and negligent". *APC-V.24, 117.*

Jesus. Of London.

This ship is mentioned in an inventory of 1546 as 700 tons with 118 soldiers, 158 mariners and 24 gunners. An inventory of 1557 mentions 50 hackbutters, 80 soldiers, 190 mariners and 30 gunners.

1) 19 December 1551. Requesting information to determine if this ship will suit the king's services. *APC-V.3, 447.*

2) 20 March 1558. Orders to prepare to sail to the Low Countries. *APC-V.7, 69.*

3) 20 April 1559. Embargo removed and to prepare to sail. *APC-V.7, 90.*

4) 22 December 1577. This ship was ordered to depart London to Rye, East Sussex. *APC-V.10, 123.*

5) 8 November 1579. A report this ship had wrecked on the shore of Hurst Castle in Hampshire. Among the unaccountable cargo were bags of money. The crew were suspect as to the money's disappearance. *APC-V.11, 297–298.*

6) 21 September 1581. A dispute over a purchase regarding this ship and a hold on any further movement of this ship until the dispute is settled. *APC-V.13, 215.*

7) 16 March 1585. The letter is rather ambiguous, but it would appear this ship's cargo was confiscated while out of Tripoly in Barbary. Merchants affected had sought restitution. *APC-V.14, 33–34.*

Jesus. Of Newcastle.

1) 27 February 1580. Permission to depart the Thames River to home of Newcastle. *APC-V.11, 401.*

Jewell. Of London.

1) 6 June 1596. Complaint filed with the council regarding the theft of cochineal from this ship. *APC-V.25, 436.*

Joan.

Records suggest this was 80 tons.

1) 8 May 1580. Released to the sea.

John.

This ship is mentioned in the 1588 inventory against the Spanish armada at 70 tons with John Young as captain of 50 mariners. *MRP.*

1) 26 November 1565. Description of the inhabitants of the town and three ships, this being one, that was used as a fishing vessel. Was owned by Edward Kitchin. *CSP-D-Addenda. 573.*

2) 8 July 1576. A letter mentioning that pirates took 16 little barrels of butter and one hogshead of tallow and taken to the port of Weymouth and Malcomb Regis. *APC-V.9, 155.*

3) 25 March 1590. Slight mention of the loss of their cargo under suspicion of supporting King Phillip of Spain. *APC,-V.19, 3.*

4) 5 April 1590. Service for 2 months against the Spanish invasion attempt in the Narrow Seas. Fees paid for victuals, powder, munitions, and other artillery for the ship's consumption. *APC-V19, 11–12.*

5) 29 September 1590. Scottish pirates associated with Spanish soldiers were assaulted and taken by force near the Trise on the North coast. Cargo taken included 105 quarters of beans. Mention of the severe debt by the owner and to take consideration for his wife and children. Seeking punishment to those involved. *APC-V.19, 472.*

6) 11 June 1592. This ship was plundered by a French Captain Cokeyne of Dieppe of wines, oils, and other merchandise. Merchants of London seeking restitution. *APC-V.22, 525-526.*

7) 16 May 1597. Complaints filed about Captain Thomas Venables for his act of piracy of taking by force and violence from this ship. Warrant for the arrest of all involved in the plundering pirates from the *Dolphin* of Portsmouth and return of all plundered goods. *APC-V.27, 116.*

John. Of Apsam.

1) 17 April 1553, Thomas Brown was master of the ship.

2) 20 April 1553 the Privy Council ordered that Thomas Brown be apprehended as soon as he returned from Flanders.

John. Of Chepstowe.

1) 2 April 1558. Orders to John Asshe captain and John Ellyzaunder to appear at court regarding their sinking of a ship of Lubecke. *APC-V.6, 300.*

John. Of Hampton.

1) 27 March 1558. Ordered recall to Bristol. *APC-V.6, 294.*

John Brandlinges.

1) 20 March 1558. Orders to prepare to sail to the Low Countries. *APC-V.7, 69.*

John Stokes.

Records suggest this was 60 tons.

1) 1 April 1580. License to transport timber and copper to Spain for 'erecting a sugar house.' *APC-V.11, 437.*

John Trelany.

1) 6 October 1588. Orders for pay to the crew for their service to the queen. *APC-V.16, 303.*

Jonas. Of Sandwich.

Records suggest this was 10 tons.

1) 13 November 1575. Mention that this ship should be held as no license has been granted for it to leave port. *APC-V.9, 45.*

2) 27 February 1580. Permission granted to depart to Bristol. *APC-V.11, 401.*

3) 20 March 1597. This ship with two other ships was pirated by French of cargo, tackle, and furniture. *APC-V.26, 552.*

4) 24 March 1599. This ship was to be in service in Ireland for 176 days. Requested payment for that service. *APC-V.30, 191–192.*

Judith.

1) 19 February 1578. Letter indicating this ship may be sold to pay debits and crew. *APC-V.11, 52.*

2) 25 March 1578. Instructions to Martin Frobisher to begin preparations for another voyage her majesty called *meta incognita* (unknown destination) to the northwest parts and Cathey (North China). He was to acquire 90 mariners for this ship, the *Gabriel*, *Aid* and *Michael*. Furthermore, to hire 130 pioneers and 50 soldiers for 6 additional vessels. Victuals for 90 persons for 7 months to be loaded and to prepare to sail before 1 May and return with 800 tons of ore. Additional note indicated this crew was to include 40 mariners,

gunners, shipwrights, carpenters, 30 soldiers, 30 pioneers with victuals for 18 months. *CSP-C, 1513–1616. 35–36.*

3) 1 June 1578. Orders and articles to be observed by the fleet from Captain Frobisher and delivered to every ship under his command. "To banish swearing, dice, cards, playing and all filthy talk, and to serve God twice a day and to clear the glass every night according to the old order of England. Signals in case of fogs, trumpets, drums, etc. to be sounded, or contrary winds. Watch words 'Before the world was God' the answer 'After God came Christ his Son.'" *CSP-C, 1513–1516, 37.*

4) 28 January 1598. James Beauvoir seeking restitution for the plunder of twenty thousand fish from Newfoundland. *APC-V.28, 285–286.*

Julian.

1) Ordered to transport soldiers on 7 February 1551 for 20 days. *APC-V.3, 43.*

2) Reported as plundered by the French on 22 February 1554 returning from Spain with "Cordovan skins, silks, and other rich merchandise, so lifted that nothing was left in her but a few articles of no value." This occurred near Brest.

3) 18 October 1579. Orders to owners Jacques Lake and John de Brys to set sail for the apprehension of pirates. *APC-V.11, 286.*

4) 31 October 1601. During the month of August, this ship received orders to sail and patrol the seas for Spanish ships. Request for payment for services. *APC-V.32, 325.*

Katherine.

This ship is mentioned in the 1588 inventory against the Spanish armada as 60 tons with 30 mariners. *MRP.*

1) 27 March 1559. Orders to prepare to sail. *APC-V.7, 73.*

2) 30 January 1597. An order to John James to carry munitions to Ireland. *APC-V.26, 152.*

Leader.

1) 12 November 1558. Pay record to William Stephan, shipwright for building this barge. *APC-V.6, 426.*

Less Bark.

This ship is mentioned in an inventory of 1548 as 400 tons with 250 mariners and soldiers, 11 pieces of brass ordnance and 98 iron ordnance. *MRP.*

1) 14 June 1551. Ordered into dock for repairs.

Leicester.

This ship is mentioned as the Galleon *Leicester* in the 1588 inventory against the Spanish armada as 400 tons with Captain George Fenner as captain of 160 mariners under the command of Sir Francis Drake. *MRP.*

1) 14 May 1593. Complaints by members of the crew that they did not receive a proper share of the prizes taken at sea while in the seas of the Low Countries. *APC-V.24, 232.*

Lion.

This ship is mentioned in a 1546 inventory as 140 tons with 88 mariners and 12 gunners. *MRP.*

1) 9 November 1553. Reported as a barge and payment made for her repairs.

2) 1 September 1576. Orders to accompany the fleet from Flanders to Dunkirk. *APC-V.9, 198.*

3) 8 March 1569. Note of all materials to be provided for the fitting out of this ship. No additional information is shared. *CSP-D-1547–1580.*

4) 27 February 1580. Robert Hook was ordered to delivery corn to Vean, Portugal and licensed to depart. An additional complaint was made regarding four hundred quarters 'of corrupt and musty wheat' because the ship had remained at sea too long. *APC-V.11, 401.*

5) 17 July 1589. Settled the account of this ship's service for conveying letters and 'five pilots to aid and assist for the return of the hulks and soldiers employed by Sir Francis Drake'. *APC-V.17, 393.*

6) 3–4 September 1591. Shortly after the *Revenge* was captured by the Spanish. This ship had captured a Spanish captain responsible for her capture and he was brought as a prisoner to England. *SFLB-35*

7) 16 April 1592. Notice to officials that this ship was in the Dartmouth harbor preparing to sail to Newfoundland for fishing. Notice that if any foreigner was to attempt to hire this ship, to arrest them. *APC-V.22, 401–402.*

8) 22 April 1592. Permission for this ship to begin its voyage to fishing in Newfoundland. *APC-V.22, 402.*

9) 24 April 1597. Orders to store victuals for 220 men and be ready to sail. *APC-V.27, 65.*

10) 22 March 1601. Request for payment of services in transporting victuals to support English troops in Ireland for the period of 7 weeks. *APC-V.31, 232.*

11) 16 May 1601. The council received the names and addresses of 16 fugitives taken by this ship in Tilbury Hope. It is difficult to extract useful

information from the snippet. It would appear they were to be transported to Calais. *CSP-D, 1601–1603, 41.*

Lion's Whelp.
Records indicate this was a pinnace.
1) 23 September 1601. Instructions from the queen that Sir Richard Leveson would command a fleet of ships in response to the continual possible threats from the king of Spain. This ship and with others would patrol the coast and prevent or defeat any forces against England. *CSP-D, 1601–1603, 101.*
2) 9 July 1602. This ship was under the command of Sir William Monson, vice-admiral of the fleet for the coast of Spain and received the same instructions as the *Adventure. CSP-D, 1601–1603, 220–221.*

Magdalen.
1) 31 August 1591. Warrant to apprehend John Harman in Sussex and Edward Heath, masters of this ship, wherever they may be found. *APC-V.21, 418.*

Makespeed.
1) 29 November 1573. Released from arrest. *APC-V.8, 151.*

Mannet.
1) 7 October 1578. Letter describing that this ship was recently built at Southampton. Captain John Martin was to receive 4 tons of ordnance at the Tower Wharf in London and to prepare to sail. *APC-V.10, 338.*

Margaret. Of Chester.
1) 15 December 1601. Orders to transport frame timbers to Ireland. *APC-V.32, 429.*

Margaret. Of Pennarke.
1) 26 November 1556. Record of goods removed from this ship. *APC-V.6, 24.*
2) 20 April 1559. Embargo removed and to prepared to sail. *APC-V.7, 90.*

Margaret. Of Milford.
1) 22 April 1567. Orders to transport provisions. *APC-V.7, 345–346.*
2) 30 March 1592. A matter between merchants of Holland and Zealand and this ship had been settled with the merchants to be paid a small amount of money. This ship was free to depart. *APC-V.22, 381–3812.*

Margaret Bonaventure.
1) Mention of 26 January 1554. Sea worthy not reliable per correspondence.

Margaret and John.

This ship is mentioned in the 1588 inventory against the Spanish armada as 200 tons with John Fisher as captain of 90 mariners that was fitted out in London. *MRP.*

1) 14 September 1600. Orders to arrest and confiscate all goods, wares, and merchandise that this ship brought into Portsmouth. *APC-V.30, 619.*

2) 6 October 1600. Additional information is shared in this letter that this ship plundered cargo from the *Salamander* of France and taken while at sea. *APC-V-30, 715.*

Marie James.

1) Ordered to transport soldiers on 7 February 1551 for 20 days. *APC-V.3, 43.*

Marie Jermin.

1) 5 July 1551. Payment made to Richard Duke for his service at Holly Islands. *APC-V.3, 294.*

Marie Susan.

Records indicate this was 120 tons.

1) 25 March 1579. Orders to release this ship and proceed on her voyage. *APC-V.11, 430.*

Marigold.

Records indicate this was 30 tons.

1) 13 December 1578. This ship was used by Sir Francis Drake in his important expedition into the South Seas. *NHGB-11.*

2) 19 March 1580. Orders to return to London. *APC-V.11, 423.*

3) 19 June 1601. Record indicated that John Bourn was master. *APC-V.31, 442.*

4) October 1601. Captain Lee requested directions for his voyage off the coast of Spain including what he would do if he sank a ship carrying munitions, powder, corn, or naval provisions. *CSP-D, 1601–1603, 118–119.*

5) 29 October 1602. The court of the admiralty reviewed a complaint from merchants of Amsterdam and Hamburg that Charles Leigh, late captain of this ship, had plundered a cargo of 20 bales of indigo, wool, and other things. The merchants sought restitution. *CSP-D, 1601–1603, 252.*

Marlion.

1) 8 December 1589. Charges that Captain Sachfield, who died on the Portuguese voyage, had robbed a Scottish vessel and had imprisoned a man Adams who was the new captain and all others that participated in the piracy as soon as the ship arrived in port. *APC-V.18, 253.*

Martin.

This ship is mentioned in the 1588 inventory against the Spanish armada as 50 tons with Walter Gower as captain of 35 mariners that served under Charles Howard of Effingham. *MRP.*

1) 8 June 1598. Orders to sail for service on the Irish coast between Ireland and Scotland to hinder the rebels. *APC-V.28, 496.*

Mary Edwards.

1) 7 May 1602. Fernandez Perera sent the following to Thomas Bradshaw. "I want help. I wish my friend to have a copy of our cipher that he may write his mind large at all times. When at liberty, I shall be able to affect all that is required of me. I coven to shoot as near as I can when once I bend my bow, but I must have strings to my bow, therefore I beg you to send provisions". This looks to be a cipher. *CSP-D, 1601–1603, 186.*

Mary Flower.

1) 20 March 1558. Orders to prepare to sail to the Low Countries. *APC-V.7, 69.*

2) 19 August 1575. Letter mentioning the restitution of merchandise taken from this ship as she came from Sluse. *APC-V.9, 15.*

3) 10 April 1581. Thomas Tucker was master. Two London merchants delivered items to be transported to Ligurno, Italy. A complaint was issued because the delivery was not correct. Three days later, the matter had not been resolved and the cargo could perish. Restitution was made and the ship was released. *APC-V.13, 16–17, 21, 27, 103, 171.*

4) 5 October 1590. A command to hold this ship laden with corn and "other prohibited merchandises. When the ship is stopped, to determine their purpose". *APC-V.20, 8.*

Mary Fortune.

1) Mention of 26 January 1554.

2) 27 March 1559. Orders to prepare to sail. *APC-V.7, 73.*

3) 20 July 1576. Letter mentioning the loss of merchandise. *APC-V.9, 169.*

4) 28 May 1579. The ship was threatened to be taken by individuals preventing her from departing. The letter was to assure the captain and crew that she would have safe passage. *APC-V.11, 144.*

5) 30 August 1596. A search of this ship by authorities was encountered by a captain and master of this ship displaying lewd behavior. The day after the ship was captured, pirates came with small boats and began removing "divers chest and trunks" having been told it was a lawful prize, loaded

the small boats with items of great value. The crew was threatened if they resisted. *APC-V.26, 136*

Mary Gallant.
Records suggest this was a crayer of 20–50 tons.
1) Undated letter during the reign of King Edward VI. Short account that munitions had been received at Newcastle. *CSP-D-Addenda. 427.*
2) On 18 July 1553 was reported at Orwell Haven laden with salmon with instructions that 3 barrels were for the queen.

Mary Grace.
1) 27 March 1559. Orders to prepare to sail. *APC-V.7, 73.*
2) 18 July 1592. Preparations were made with victuals and furniture to set sail 'in a warlike manner'. After the ship had sailed, this ship and the *Mary Grace* captured the *Whalefish* loaded with salt and other merchandise. *APC-V.23, 36–37.*

Mary. Of London.
1) 29 May 1571. Orders to John Ravez and Robert Wolly to return all the ship's tack and apparel to the way they found her. *APC-V.8, 27.*
2) 28 January 1577. This ship was pirated by a Scotsman, John Anderton. Warrant was issued to apprehend Anderton upon arrival in any of her majesty's ports. *APC-V.10, 153.*
3) 14 June 1592. In August of 1591, this ship was pirated by the *Salamander* of Dieppe of salt, pepper, suckets, marmalade, calicut, sugars, cloves, nutmeg, ginger, gold wire, silk lace and other merchandise. The French left the ship at about sixty leagues from Cape Finisterre with only 16 men onboard with only a basket of broken bread and a small rondelet of cider mixed with water where they had to sustain themselves for 25 days. Two men died from hunger and the remaining were desperate from famine. *APC-V.22, 533.*

Mary Catherine.
1) 12 May 1573. Orders to prepare the ship to transport 200 quarters of grain, half wheat, half malt to Ireland. *APC-V.5, 105.*

Mary and John.
1) 25 March 1579. Orders to release this ship and proceed on her voyage. *APC-V.11, 430.*
2) 7 March 1586. John Gross, owner, was transporting French wines at the port of Yarmouth when a storm forced him into the port of Dartmouth

where the cargo was plundered by inhabitants living there. The French merchant was seeking restitution. *APC-V.14, 380.*

Mary Martin.
Records suggest this was a 160 ton.
1) 20 July 1576. Letter of restitution regarding the loss of their merchandise belonging to London merchants. *APC-V.9, 169.*

Mary Ocian.
1) Undated letter during the reign of King Edward VI. Short account that munitions had been received at Newcastle. *CSP-D-Addenda. 427.*

Mary Rose.
This ship is mentioned in a 1546 inventory as 700 tons with 185 soldiers, 200 mariners and 30 gunners.
1) 8 March 1602. This ship was reported to have taken in victuals but was waiting for a crew. *CSP-D, 1601–1603, 161.*
2) 9 July 1602. This ship was under the command of Sir William Monson, vice-admiral of the fleet for the coast of Spain and received the same instructions as the *Adventure. CSP-D, 1601–1603, 220–221.*

Mary Willoughby.
This ship is mentioned in a 1548 inventory as 140 tons with 160 soldiers and mariners and 23 pieces of ordnance. A 1557 inventory mentions her as 160 tons with 10 hackbutters, 20 soldiers, 84 mariners and 16 gunners.
1) 6 March 1552. Ordered to prepare to sail to the coast of Ireland to apprehend a pirate Strangyshe.

Mathew.
This ship is described in a 1546 inventory as 600 tons with 138 soldiers, 138 mariners and 24 gunners.
1) 24 May 1577. The owner David Wiottie, a Scotsman, was accused of piracy. He was cleared and the ship was released. *APC-V.9, 346.*
2) 20 March 1597. This ship with two other ships were pirated by French of cargo, tackle, and furniture. *APC-V.26, 552.*

The Mathew
[*Ships & Ways of Other Days.*]

Mathew Gonson.

Records suggest that this was a 600-ton Merchant.

1) On 6 November, the Privy Council indicated that she should be restored to original condition or pay a fine.

Marleon.

1) 13 April 1589. Orders to Captain Sir John Williams that upon receipt of the letter to make preparation to sail and join the fleet against the Spanish with Sir Frances Drake. *APC-V.17, 131.*

Martin.

This ship is mentioned in the 1588 inventory against the Spanish armada as 50 tons with Walter Gower as captain of 35 mariners under the command of Charles Howard of Effingham. *MRP.*

1) 20 March 1558. Orders to prepare to sail to the Low Countries. *APC-V.7, 69.*

2) 19 February 1580. Having returned from Ireland, a request was made to the lord treasurer to pay the mariners. *APC-V.12, 337.*

Mayflower.

This ship is first reported in the inventory of 1588 at 200 tons with Edward Banks as captain with 90 mariners.

1) 10 December 1588. Captain Alexander Musgrave was informed that certain individuals were not willing to contribute to the support of this

ship for the queen's service. The amount based on the tonnage was not an acceptable charge. *APC-V.16, 376.*

2) 27 April 1589. Request to officials that this ship laden with cloth, lead and tin may take in a load of pilchards (small fish) at Falmouth. *APC-V. 17, 429.*

3) 29 September 1589. Letter to Sir Francis Drake requesting wages to be paid for the ships time of service into Portugal. *APC-V.18, 155–156.*

Merehonour.

1) 23 September 1601. Instructions from the queen that Sir Richard Leveson would command a fleet of ships in a response to the continual possible threats from the king of Spain. This ship and with others would patrol the coast and prevent or defeat any forces against England. *CSP-D, 1601–1603, 101.*

Merchant Royal.

This ship is mentioned in the 1588 inventory against the Spanish armada as 400 tons with Robert Flyke as captain of 60 mariners under the command of Sir Francis Drake. *MRP.*

1) 1 September 1578. Letter describing the unpaid crew of this ship to the admiral. *APC-V.10, 317.*

2) 13 April 1589. Charges brought against this ship by the Dutch that their cargo was plundered and sought restitution. *APC-V.17, 126.*

Mercury.

This ship is only mentioned in an inventory of ordnance with 1 culverin, 1 saker and 4 fowler chambers.

1) 24 April 1597. Orders to store victuals for 160 men and be ready to sail. *APC-V.27, 65.*

Mere Honora.

1) 24 April 1597. Orders to store victuals for 400 men and be ready to sail. *APC-V.27, 65.*

Michael.

1) 20 March 1558. Orders to prepare to sail to the Low Countries. *APC-V.7, 69.*

2) September (?) 1577. The *Aid* and the *Gabriel* arrived from their first voyage to the northwest parts at Bristol and the council suggested Martin Frobisher to unload the ore there and keep it safe in the castle. The *Michael* arrived in the Thames and the ore was to be unloaded and kept safe under

guard. The council expressed a strong desire "on the speedy melting of the ore." *CSP-C, 1513–1616. 20–21.*

3) 17 October 1577. Letter describing the ore from this ship and how the gold and other ore was to be melted and distributed. *APC-V.10, 55.*

4) 17 October 1577. Letter concerning the payment of wages of soldiers and mariners of this ship and of the victuals that will not keep and to be moored and tack undisturbed. *APC-V10, 56.*

5) 25 March 1578. Instructions to Martin Frobisher to begin preparations for another voyage her majesty called *meta incognita* (unknown destination) to the northwest parts and Cathey (North China). He was to acquire 90 mariners for this ship, the *Gabriel, Aid* and *Judith*. Furthermore, to hire 130 pioneers and 50 soldiers for 6 additional vessels. Victuals for 90 persons for 7 months to be loaded and to prepare to sail before 1 May and return with 800 tons of ore. Additional note indicated this crew was to include 40 mariners, gunners, shipwrights, carpenters, 30 soldiers, 30 pioneers with victuals for 18 months. *CSP-C, 1513–1616. 35–36.*

6) 1 June 1578. Orders and articles to be observed by the fleet from Captain Frobisher and delivered to every ship under his command. "To banish swearing, dice, cards, playing and all filthy talk, and to serve God twice a day and to clear the glass every night according to the old order of England. Signals in case of fogs, trumpets, drums, etc. to be sounded, or contrary winds. Watch words 'Before the world was God' the answer 'After God came Christ his Son.'" *CSP-C, 1513–1516, 37.*

7) 25 May 1600. The council was informed that Richard Tasker, master of this ship, had transported soldiers out of Ireland without permission. The transported soldiers were regarded as traitors. The council ordered Tasker to appear, but he had not. *APC-V.30, 338.*

Minion.

This ship is mentioned in a 1546 inventory as 300 tons with 100 soldiers, 100 mariners and 20 gunners. *MRP.*

1) The ship was to be delivered to the Master of the Horse on 18 June 1550. It would appear the ship had been commissioned in June. *APC-V.3, 43.*

2) Ordered to transport soldiers on 7 February 1551 for 20 days. *APC-V.3, 43.*

3) 22 January 1557. Orders to remain at Plymouth until the queen needed it. *APC-V.6, 247.*

4) 20 July 1576. Letter of restitution regarding the loss of wine. *APC-V.9, 169.*

5) 10 November 1577. Letter to the officers of the port of London to release this ship and allow it to travel to Spain. *APC-V.10, 81.*

6) 25 March 1579. Orders to release this ship and proceed on her voyage. *APC-V.11, 430.*

7) 4 March 1580. Some of the plundered cargo had been recovered and the ship was released to complete its original voyage. *APC-V.11, 408.*

8) 15 January 1581. While at Bristol, this ship was released from her majesty's duty and could be employed if a merchant needs it. *APC-V.12, 312.*

9) May 1590. A rather confusing letter indicating that Nicholas Debois, master, and Peter Lurash, master's mate, were arrested by Barbary merchants while traveling from Dunkirk to Alarada to Newhaven. *APC-V.19, 113.*

10) 29 June 1596. Complaint about Captain Thomas Webb who plundered a Danish ship in an "inhumane and unchristian manner and tortured and cruelly handled the master and mariners of the said ship." He also took the anchors, cables, and other necessary furniture. The master and 14 mariners "were cast away and perished." Seeking punishment under the full extent of the law. *APC-V.25, 491–492.*

Mirable. Of London.

Records indicate this was a barque.

1) License to Patrick Strange to transport 300 quarters of wheat to Waterford. Rowland Huxley was master. *APC-V.27, 141.*

Moon.

This ship is mentioned in the 1588 inventory against the Spanish armada as 600 tons with Alexander Clifford as captain of 40 mariners under the command of Charles Howard of Effingham. *MRP.*

1) 23 February 1597. A request for assistance for David Duffield who joined her majesty's navy while serving on this ship, lost his sight and was disabled. Seeking assistance for the man. *APC-V.26, 513–514.*

2) 12 July 1597. This ship was charged with plundering cargo from the *Four Sons* of Amsterdam off the coast of Spain and sold and dispersed at Plymouth. *APC-V.27, 286.*

3) 23 June 1600. Orders to store enough victuals for a 2-month voyage to Ireland. *APC-V.30, 421.*

4) 9 August 1600. The *Poppingay* was deemed unfit for service to Ireland and this ship was ordered to transfer ordnance to her and prepare to travel to and from Ireland as required. *APC-V.30, 586.*

5) 15 March 1601. Orders to prepare this ship with victuals and 134 men to serve on the coast of England for 4 months. *APC-V.31, 225–226.*

6) 11 July 1601. Orders to serve an additional 3 months on the coast of Ireland. *APC-V.32, 42–43.*

7) 24 December 1601. Orders to remain on the Irish coast. *APC-V.32, 451.*

Moonshine.

This ship is mentioned in the 1588 inventory against the Spanish armada at 60 tons with John Brough as captain of 30 mariners. This ship was fitted out in London. *MRP.*

1) 9 August 1591. John Middleton had plundered a French ship laden with fish and arrived at Portsmouth. Martin Dartiago of St John de Luce is seeking to have the matter resolved. *APC-V.21, 376.*

Neptune.

1) 28 January 1598. Complaints from a Dutch merchant that this ship had plundered a cargo of 120 thousand fish and two dry fates of linen cloth. *APC-V.28, 283.*

New Year's Gift. Of Plymouth.

1) 31 July 1601. Orders to the victualer of the navy to deliver victuals for 16 men for 56 days to be laden in this ship. *CSP-D, 1601–1603, 77.*

2) 19 August 1601. Captain Whorwood departed to discover what the Spaniards were doing, but had encountered bad weather and was abandoned at sea when it she was half full of water. The captain and crew were saved by a Plymouth ship. *CSP-D, 1601–1603, 85.*

3) December (?) 1601. Request for an evaluation of value of this ship cast away in her majesty's service. *CSP-D, 1601–1603, 140.*

Nicholas. Of Feckenham.

Records suggest that this was 70 tons.

1) 29 December 1574. This one is rather tricky. A French merchant complained that this ship laden with wine and sugar was arrested by the captain of the *Isle of Wight* and *Bailey* and *White* also of the Isle of Wight. I can find nothing else to clarify this. *APC-V.8, 329.*

Nightingale.

This ship is mentioned in the 1588 inventory against the Spanish armada at 160 tons with John Doate as captain of 16 mariners under the command of Charles Howard of Effingham. *MRP.*

1) 1 June 1576. Orders to release 5 crewmembers of this ship detained in Dover. *APC-V.9, 133.*

2) 1 April 1580. Loaded with cargo for Prussia and released to sail. *APC-V.11, 436.*

3) 6 May 1593. First report this ship was lost due to fire in the Gironde, the river mouth leading to Bordeaux, France. There was a loss of 4 members of the crew and ship.

4) 6 May 1593. Captain William Winter filed a complaint regarding Sir John Arundel "wrongfully detained from him a barque called the *Nightingale* about 4 years ago, since mortgaged and since redeemed and having recovered diver's prizes and Mr. Winter claims one-third ownership." *APC-V.24, 210–211.*

5) 19 June 1593. The council received a request from "the poor and comfortless women" to ensure that the sailor's widows and their husbands received their wages. *APC-V.24, 319–320.*

6) 24 August 1596. Complaints by English merchants of Scottish plundering when they were violently taken and goods taken away. Seeking restitution from the Scottish king. *APC-V.26, 127–128.*

7) 17 September 1600. Orders to transport victuals while in Ireland and remain in service until June of 1601. *APC-V.30, 645.*

Nonpareil.

This ship is mentioned in an inventory of 1603 at the time of Elizabeth's death as 500 tons, 150 mariners, 30 gunners and 70 soldiers. *MRP.*

1) 29 July 1602. This document reads very similar to 30 October 1592 entry of the *Garland.* Three ships had received the cargo of a great carrack and the remainder is in three merchant ships. The ballast from the carrack is also being unloaded and inspected for hidden treasures. The carrack and these three ships were in Plymouth. The carrack was to be held until her majesty determined how to dispose of it. *CSP-D, 1601–1603, 226–227.*

2) 14 December 1602. A warrant was issued to the treasurer of the navy for the estimated "new building" of this ship. This must be a refitting and or repair. *CSP-D, 1601–1603, 269.*

Northstar.

Record indicates this is a pinnace.

1) 1587. This ship and the *Sunshine* were part of the fleet of M. John Davis that set out looking for a passage between Greenland and Iceland. *HCEV-V.3, 146.*

Our Lady.

1) 11 August 1577. This ship laden with iron ore was taken on the coast of Galicia, Spain, by Captain Hix. A warrant was issued to search the ship as it was in Saltash, England. *APC-V.10, 14.*

Pansy.
1) 19 June 1601. Record indicated that Abraham Bonner was master. *APC-V.31, 442.*

Partridge.
Records suggest this was 60 tons.
1) 2 March 1579. Ship was released to deliver gunpowder to Hamburg. *APC-V.11, 404.*

Paragon. Of London.
1) 9 July 1602. This ship was under the command of Sir William Monson, vice-admiral of the fleet for the coast of Spain and received the same instructions as the *Adventure. CSP-D, 1601–1603, 220–221.*

Parnell.
This ship is mentioned in the 1588 inventory against the Spanish armada at 220 tons with Nicholas Gorge as captain of 80 mariners. This ship was fitted out in London. *NRP.*
1) 18 January 1590. Having completed its service with the admiral against the Spanish, the ship is released to travel to St. Jean de Lux in Southwest France. *APC-V.18, 314.*

Pelican.
Records suggest that this was a 400 ton. In 1577, it was a 100 ton. This ship was not included in inventories.
1) 11 April 1551. Reported to have delivered grain. *APC-V.5, 255.*
2) 24 February 1557. Orders to Henry Kite informing him this ship would be used for the king's needs. *APC-V.6, 274–275.*
3) 20 April 1559. Embargo removed and to prepare to sail. *APC-V.7, 90.*
4) 13 December 1578. This ship was used by Sir Francis Drake in his important expedition into the South Seas. Record indicates he commanded this ship himself. *NHGB-11.*
5) 11 January 1580. Plundered by John Granger, pirate. *APC-V.12, 307.*
6) 29 September 1596. Charges filed against this ship for plundering a ship leaving Cane in Normandy. Seeking restitution. *APC-V.26, 210.*
7) 21 November 1596. Orders to restore all that was plundered. *APC-V.26, 315.*

Peter.
This ship is mentioned in a 1546 inventory as 600 tons with 185 soldiers, 185 mariners and 30 gunners. *MRP.*

1) 1 May 1576. A report that this ship was lost in a storm on the coast of Somerset, Cornwall, and South Wales, with only 4 crew saved. A request was made for assistance in recovery of the merchandise lost. *APC-V.9, 113–114.*

Peter Pomgranate.
1) 30 March 1556. Was in port for repairs. *APC-V-5, 258.*
2) 20 March 1558. Orders to prepare to sail to the Low Countries. *APC-V.7, 69.*

Peter. Waterford.
Records suggest this was 40 tons.
1) 6 March 1552. Ordered to prepare to sail to the coast of Ireland to apprehend a pirate Strangyshe.
2) 1 April 1565. Mention of an inventory of the ship and goods that arrived at Holy Island 30 August and was there arrested on suspicion of piracy. *CSP-D-Addenda, 562.*
3) 26 November 1565. Description of Hartlepool, the fishing town that was the home port of this ship that belonged to John Brown and George Smith. *CSP-D-Addenda, 573.*
4) 20 August 1587. A warrant was issued for those responsible after this hoy was robbed of certain apparel, jewels, and money the postmaster was attempting to deliver to Wivenhoe, Essex to London. *APC-V.15, 252.*
5) 26 April 1590. Loaded in Spain with wines, the ship was brought to Plymouth. Upon further inspection, Nicholas Strong was found to have had correspondence with Spaniards regarding matters of intelligence concerning affairs of state. Additional correspondence was located from rebels in Spain to Ireland. Nicholas Strong was placed in custody. *APC-V.19, 83–84.*
6) 14 June 1592. In October, 1591, this ship was captured and plundered of her cargo of frizes, hides, linen cloth, leather mantels, blankets, and other goods by a French ship, with Le Fort of Cane as captain. Merchants of London who lost merchandise complained of the lack of justice. *APC-V.22, 533–534.*

Philip and Mary.
This ship is mentioned in a 1578 inventory as 600 tons with 160 mariners, 30 gunners and 110 soldiers. *MPR.*
1) 6 January 1557. Orders for Gore Ende to assume command as captain and to prepare for sea. *APC-V.6, 232.*
2) 8 March 1569. Note of all materials to be provided for the fitting out of this ship. No additional information is shared. *CSP-D–1547–1580.*

Phoenix.

This ship is mentioned in a 1546 inventory as 40 tons with 46 mariners and 4 gunners.

1) 11 January 1553. This ship was ordered to be ready to sail to Spain.

2) 17 November 1554. Received 'five demi barrels of serpentine powder.' *APC-V.5, 86.*

3) 16 August 1558. Charges brought by Peter Urtiz de Uribarry against some crew members. *APC-V.6, 376.*

4) 24 June 1587. It was reported that this ship was plundered by a French galleass and merchant's cargo of 'seckes and linen clothe' taken. A French ship was detained in Dartmouth and 2 others to inspect for the stolen cargo. The letter mentions that the king had 'granted a letter of marte against English men's goods'. *APC-V.15, 138.*

Pilgrim.

1) 31 August 1591. This ship attempted to help the *Revenge* when the Spanish had decimated her while commanded by Jacob Whiddon. *SFLB. 31.*

Pleasure.

1) 13 February 1597. Request for payment for services in a late action at Calais. This ship was the largest of those involved and the first to receive compensation. *APC-V.26, 491.*

Poppingay.

1) 28 December 1589. Letter to the admiral requiring a replacement of worn cables, cordage, and furniture to ensure the ship can serve in a voyage to Ireland. *APC-V.18, 282–283.*

2) 8 March 1590. Additional information regarding the expedition to Connaught Ireland to include transporting 600 soldiers with 200 to be supplied by Sir Walter Raleigh. *APC-V.18, 403.*

3) 30 April 1590. Orders to transport Sir John Norris and his company to Ireland. *APC-V.19, 100.*

4) 16 June 1590. While in Ireland, several of the men that accompanied Sir John Morris had mutinied. If any of the officers arrived at the gate of the castle in Dublin, they deserved hanging. Others would be imprisoned. *APC-V.19, 226–227.*

5) 28 February 1591. Request to repay Captain Thornton for his time served off the coast of Ireland against the Spanish and for charges of 'repairing and graving' the galleon and for additional charges for 'strengthening the timbers.' *APC-V.20, 314.*

6) 8 August 1596. Orders to transport munitions from the Tower of London to Dublin, Ireland for garrisons there. In addition, there were 36 horses. *APC-V.26, 92.*

7) 9 August 1600. In a letter ordering the *Moon* to assume the responsibility of this ship because it was unfit for service. *APC-V.30, 586.*

8) 29 June 1601. Having been recently employed for support of English troops in Ireland, the ship had been certified unserviceable and was at "the kaye at Dublin". It was also determined that it was unfit for sale. *APC-V.31, 474–475.*

Pool.

1) Ordered to transport soldiers on 7 February 1551 for 20 days. *APC-V.3, 43.*

Primrose.

The Primrose is mentioned in a 1578 inventory as 803 tons with 330 mariners, 40 gunners and 100 soldiers. Furthermore, this ship is mentioned in the 1588 inventory against the Spanish armada as 200 tons with Robert Bingborn as captain of 90 mariners. This ship was fitted out in London. *MRP.*

1) 11 March 1551. Orders to prepare ship for sea.

2) 8 March 1569. Note of all materials to be provided for the fitting out of this ship. No additional information is shared. *CSP-D-1547–1580.*

3) 17 March 1579. Orders to release this ship and prepare to sail. *APC-V.11, 419.*

4) 16 November 1579. Dispute regarding disposition of certain cargo. *APC-V.11, 309.*

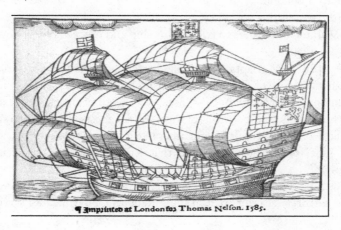

¶ Imprinted at London for Thomas Nelson. 1585.

Primrose. *Of London.*

[*Primrose of London, With Her Valiant Adventure on the Spanish Coast. London, 1585.*]

5) 8 May 1580. Orders to release the ship for a voyage to Elbing, Poland. *APC-V.12, 6.*

6) 12 May 1588. This ship, despite the queen's orders, sent out for the 'new found land' and apparently had attempted to seek support from others. Recommendations to imprison Peter Cox for his actions. *APC-V.16, 59.*

7) 5 June 1588. Peter Cox was before the court and though imprisoned, he was released. It appears that his age prevented his travel. *APC-V.16, 110.*

8) 5 November 1589. A concern regarding an unpaid account to the captain and crew of this ship to be armed, victualled, furnished, and set out to sea in the Narrow Seas against the Spaniards. *APC-V.18, 207–208*

9) 5 September 1596. Warrant to the master for restitution of 8 pieces of armor taken from soldiers. *APC-V.26, 139.*

Prosperity.

1) 13 May 1580. Philip Boite captain. French complained of plundering by this ship. *APC-V.12, 16.*

Prosperous.

1) 24 February 1598. Letter to the council on behalf of Robert Middleton, Henry Hilton and Thomas Swinborn who were severely injured and maimed during the voyage against Spain in a fight with the Spanish prizes while serving on this ship. *APC-V.28, 341.*

Prudence. Of London.

Records suggest this was 150 tons.

1) 25 March 1579. Orders to release this ship and proceed on her voyage. *APC-V.11, 430.*

2) 30 April 1592. Captain William Batten had pirated the *Jonas* of Amsterdam of 20 tons of syrup in divers casks, 9 tons in several casks and 17 bags of almonds, 50 packs of buck skins, 77 hogsheads of alleles, 30 chests of sugar, 99 hogsheads and six barrels of sugar, 17 half chests of sugar, 685 skins full of anneal, one barrel of dates and other like goods. *APC-V.22, 417.*

3) 19 June 1601. Record indicated that Richard Chester was master. *APC-V.31, 442.*

4) 31 October 1601. During the month of August, this ship received orders to sail and patrol the seas for Spanish ships. Request for payment for services. *APC-V.32, 325.*

Quittance.

This ship is mentioned in the 1603 inventory at the time of Elizabeth's death as 200 tons with 70 mariners, 10 gunners and 20 soldiers. *MRP.*

1) 23 September 1601. Instructions from the queen that Sir Richard Leveson would command a fleet of ships in a response to the continual possible threats from the king of Spain. This ship and others would patrol the coast and prevent or defeat any forces against England. *CSP-D, 1601–1603, 101.*

2) 9 July 1602. This ship was under the command of Sir William Monson, vice-admiral of the fleet for the coast of Spain and received the same instructions as the *Adventure. CSP-D, 1601–1603, 220–221.*

Rainbow.

This ship is mentioned in the 1588 inventory against the Spanish armada as 500 tons with Henry Seymour as captain of 250 mariners. *MRP.*

1) 22 October 1587. Orders to remain at sea in a 'warlike manner' for six weeks, beginning 13 October to 2 November. *APC-V.15, 267.*

2) 7 December 1587. Orders to remain at sea in a 'warlike manner' for six weeks, beginning 14 December to 23 January. *APC-V.15, 293.*

3) 31 December 1589. Orders for a month worth of victuals and make preparations to sail into the West Countries. *APC-V.18, 289.*

4) 25 January 1592. Letter to Sir Henry Palmer, admiral of the Narrow seas. Reports that 1500 Spaniards are about St. Mallows. The admiral was on this ship accompanied by 2 others, *Vantage* and *Answer* and were to determine the purpose of the Spaniards between Newhaven and Hage for a period of 14–15 days. The admiral had permission to take in any merchant or war ship if he felt it necessary. *APC-V.22, 206–207.*

5) 19 September 1592. Orders to prepare to sail to the Narrow seas and assemble a crew had been canceled. Orders included discharging any of the crew that had arrived. *APC-V.23, 204.*

6) 6 September 1596. Captain Parker. This ship had returned with 6 pieces of ordnance seized at Calais. The council wanted to ensure they were to be used in her majesty's service. *APC-V.26, 142.*

7) 23 September 1601. Instructions from the queen that Sir Richard Leveson would command a fleet of ships in a response to the continual possible threats from the king of Spain. This ship and others would patrol the coast and prevent or defeat any forces against England. *CSP-D, 1601–1603, 101.*

8) 14 December 1602. A warrant was issued to the treasurer of the navy for the estimated repairs of this ship. *CSP-D, 1601–1603, 269.*

Red Lion. London.

This ship is mentioned in the 1588 inventory against the Spanish armada as 200 tons with Jarvis Wild as captain of 90 mariners. *MRP.*

1) 12 August 1593. The council addressed an issue from November and December 1592, regarding this ship loaded with packs of wax, linen cloth, sails, grogram's and other merchandise, that hit the sandbank in Goodwin Sands and its cargo was plundered by local inhabitants. Seeking restitution. *APC-V.24, 456–457.*

Refusal.

1) 2 March 1599. Orders for the arrest of Captain Crocker with the master and chief officers for their involvement in an act of piracy on a Dutch ship. *APC-V.30, 134.*

2) 16 March 1602. This ship with three other English ships had chased 4 Portuguese ships. One ship surrendered and was left to drift without a crew. The fight with the other three ships lasted two to three hours then all captured. *CSP-D, 1601–1603, 163.*

Revenge.

This name turns up twice in the 1588 inventory against the Spanish armada. This is the first and I believe the entries for all below as 500 tons with 250 mariners with Sir Francis Drake as captain. The other mention is at 60 tons with Richard Bedford as captain of 30 mariners. *MRP.* An original source document from 1591 indicates the *Revenge* was perhaps built in 1579 at Chatham by Sir J. Hawkins.

1) 30 December 1580. Request for payment for wages for mariners, gunners and soldiers that served while off the coast of Ireland. *APC-V.12, 297.*

2) 20 January 1590. Letter thanking them for their labors and discretion used in recovering this ship "overthrown and drowned" by a recent tempest. They further indicate "should be perfectly recovered and that there should be no great loss by that mischance." *APC-V.18, 324.*

3) 15 December 1591. Note regarding the wife of John Carew, who served as a mariner aboard this ship and was was slain during the Spanish invasion. "She, left poor, with child and without relief" does desire to receive her husband's wages. The council agreed with her request. *APC-V.22, 120–121.*

4) 11 January 1595. Seeking relief for Thomas Benson, a cannoneer that had served her majesty's service many years and received many wounds, was maimed in one of his hands. *APC-V.25, 148.*

Richard Arundel.
Records suggest this was 90 tons.
1) 8 May 1580. Orders to release the ship for a voyage to Elbing, Poland. *APC-V.12, 6.*

Richard and Jane. London.
Record indicates this was 100 tons.
1) 7 March 1597. At this time, the ship had 20 mariners, a master, and a boy. The ship was blown into Falmouth by contrary winds. Permission was granted to allow the ship to continue its voyage to Spain and Portugal. *APC-V.27, 284.*

Roebuck.
This ship is mentioned in the 1588 inventory against the Spanish armada as 300 tons with Jacob Whitton as captain of 120 mariners. *MRP.*
1) 22 July 1557. On 7 June, this ship captured a Guernsey ship near Sark, France, loaded with French wines. A dispute over the ownership of the wines and merchandise was settled. It was pointed out, that the captain exerted great restrain over the crew that felt the cargo now belonged to them. *CSP-D-Addenda, 455.*
2) 17 November 1588. The letter indicates that this was Sir Walter Raleigh's ship. Ordinance was removed from the Carrack to furnish this ship against the Spanish. *APC-V.16, 347.*
3) 1 December 1588. Complaints by the Spanish because Jacob Whiden, captain of this ship, plundered 'cloth of gold and other rich furniture' from Don Petro de Valdeas. Seeking compensation or the return of the goods pirated. *APC-V.16, 363.*
4) 13 September 1590. Complaint filed against John Cock, captain, for plundering Spanish wines and other merchandise while at sea. *APC-V.18, 465.*
5) 30 October 1592. This ship was one of three that received the cargo from the 'great Carrack'. Notice was given to this ship to take care while transporting the cargo along the Thames River. There is mention that some items went missing from the Carrack before being transferred. *APC-V.23, 275.*

Rose. Of Dover.
Three ships of this derivative are noted in the ship inventories but I do not have enough information to speculate whether this ship is of them.
1) 22 March 1597. Orders to master Cobham Dones to transport 300 quarters of wheat to Carlingford Ireland for her majesty's army there. *APC-V.28, 369–370.*

Royal Merchant.

1) 6 November 1580. To be loaded for Levant France. 'Should a merchant desire their ship, to serve them.' *APC-V.12, 258–259.*

Ruby.

1) 30 September 1588. Very short mention of her service to her majesty. *APC-V.16, 295.*

2) 6 September 1596. Captain Thomas Woodhouse. This ship returned with 6 pieces of ordnance seized at Calais. The council wanted to ensure they were to be used in her majesty's service. *APC-V.26, 142.*

Saker.

This ship is mentioned in a 1548 inventory as 40 tons with 50 soldiers, 2 brass ordnance and 18 iron ordnance. This ship is also mentioned in a 1557 inventory as 60 tons with 4 hackbutters, 8 soldiers, 44 mariners and 8 gunners. *MRP.*

1) 4 June 1551. Report of payment to the late Captain John Walwin. *APC-V.3, 291.*

Salamander. Bristol.

This ship is mentioned in a 1546 inventory as 300 tons with 200 mariners and 20 gunners. This ship is also mentioned in the 1588 inventory against the Spanish armada as 120 tons with Captain Samford of 60 mariners and fitted out in London. *MRP.*

1) 18 June 1592. Notice of warrants for the arrest of several crew members of this ship that robbed a Danish ship. *APC-V.22, 536–537.*

2) 18 July 1592. Preparations were made with victuals and furniture to set sail 'in a warlike manner'. After the ship had sailed, this ship and the *Mary Grace* captured the *Whalefish* loaded with salt and other merchandise. *APC-V.23, 36–37.*

Salvator.

1) 12 April 1571. Orders to Anthony Willemson to return 'wares and merchandises' to the company of the *Stillard. APC-V.8, 24.*

Salmon.

1) 27 March 1559. Orders to prepare to sail. *APC-V.7, 73.*

2) 25 March 1579. After returning from a voyage from the Northwest, ship owner Hugh Randolph had not paid all debits and London was pushing him for restitution of those debts. *APC-V.11, 89.*

3) ? September 1588. A request to pay the crew their wages and discharge them. *APC-V.16, 269.*

4) 19 December 1591. A complaint about a cargo seized in 1585 by the duke of Prussia. Seeking restitution. *APC-V.22, 133.*

Samaritan.

1) 17 April 1580. Captain Michael Demundes was licensed to the company of Moscovia to depart London for a fishing voyage in Lappa. *APC-V.11, 449.*

2) 17 November 1588. It was reported that 14 barrels of gunpowder were on this ship and to leave all the barrels with the mayor of Plymouth for safe keeping in case they are needed by the fleet against the Spanish. *APC-V.16, 346.*

3) 27 July 1589. Letter to Sir Francis Drake requesting payment for services in a voyage to Portugal from funds to be made from the sale of corn. *APC-V.17, 428.*

4) 17 September 1600. Orders for this ship to transport items to support English troops in Ireland for the period of 6 months. *APC-V.30, 648.*

5) 15 March 1601. Orders to prepare this ship with victuals and 134 men to serve on the coast of England for 4 months. *APC-V.31, 225–226.*

Samewell.

1) 13 May 1580. Philip Boite captain. French complained of plundering by this ship. *APC-V.12, 16.*

Sampson.

1) 30 March 1592. A matter between merchants of Holland and Zealand and this ship had been settled with the merchants to be paid a small amount of money. This ship was free to depart. *APC-V.22, 381–382.*

Scout.

This ship is mentioned in the 1588 inventory against the Spanish armada as 120 tons with Henry Ashley as captain of 73 mariners. *MRP.*

1) 24 March 1580. Stored victuals and prepared for a voyage to the North Sea and to transport French commissioners. *APC-V.12, 362.*

2) 7 December 1587. Orders to remain at sea in a 'warlike manner' for six weeks, beginning 14 December to 23 January. *APC-V.15, 293.*

3) 5 May 1587. Orders to remain at sea from 23 March until 15 June. *APC-V.15, 108.*

Scorpion.

1) 24 December 1550. Request to send this ship to the Brethren gun founders to determine the pieces for this ship and to protect them from loss. *CSP-D-Addenda,* 406.

Sea Bright.

Records suggest this was a bark.

1) 10 November 1579. Sir John Perrotte was employed to transport munitions for the queen's ships sent to Ireland. *APC-V.12,* 303.

Sea Cock.

1) 29 January 1597. This ship was reported to have wrecked on the coast of Cardigan, Wales, on her course from St. Lucar, Spain to Zeeland, due in part to the pilot. A great quantity of goods had washed on shore and were taken by local inhabitants. *APC-V.28,* 284–285.

Sea Dragon.

1) 7 December 1589. Captain John Froume and Rober Naylour allegedly took ten tons of wine and sugar by "forcible composition" from a French ship from Audierne Brittany. The master of the French ship was seeking restitution. *APC-V.18,* 252.

Seven Stars.

Records suggest that this was a Sixth-Rate 40–60 ton.

1) 17 November 1554. Received 'three half barrels of serpentine powder.' *APC-V.5,* 86.

Sonne. (Sun)

This ship is mentioned in a 1546 inventory as 20 tons with 36 mariners and 4 gunners. Though it is possible that this ship was in service over 60 years, it is more likely that two ships bore the same name. It is mentioned in a 1603 inventory at the time of Elizabeth's death but as 40 tons with 24 mariners, 4 gunners and 2 soldiers. *MRP.*

1) 17 November 1554. Served the king and queen in the Narrow Seas for 2 months and three weeks. *APC-V.5,* 82.

2) 5 May 1587. Orders to remain at sea from 23 March until 15 June. *APC-V.15,* 108.

3) 24 April 1597. Orders to store victuals for 40 men and be ready to sail. *APC-V.27,* 65.

Sonnvettes.

1) 20 April 1559. Embargo removed and prepared to sail. *APC-V.7, 90.*

Spaniard.

1) Ordered to transport soldiers on 7 February 1551 for 20 days. *APC-V.3, 43.*
Sparrow Hawk.

1) 18 September 1576. Orders to release this ship in Rotterdam. *APC-V.9, 205.*

2) 19 September 1576. Ordered to release the ship then go to Scotland. *APC-V.9, 205.*

Spy.

This ship is mentioned in the 1588 inventory against the Spanish armada as 50 tons with Ambrose Ward as captain of 40 mariners. *MRP.*

1) 24 April 1597. Orders to store victuals for 40 men and be ready to sail. *APC-V.27, 65.*

2) 8 June 1598. Orders to sail to service on the Irish coast between Ireland and Scotland to hinder the rebels. *APC-V.28, 496.*

St. Andrew.

This ship is mentioned in the 1603 inventory at the death of Elizabeth as 900 tons with 268 mariners, 32 gunners and 100 soldiers. *MRP.*

1) 24 April 1597. Orders to store victuals and prepare to be at sea for 28 days for 3 months with 400 men. *APC-V.27, 65.*

2) 3 November 1597. Orders to Portsmouth to transport 200 men to Ostend Ireland for defense of that place. *APC-V.28, 96.*

St. Mathew.

This ship is mentioned in the 1603 inventory at the death of Elizabeth as 1000 tons with 340 mariners, 40 gunners and 120 soldiers. *MRP.* An early account believes this was a Spanish ship taken by the English.

1) 24 April 1597. Orders to store victuals for 400 men and be ready to sail. *APC-V.27, 65.*

Steads.

1) 15 May 1558. Ship was at Portsmouth. *APC-V.6, 315.*

Strews.

1) 18 February 1551. Letter to the officers to determine if ship should be sold and for how much. *APC-V.3, 480.*

Sunshine.

Record indicates this barque is 50 tons.

1) 1587. This ship and the *Northstar* were part of the fleet of M. John Davis that set out looking for a passage between Greenland and Iceland. *HCEV-V.3, 146.*

Susan and Harry.

1) 6 November 1580. To be loaded for Levant France in the event a merchant should desire to hire them. *APC-V.12, 258–259.*

2) 18 January 1590. Having completed its service with the admiral against the Spanish, the ship was released to travel to St. Jean de Lux in Southwest France. *APC-V.18, 314.*

3) 13 August 1592. Request sent to Sir Walter Raleigh for payment of wages for mariners of this ship. *APC-V.23, 117–118.*

Sutton.

1) 2 June 1588. Ordered to man, rig and join her majesty's forces at sea. *APC-V.16, 99.*

2) 9 December 1588. Captain Nicholas Webb. Payment of money for the services of this ship. Commendations to the captain for his service. *APC-V.16, 387, 405.*

Swallow.

This ship is mentioned in a 1546 inventory as 240 tons with 130 mariners and 30 gunners. *MRP.* A reference in 1588 indicated this was 360 tons with 160 men. *APC.*

1) 29 July 1563. Excerpt from a letter of Captain Basing of this ship, that he heard from a passing crayer from Newhaven that 2 or 3 men were shot in passing out of Portsmouth. *CSP-D-Addenda, 539.*

Swan.

1) 16 August 1556. Issuance of a bond to deliver 19 casks of herrings to Yarmouth before 2 February 1557. *CSP-D-Addenda, 443.*

2) 12 June 1596. This was one of three ships that acted as a lookout for Spanish ships. They encountered a flyboat, "which made resistance and escaped." *NGCV.*

3) 6 September 1596. This ship returned to Portsmouth with several pieces of ordnance seized at Calais. The council wanted to ensure they were to be used in her majesty's service. *APC-V.26, 142.*

4) 17 December 1598. Orders to Daniel Cornelius, master, to transport 1000 English soldiers to Ireland. *APC-V.29, 368.*

Swiftsure.

This ship is mentioned in a 1578 inventory as 400 tons with 140 mariners, 20 gunners and 80 Soldiers. *MRP.* This ship also served against the Spanish armada of 1588 as 400 tons with Edward Fennar as captain of 200 mariners. *MRP.*

1) 30 July 1576. Orders that Mr. Nicholas Gorge was appointed captain and to prepare himself to take charge of the ship by 10 August. Furthermore, he was to report to the new admiral Mr. William Holstock. *APC-V.9, 175.*

2) 30 September 1577. Orders to receive victuals for 6 weeks and to return to sea as soon as possible. *APC-V.10, 42.*

3) 19 February 1580. Having returned from Ireland, a request to the lord treasurer to pay the mariners. *APC-V.12, 337.*

4) 14 August 1580. Mariners, gunners, and soldiers assigned to this ship were supplied with hose (stockings), shoes, shirts, caps, canvas for breeches and doublets, cotton, and other provisions in preparation for a voyage to Ireland. *APC-V.12, 154.*

5) 13 April 1589. Orders to Captain Goringe that upon receipt of a letter to make preparation to sail and join the fleet against the Spanish with Sir Frances Drake. *APC-V.17, 131.*

6) 29 May 1593. This ship was held, as was Captain George Raiman, for allegedly plundering a French ship. The council informed the mayor of Southampton to release this ship. *APC-V.24, 261.*

7) 13 October 1601. Orders to transport 300 men and winter apparel to English troops in Ireland. The apparel list as follows: A cassock of broad cloth, a pair of venetians, a doublet of canvas, a hat cap, 2 shirts of linen cloth, 2 bands of Holland cloth, 3 pair of Carlisle socks, 3 pair of boots. *APC-V.32, 274–275.*

8) 24 December 1601. Orders to remain on the Irish coast. *APC-V.32, 451.*

9) 9 July 1602. This ship was under the command of Sir William Monson, vice-admiral of the fleet for the coast of Spain and received the same instructions as the *Adventure. CSP-D, 1601–1603, 220–221.*

Thomas.

1) 28 October 1578. The queen was upset with Captain Tamfield for abandoning the fleet on their voyage to the North West parts. Captain Tamfield said the fleet was miscarried. *APC-V.10, 358–359.*

2) 26 February 1579. Owner Thomas Bonham and crew were charged with misdemeanors during their voyage to the Northwest. Recommendations were made for more severe punishment other than wages. *APC-V.11, 59.*

3) 20 August 1598. Warrant issued for the arrest of Thomas Whitbrook who served as captain during an act of piracy of valuable goods. *APC-V.29, 67.*

Thornback.

1) 19 October 1575. This ship had been captured by a pirate ship manned by Englishmen off the coast of Dunkirk. The report mentions other ships under the same circumstances. *APC-V.9, 29.*

Three Moons.

1) 8 July 1580. While travelling to Civil Spain, was overtaken in the Straits of Gibraltar by the Turks. George Clement was held hostage for ransom. At that time, money was being collected for his release. *APC-V.12, 90.*

2) 7 December 1587. Orders to remain at sea in a 'warlike manner' for six weeks, beginning 14 December to 23 January. *APC-V.15, 293.*

3) 5 May 1587. Orders to remain at sea from 23 March until 15 June. *APC-V.15, 108.*

Tiger.

This ship is mentioned in a 1546 inventory as 200 tons with 100 mariners and 20 gunners. This ship is also mentioned in the 1588 inventory against the Spanish armada, at 200 tons, with John Bostock as captain of 100 mariners. This ship is also mentioned in the 1603 inventory at the death of Elizabeth as 200 tons and 70 mariners, 10 gunners and 40 soldiers. *MRP.*

1) 4 December 1556. Report that the ship was unfit for service and recommended it be brought into Harborough for repairs. *APC-V-6, 28.*

2) 8 January 1557. Orders to temporarily accommodate 200 men. *APC-V.6, 235.*

3) 22 January 1557. Orders to remain at Plymouth until the queen needed it. *APC-V.6, 247.*

4) 19 February 1580. Having returned from Ireland, a request to the lord treasurer to pay the mariners. *APC-V.12, 337.*

5) 7 December 1587. Orders to remain at sea in a 'warlike manner' for six weeks, beginning 14 December to 23 January. *APC-V.15, 293.*

6) 18 September 1588. Proposed expedition into Ireland and the provision of victuals. *APC-V.16, 280.*

7) 30 March 1592. A matter between merchants of Holland and Zealand and this ship had been settled with the merchants to be paid a small amount of money. This ship was free to depart. *APC-v.22, 381–3812.*

8) 10 April 1597. In 1593, this ship plundered a ship from Holland. William Holliday was captain at the time and served a prison time for his actions. The Holland merchants were seeking restitution in the value of the lost goods. *APC-V.27, 31–32.*

Toby.

Ship inventory of 1588 indicated this ship was fitted in London at 250 tons and the captain was Robert Barret with 100 mariners.

1) 15 January 1581. While at Bristol, there appears to be a release from her majesty's duty and could be employed if a merchant needed it. *APC-V.12, 312.*

Tramontana.

This ship is mentioned in the inventory of 1588 against the Spanish armada as 150 tons with 70 mariners. This ship is also mentioned in the 1603 inventory at the death of Elizabeth as 140 tons with 52 mariners, 8 gunners and 10 soldiers. *MRP.*

1) 21 September 1597. Basically, this ship received orders to stop any ship carrying corn from the East Countries or Low Countries to Spain. The queen is quoted as comanding "that you shall with all diligence lie in wait for them." *APC-V.28, 8.*

2) 16 April 1601. 'Taken in her victuals to last until 5 August' and was ready to depart with the first good wind. *CSP-D, 1601–1603, 28.*

3) 24 December 1601. Ordered to remain on the Irish coast. *APC-V.32, 451.*

4) 30 August 1603. Ordered to transport the Earl of Tyrone and his servants to Ireland. *APC-V.32, 502.*

Trial. Of London.

1) 17 September 1600. This ship was in service to Ireland from 10 April to 18 July and requested payment for their services. *APC-V.30, 646.*

Trinity.

This ship is mentioned in a 1557 inventory as 300 tons was 20 hackbutters, 40 soldiers, 140 mariners and 20 gunners. *MRP.*

1) 28 April 1553. Ordered to pay William Sherwood of Newcastle for the service of this ship 3 years ago. *CSP-D-Addenda, 423.*

2) 20 March 1558. Ordered to prepare to sail to the Low Countries. *APC-V.7, 69.*

3) 20 April 1559. Embargo removed and prepared to sail. *APC-V.7, 90.*

4) 24 September 1576. Report of spoil while at anchor under the castle of Dealve by Nicolson of Flushing and that he be apprehended under the law. *APC-V.9, 208.*

5) 29 April 1577. Detained after their arrival from Spain laden with spices, oils, and olives to be released. *APC-V.9, 333.*

6) 10 November 1577. Letter to the officers of the port of London to release this ship and allow it to travel to Spain. *APC-V.10, 81.*

7) 8 May 1580. Orders to release the ship for a voyage to Elbing, Poland. *APC-V.12, 6.*

Triumph.

This ship is mentioned in the 1578 inventory as 1000 ton with 450 mariners, 50 gunners and 200 soldiers. *MPR.* This ship is mentioned in the 1588 inventory against the Spanish armada as 1100 tons with Martin Frobisher as captain of 500 mariners. *MRP.*

1) 22 April 1593. A fund was collected and distributed for the relief of maimed soldiers when a carriage of a piece of ordnance broke. *APC-V.24, 200.*

2) 24 April 1597. Ordered to store victuals and be ready to sail.

3) 1 May 1601. This ship was prepared and victuals stored for 6 months with 70 men to serve in Ireland. *APC-V.31, 323.*

Unicorn.

This ship is mentioned in a 1546 inventory as 240 tons with 130 mariners and 16 gunners. This ship is also mentioned in the 1588 inventory against the Spanish armada as 130 tons with James Laughton as captain of 66 mariners. This ship served as a 'coaster' and was out of Bristol. *MRP.*

1) 9 December 1588. Orders for Rasse Hawse to serve her majesty against the Spanish fleet for 2 months and 4 days. A salary was agreed on. *APC-V.16, 404.*

Unity.

This ship is mentioned in the 1588 inventory against the Spanish armada as 80 tons with Humphrey Sidman as captain of 70 mariners. *MRP.*

1) 5 August 1589. Report that this ship was expected to return to London with master Richard Brook and Captain Henry Bird possessing Spanish gold and 'double pistolettes' plundered from a Spanish ship. The gold was brought on shore at Plymouth to the house of James Barnes and from there loaded aboard a ship hidden in chests of powder and munitions. Furthermore, a waistcoat of carnation embroidered in gold was also taken. It was requested by council that the ship be searched upon arrival and the captain, master and mariners be questioned. *APC-V18, 11–13.*

2) 10 August 1589. An additional search is requested of the ship to locate the above-mentioned stolen cargo. *APC-V.18, 28–29*

Uswen. South Shields.

1) 26 November 1565. Description of the inhabitants of the town and three ships, this being one, that was used as a fishing vessel. Was owned by John Bowmaker. *CSP-D-Addenda. 573.*

Vanguard.

This ship is mentioned in the 1588 inventory against the Spanish armada as 500 tons with William Winter as captain of 250 mariners and soldiers. *MRP.*

1) 2 January 1590. Orders that the ship be made ready to sail and transport Lord Willoughby and his forces to aid the French King. Willoughby's forces will be transported to Cherbourg near Cane in Normandy. *APC-V.18, 302.*

2) 31 December 1589. Orders for a month's victuals and made preparations to sail into the West Countries. *APC-V.18, 289.*

3) 30 October 1592. This ship was one of three that received the cargo from the 'great Carrack'. Notice was given to this ship to take care while transporting the cargo along the Thames River. There is mention that some items went missing from the Carrack before being transferred. *APC-V.23, 275.*

Vantage.

1) 25 January 1592. Letter to Sir Henry Palmer admiral of the Narrow seas. Reports that 1500 Spaniards are about St. Mallows. The admiral was on the *Rainbow* accompanied by the *Answer* to determine the purpose of the Spaniards between Newhaven and Hage for a period of 14–15 days. The admiral had permission to take in any merchant or war ship if he felt it necessary. *APC-V.22, 206–207*

Victory.

This ship is mentioned in the 1578 inventory as 803 tons with 330 mariners, 40 gunners and 100 soldiers. This ship is also mentioned in the 1588 inventory against the Spanish armada as 800 tons with John Hawkins as captain of 400 mariners and soldiers. John Hawkins was also rear admiral at that time. *MRP.*

1) 24 April 1597. Orders to store victuals for 400 men and be ready to sail. *APC-V.27, 65.*

Warspight.

This ship is mentioned in the 1603 inventory at the death of Elizabeth as 600 tons with 190 mariners, 30 gunners and 80 soldiers. *MRP.*

1) 28 December 1601. Request for additional victuals while this ship remained on the coast of Ireland. *APC-V.32, 464–465.*

2) 13 October 1601. Orders to transport 200 men and winter apparel to English troops in Ireland. The apparel list as follows: A cassock of broad cloth, a pair of venetians, a doublet of canvas, a hat cap, 2 shirts of linen cloth, 2 bands of Holland cloth, 3 pair of Carlisle socks, 3 pair of boots. *APC-V.32, 274–275.*

3) 23 September 1601. Instructions from the queen that Sir Richard Leveson would command a fleet of ships in a response to the continual possible threats from the king of Spain. This ship and with others would

patrol the coast and prevent or defeat any forces against England. *CSP-D, 1601–1603, 101.*

Watt.

1) 16 March 1602. This ship with three other English ships had chased 4 Portuguese ships. One ship surrendered and was left to drift without a crew. The fight with the other three ships lasted two to three hours then all captured. *CSP-D, 1601–1603, 163.*

William Bonadventure.

1) 20 April 1559. Embargo removed and to prepared to sail. *APC-V.7, 90.*

2) 22 December 1577. This ship was ordered to depart London to Rye East Sussex. *APC-V.10, 123.*

3) 2 February 1591. Requesting to be paid for their services in 1588 against the Spanish. Previous requests for payment had been unaddressed. *APC-V.22, 222.*

4) 24 June 1601. Master Richard Morecock. This ship was loaded and ready to transport merchandise to Hamburg. *APC-V.31, 451.*

William and John.

1) 5 September 1589. Inventory of received cargo of 200 sacks of wheat and 200 sacks of rye. *APC-V.18, 82.*

2) 28 November 1596. Sir Walter Raleigh received a petition from Nicholas Simonson, shipwright for work making this ship serviceable. *APC-V.26, 334.*

White Bear.

This ship is mentioned in the 1578 inventory as 900 tons with 300 mariners, 50 gunners and 200 soldiers. This ship is also mentioned in the 1588 inventory against the Spanish armada as 1000 tons with Edmund Sheffield as captain of 500 mariners and soldiers. *MRP.*

1) 16 June 1591. Requesting payment for an absent official during his time under Lord Sheffield against the Spaniards. *APC-V.21, 203.*

White Falcon.

1) 19 July 1589. A request was made for a full inventory of this ship including powder, shot, armor and other munitions. *APC-V.17, 409.*

White Hart.

1) 16 August 1577. Letter to Spain to arrest this ship and the captain and all her tackle. No reason could be found why. *APC-V.10, 17.*

White Lion.

1) 23 March 1589. Orders to delay the ship belonging to Pole Wheel while in Portsmouth and an inventory conducted. There was concern that a delay would spoil the cargo. *APC-V.18, 439–440.*

2) 20 April 1590. Request for inventory of this ship while in Weymouth. *APC-V.19, 71.*

3) 21 April 1590. Mistress Chidley whose husband died while at sea, served a warrant to seize the ship from the lord admiral. Orders were passed not to sell any part of the ship including tackle, furniture or anything until the matter was decided by a court of law. *APC-V.19, 75.*

4) 19 July 1590. Request for the inventory of the items sold and items in the possession of Mistress Chidley. It would appear the matter was settled. *APC-V.19, 330.*

5) 14 December 1590. The complaint by Mistress Chidley held this ship at Weymouth. It was well noted that it was at great expense of the widow to maintain the ship while it was determined of the ownership. The 'mistress had made no sales yet'. *APC-V.20, 114.*

6) 21 December 1590. Mistress Chidley made a claim to 2 brass culverins that belonged to the ship her late husband owned. It would appear a few pieces of ordnance were removed and melted down. *APC-V.20, 144.*

7) 27 June 1591. No solution as to the ownership of the cannons yet. *APC-V.21, 237–238.*

8) 13 May 1593. Petition to the council on behalf of Oliver Skinner merchant of London for the possession of one half of this ship. *APC-V.24, 229–230.*

Young.

1) 14 December 1579. Dispute over payment of a load of fish and the ship had been detained until the matter can be settled. *APC-V.11, 342*

Sources used in this part:

APC: Acts of the Privy Council of England. 32 Volumes.

CSP-C: Calendar of State Papers, Colonial Series. Various volumes.

CSP-D: *Calendar of State Papers Relating to England, Domestic Series.* Various volumes.

CSP-F: *Calendar of State Papers Relating to England, Foreign Series.* Various volumes.

HCEV-*Hakluyt's Collection of the Early Voyages, Travels, and Discoveries.* London, 1810.

MRP-*Memoirs of the Rise and Progress of the Royal Navy.* London, 1806.

NHGB-*The Naval History of Great Britain.* London, 1761.

NGCV- *New General Collection of Voyages and Travels,* Volume 1, London, 1744.

SFLB-*Sea Fights and Land Battles from Alfred to Victoria.* London, 1869.

1-3. Event Records of French Ships.

Barge. Of Dieppe.
1) 10 March 1577. This ship was plundered by English pirates while en route to Dieppe with a cargo of herring and tanned hides about 8 January 1576. *APC-V.10, 181.*

Bonvoloire. Of Normandy.
Records suggest this was 30 tons.
1) 22 February 1577. Complains of English pirates plundering cargo of wine. Two other incidents are mentioned, but no ship names. *APC-V.10, 173*

Bon Adventure.
Records indicate this was 50 tons.
1) 21 November 1551. Jacques Masse of Fecamp was reported as captain. *APC-V.3, 422.*
2) 11 December 1575. Letter to the owners of the ship to question all crew regarding an incident. I am unable to determine what it was. *APC-V.9, 60.*
3) 24 December 1575. Letter to the owners, Vigvier and Tiratt that were under suspicion of being pirates and had sold 'some of her majesty's subjects to the Turks'. *APC-V.9, 65.*

4) 29 June 1576. Flushing pirates had overtaken this ship and sought restitution. *APC-V.9, 151–152.*

5) 4 March 1592. Captain Jehan Mallibre. This ship was captured by English and taken to the port of Plymouth. The council ordered her release without plunder and allowed to return to France. *APC-V.24, 98–99.*

Brave.
Records suggest that this was a ship of war.
1) Ordered to account for goods taken from two Norwegian hoys. *APC-V.7, 360.*

Catalina de St. Vincent.
1) 22 October 1591. This ship was captured by Edward Lewis, captain of the *Golden Hine* of Weymouth. Restitution was requested of the return or compensation for the munitions, furniture, and cargo. *APC-V.22, 35.*

Catherine. Or Katherine.
1) 28 May 1553, this ship was reported to have been owned by Pierre Catell. Several of his crew were charged with the murder and robbery of Englishmen. This may be in conjunction with the capture of the *Aucher*.

2) 28 December 1576. Captain Peron Alhand. Orders from England to all English ships to allow this ship to pass as it contained cargo of the French King to London. *APC-V.9, 260.*

3) 11 December 1592. This ship was captured by an English ship and brought into Portsmouth. Charges were filed against the French captain Mark Prigent after refusing to acknowledge the loss of merchandise belonging to French merchants and had to sue him. *APC-V.23, 358.*

4) 24 March 1601. It was reported that this ship was wrecked on the coastal entrance to Shoreham England containing wine, oil, wool, and other goods. *APC-V.31, 372.*

Charles de Grand.
1) 2 February 1588. Petition to England to allow this ship with a cargo of corn from Dieppe to stop in Southampton then to Middleburgh in Zealand. *APC-V.17, 68.*

Collett.
1) 17 September 1598. Complaint against an English pirate that took a Spanish horse that belonged to the governor of Brest, and other goods belonging to the master of the ship including the ship's tackle. *APC-V.29, 170.*

Constance.

1) 17 January 1598. Letter of complaint regarding an incident of 3 years ago still seeking redemption from the owners of this ship. *APC-V.28, 247–248.*

Crescent. Middlesbrough.

1) 24 October 1592. Letter to Sir Walter Raleigh regarding this ship that had been captured with a cargo of salt and other merchandise and brought into Dartmouth, to be released and their captors apprehended. *APC-V.23, 237.*

Diamond. Rye.

1) 11 July 1591. Cutbert Carr, master of this ship filed a complaint regarding English plundering of cargo seven leagues from the Isle Use. Seeking restitution of the great loss. *APC-V.21, 271–272.*

Eagle. Of Ingerville.

1) 18 January 1581. Complained to London that this ship was plundered by Englishmen on 20 December 1580. The cargo stolen was wine and taken to the Isle of Wight for ransom. Requested restitution and punishment. *APC-V.12, 316.*

Ermine.

1) 10 December 1588. Complaints of plundering their cargo of corn and meal loaded in Calais for Villa Nova in Portugal and taken by English pirates into Cornwall and sold to local inhabitants. Seeking restitution. *APC-V. 16, 414–415.*

Esperance. Of Conquet.

1) 25 May 1574. Orders to hold this ship and to apprehend Rowland Torner and everything be removed. *APC-V.8, 144.*

2) 22 January 1589. It was reported that this ship was carrying cargo to Scotland from Dieppe and on New Year's Day was driven on the coast between Cromer and Bieston in the county of Norfolk and wrecked. Most of the cargo was taken by local inhabitants and the owner was seeking restitution for partial loss. I was unable to locate Bieston in Norfolk, ancient or recent, with similar spelling, so it will not be in part 3. *APC-V.17, 41–42.*

Esperance. Of St. Malo.

1) 16 May 1596. Complaint filed against Nicholas Saunders and Benjamin Nutking who had violently boarded this ship and took "certain ballutes of linen cloth" belonging to French Merchants. Seeking restitution. *APC-V.25, 399.*

Faulcon.

1) 28 May 1553. This ship was reported to have taken an English ship the *Aucher. APC-V.4, 273.*

Fleme des Les.

1) 14 June 1573. Captured by a Captain Butler and Garret between Dieppe and Spain. *APC-V.8, 113.*

Fleur de Lys. Flower de Lyce.

1) 27 April 1557. Correspondence indicates that the captain was John Rybawde.

2) 24 August 1589. This ship was captured in the Portuguese voyage. Martin Heithuses was master of the ship and requested to be released from Plymouth with a cargo of pilchard (fish) now hired by Philippe Corsini for a voyage to Italy. *APC-V.18, 67.*

Francis. Of Dieppe.

1) 28 November 1589. Orders for the restitution of all tackle, apparel, and furniture. *APC-V.18, 242.*

2) 6 January 1597. Newcastle English merchants seeking restitution for an act of piracy from this ship. *APC-V.28, 220.*

3) 29 October 1598. Additional information regarding the piracy. The ship the *Flying Dragon* was to be arrested and all her ordnance, munitions, sails, and tackle held for inspection. *APC-V.29, 247.*

Gift of God. Of Dieppe.

1) 6 January 1597. Newcastle English merchants seeking restitution for an act of piracy from this ship. *APC-V.28, 220.*

Greyhound.

1) 14 May 1587. Master John Hesbert was seeking restitution for the plunder of a cargo out of Spain by Sir Thomas Leighton, knight, captain of the Isle of Garnesey. The master requested either the cargo be returned or financial restitution. *APC-V.15, 77.*

2) 11 June 1587. Orders to compensate the loss of cargo plundered by Sir Thomas Leighton. *APC-V.15, 125–126.*

Guallander-Alias Sea Gull.

1) 10 September 1598. Complaint against English pirates for plundering cargo, furniture, victuals, salt, and other items required for fishing in Newfoundland. Seeking restitution. *APC-V.29, 152.*

Guilliame.

1) 15 December 1577. This was one of four ships detained at Dartmouth and Plymouth England under suspicion that their cargo belonged to Spain consigned to the Low Countries and Roan. The ship was released after determining the cargo was correct. *APC-V.10, 119.*

Hare.

1) 19 April 1581. Nicholas and Robert Belleur of Dieppe requested retribution for piracy committed by Captain Derick. *APC-V.13, 32.*

Holy Ghost.

1) 17 November 1591. Cargo of fish and oil plundered by Englishmen Captain Thinn and Captain Cross. Seeking restitution. *APC-V.22, 66.*

Hope.

1) 22 April 1587. Complaints of plundering by Englishmen after this ship departed Calais with a cargo of salt. Seeking restitution of cargo or financial compensation. *APC-V.15, 44.*

2) 12 August 1590. Captured by Sir John Hawkins and Sir Martin Frobisher under orders from her majesty during the Spanish campaign. Cargo was inspected. It would appear some of the cargo was sold before the inventory was made. *APC-V.19, 384.*

John. Abbevill.

1) 25 September 1596. Request for assistance for the recovery of plundered items from this ship by English. Seeking restitution. *APC-V.26, 200–201.*

La Bende.

1) 28 December 1576. Was attacked and everything taken by pirates. "Having only recovered the bare hull." The owner requested to be allowed to restock in England. *APC-V.9, 259.*

La Doming.

1) 4 March 1592. This ship was arrested and taken to Newhaven carrying wine and the cargo taken. The owners were seeking restitution for the loss. *APC-V.24, 95.*

La Esperance.

1) 20 February 1576. 39 tons of Gascoigne wine was stolen from this ship by John Callis, Englishman. *APC-V.9, 293.*

Le Favori.

Records indicate this was a 60 tons barque.

1) 4 March 1592. Captain Pierre Tesson. This ship was captured by English and taken to the port of Plymouth. The council ordered her release without plunder and allowed to return to France. *APC-V.24, 98–99.*

La Grande Aventureuse.

1) 22 June 1570. License to allow this ship to ground itself for repairs in the river of Newport. "Weather beaten upon the seas." *APC-V.7, 369.*

La Jaune.

1) 4 March 1592. This ship was arrested and taken to Newhaven carrying wine and the cargo taken. The owners were seeking restitution for the loss. *APC-V.24, 95.*

Le Jaques.

Records indicate this was a 50-ton barque.

1) 4 March 1592. Captain was Robert du Puis. This ship was captured by the English and taken to the port of Plymouth. The council ordered her release without plunder and allowed to return to France. *APC-V.24, 98–99.*

Lanechepint.

1) 27 September 1590. A merchant of Calais complained about the plundering of 9 bags of wool, 16 bags of gallnuts, 6 pipes of oil and 2 bags of cotton by Captain Turner and taken to Plymouth. *APC-V.19, 462.*

La Petite Aventureuse.

1) 22 June 1570. License to allow this ship to ground itself for repairs in the river of Newport. "Weather beaten upon the seas." *APC-V.7, 369.*

Lazarus.

1) 15 August 1588. A letter of complaint regarding an English pirate Robert Smith who plundered 49 tons of cognac and sold it. The council requested that as much of the wine be recovered as possible. *APC-V.16, 236.*

2) 13 May 1590. Complaints of piracy by Robert Smith who plundered a cargo of wine and ship, tackle and furniture were sold in England and Ireland. Seeking restitution in payment or recovery of plundered items. *APC-V.19, 123–124.*

3) 9 June 1590. Warrant issued for the arrest of Englishman John Smith and others who plundered this ship in 1588. *APC-V.19, 203.*

Le Bon Voulloir.
1) 5 March 1577. This ship was plundered by English pirates between Calais and Dover of a cargo of wine by Robert Scarborough. Seeking restitution. *APC-V.10, 179.*

Levan.
1) 13 September 1587. Complaints of plundering by Englishmen of a cargo that departed France to Ireland. *APC-V.15, 236.*

Little Salamander.
Record indicates 50 ton.
1) 5 November 1592. Owner James Martell complained of the loss of a cargo of coal and worried about those who greatly needed it. *APC-V.23, 284.*

Lyon.
1) 26 March 1573. Orders to deliver 25 tons of wine belonging to John De la Fargue of Bordeaux. *APC-V.8, 91.*

Maudlyn.
1) 26 June 1586. Owner seeking restitution for plundering of the cargo by English pirates and the dispersing of the stolen cargo in Ireland. *APC-V.14, 162.*

Margaret. Of Dieppe.
1) 21 December 1553, the Privy Council ordered this ship be returned to Jasper Goodbonte with all ordnance. *APC-V.4, 380.*
2) 7 June 1588. A letter of complaint for the apprehension of Captain Roch or any accomplices for the piracy committed by Englishmen. *APC-V.16, 117.*

Margarite. Of Brittany.
1) 5 February 1589. Complaints against piracy by English Captain Middlesden and Willian Lynce of plundering a cargo of plates (copper?) oils, ginger, pepper, and other merchandise. *APC-V.17, 69.*

Mary. Of Cane.
1) 11 August 1577. This ship was captured by pirates and brought into Somercott. The owner Robert Moulyn was seeking restitution. *APC-V.10, 14.*

Marie.

1) 18 June 1600. Complaint against an English ship the *Guyana* owned by the Earl of Cumberland had plundered cargo from this ship. *APC-V.30, 388–389.*

Mary. Of Jersey.

Barque.

1) 20 September 1589. Loaded with 55 butts of Spanish wine in St. Malo to deliver to Dieppe, was driven by "contrary winds" into the Thames River. Requested to be allowed to depart with an additional amount of corn. *APC-V.18, 97.*

2) 7 February 1590. A request to determine if Anthony had sent a ton of corn in this ship to Spain. "Please inform". *APC-V.20.278.*

Mary. Of Odyan.

1) 5 April 1547. This ship arrived in England, but their cargo was damaged by rats and moisture from lying unmoved. *CSP-D-Addenda. 322.*

Mary. Of Rosco.

Records suggest this was 60 tons.

1) 14 May 1590.Complaints of piracy of wines and other merchandise taken from the ship while returning from Spain to Calais. Warrant for seizing the plundered goods and the arrest of Henry Perry, Jacob Whidon and Captain Stransuish. The complainants were in fear for their lives and threatened by the English pirates. *APC-V.19, 150–151.*

Michael.

1) 15 December 1577. This was one of four ships detained at Dartmouth and Plymouth England under suspicion that their cargo belonged to Spain consigned to the Low Countries and Roan. The ships were released after determining the cargo was correct. *APC-V.10, 119.*

Moon.

Records indicate a barque.

1) 16 August 1590. Captured by the English ship *Fortune* and all cargo of wine, brass, pans, honey, soap and other merchandise for Galway Ireland. Seeking restitution. *APC-V.19, 392.*

Neptune.

1) 20 August 1589. A letter requesting assistance for the recovery of the cargo of salt pirated by Patrick Turner and Robert Grimes. *APC-V.18, 52.*

2) 23 August 1590. Request that all merchandise, money, and cargo plundered by Sir John Hawkins, to be returned or restitution made. *APC-V.19, 413.*

Nicholas.

1) 5 April 1547. This ship arrived in England, but its cargo was damaged by rats and moisture from lying unmoved. *CSP-D-Addenda. 322.*

2) 16 October 1589. A request to release this ship captured during the Portugal voyage now in Bridgewater to be released with all her apparel, tackle, furniture, and all belonging to the ship and to be allowed to leave and return to France. *APC-V.18, 183–184.*

3) 17 November 1591. Seeking restitution for the plundered cargo of Newfoundland fish taken at sea by Captain William Tokins of the Hampton. *APC-V.22, 66.*

New Margaret.

1) 18 September 1579. A report this ship was plundered of its cargo by an English ship. The captain informed England that the pirate ship was at Portsmouth. *APC-V.11, 268.*

Norman.

1) 15 December 1577. This was one of four ships detained at Dartmouth and Plymouth England under suspicion that their cargo belonged to Spain consigned to the Low Countries and Roan. The ship was released after determining the cargo was correct. *APC-V.10, 119.*

Peter.

1) 12 December 1556. The ship was seized at Brest in Brittany. One of the ship's owners at the time was John Hawkins.

2) 3 November 1589. A brief description of the cargo that was taken when the ship was seized which included: "small rasers or spurres. One packe of bayes found in search." *APC-V.18, 205.*

Rose (Alias le Puche)

1) 27 June 1571. Orders to return all tackle and ordnance. *APC-V.8, 32.*

Salamander. Dieppe, France.

1) 6 June 1591. Request for a passport for Captain Gonnan of Dieppe with a weight of eight tons, to serve the French king against all enemies in the channel. *APC-V.21, 176.*

2) 17 September 1592. Seeking restitution from pirating by an English ship the *Fortune* of a cargo of salt, sugar, wine, oil, and other merchandise.

Seeking the apprehension of the captain and crew of the *Fortune*. *APC-V.23, 200.*

3) 6 October 1600. This ship was taken at sea by the English ship the *Margaret* and *John* and most of the cargo was taken. Seeking the arrest of those involved and restitution. *APC-V-30, 715.*

Santa Maria.

1) 20 February 1596. This ship was captured changing orders to dispose of the goods and merchandise taken from this ship. The council determined it was not a prize and passed orders to restore all ordnance, masts, sails, anchors, cables, ropes, tackle and all furniture belonging to this ship and to make full restitution. *APC-V.26, 503–504.*

Small Henry. Dieppe.

1) 2 July 1592. Complaint filed against this ship by an Irishman whose ship was plundered of a cargo of 36 tons of sack, half a ton of oil, seven pieces of ordnance with other furniture.

St. Catherine. Marcellus.

1) 14 March 1577. A storm wrecked this ship on the Isle of Sheppey, an island off the northern coast of Kent. Peter Aillan was the master. *APC-V.10, 184–185.*

2) 23 March 1577. A letter to the dean of Canterbury to recover as much merchandise that local people took from the ship as could be recovered. *APC-V.10. 192.*

St. Jehan.

Records indicate this was a barque of 50 tons.

1) 4 March 1593. This ship was captured by English and taken to Sandwich by Captain Bostock and unloaded of its cargo of salt. Orders from the council to release this ship and allow it to continue. *APC-V.24, 96.*

St. John. Of Abberville.

1) 17 December 1577. Letter of restitution to Nicholas Bremen owner and master, for 10 casts, 5 barrels and a half of herring and 1 barrel of white salt taken by a pirate, Phipson. *APC-V.10, 122.*

St. Peter. From Calais.

1) 12 August 1590. Captured by Sir John Hawkins and Sir Marten Furbisher [*sic*]under orders from her majesty during the Spanish campaign.

Cargo was inspected. It would appear some of the cargo was sold before inventory. *APC-V.19, 384*

St. Vincent.
1) 15 December 1577. This was one of four ships detained at Dartmouth and Plymouth England under suspicion that their cargo belonged to Spain consigned to the Low Countries and Roan. The ships were released after determining the cargo was correct. *APC-V.10, 119.*

Unicorn.
Record indicates it was 150 ton.
1) 9 May 1573. Request from the ship returning out of the Barbary to have access to access to English ports to sell their goods. *APC-V.8, 104.*

1–4. Event Records of Miscellaneous Ships.

Abraham. Ireland.
1) 14 June 1573. Letter to Ireland that this ship and Captain Garrate were wanted as pirates. *APC-V.8,113.*

Abraham. Lubeck, Germany.
Records indicate at 250 tons.
1) 15 April 1590. Complains of English piracy committed by Captain Webb and William Inganatt. "Seeking restitution". *APC-V.19, 61.*
2) 30 May 1590. Released from service. Henry Boult was master. *APC-V.19,185.*
3) 23 August 1590. Captured by English Captain Whidden with a cargo of 'pipe staves' besides the ballast confiscated under suspicion of containing 'warlike provision or munitions.' Released to depart port. *APC-V.19, 412.*
Angel. German.
1) On 9 June 1551. Captain Albert Grete given notice of charges brought against the ship for plundering an Irish ship in 1545.

Angel of Gabriel. Rostock, Germany.
Records indicate at 120 tons. Each referenced document indicted the *Angel of Gabriel* of Rostock Germany, but conflicting reports the ship sank and 'everything but the ballast' are separated by almost 15 years.

1) 3 January 1575. Requesting the recovery of this ship that sank off the coast of Isle of Sillye on her way to Flanders. Laden with spices. *APC-V.9, 70.*

2) 24 August 1589. Requested permission to depart Plymouth laden with 'deal board, wainscot and clapboard to their countries. *APC-V.18, 68.*

3) 12 April 1590. Requested compensation for losses incurred during the late Portugal voyage. Released if promised not to carry or convey munitions or war implements for Spain. *APC-V.19, 48.*

4) 15 April 1590. Taken of its cargo of tackle, furniture everything but the ballast, Hans Wegerner was released to their destination. *APC-V.19, 63.*

5) 24 December 1590. Master Urin Schult was released from Bristol promising they would not transport goods to Lisbon Portugal. *APC-V.20. 162.*

6) 25 February 1599. This ship had arrived from Hamburg and sent into Ireland for her majesty's service. The crew complained of their "Great misery and want of means to relieve themselves" in the form of payment. *APC-V.29, 599.*

Aragusy. Venice.
1) 16 June 1591. Henry Sackford requested allowances for lending certain things such as victuals, cordage, wood, and sails to this ship brought into Plymouth. Furthermore, sought pay for the crew's time. This ship may have been plundered to lose those items. *APC-V.21, 207.*

Bear. Germany.
1) 7 May 1587. Departed Lubeck for Lisbon then to Candado then loaded with sweet wine and fruit for London but was plundered by a bark called the *Fortunata* and carried to Zealand. Seeking restitution. *APC-V.15, 68–69.*

Black Raven. Dutch.
1) 31 April 1587. Loaded with a cargo from England merchants, the ship was captured and taken to Portsmouth under the pretense that the cargo was Spanish. Requests that the ship be released. *APC-V.15, 59–60.*

(Black) Bull. Hamburg, Germany.
1) 21 October 1576. Letter to Prince of Orange for restitution for merchandise on this ship belonging to merchants in London that was overtaken by a Dutch ship. This ship was in Spain at that time. *APC-V.9, 216.*

2) 15 September 1591. This was one of four of the Earl of Cumberland's prizes taken at sea during King Phillip's attempted invasion of England. The owners sought restitution. *APC-V.21, 447–448.*

Blue Dove. Hamburg.

1) 4 May 1597. Complaint filed against 3 English pirate ships that took this ship by force parcels of goods and merchandise. Requested the arrest of the pirates. *APC-V.27*, 86–87.

2) 19 June 1597. Seeking restitution for the plunder. *APC-V.27*, 219.

Blue Pigeon. Hamburg.

1) 29 May 1597. This ship was stripped of her cables, anchors, ordnance, and other munitions and taken into Plymouth. The council ordered the ship be restored. *APC-V.27*, 158.

Cat. Holland.

1) 8 March 1598. Request for payment for wheat taken from this ship for her majesty's soldiers in Ireland. *APC-V.29*, 633–634.

Christopher. Scotland.

1) 11 April 1593. William Scott of Kirkaldy Scotland, filed a complaint against certain merchants of London and was plundered of a cargo of salt and wine for the Island of Azores, Spain in 1589. Seeking restitution. *APC-V.24*, 175–176.

Daniel. Pomerania.

1) 10 September 1590. A request for the location of plundered cargo of 25 tons of oats and 5 tons of sugar taken by Captain William Morgan and brought into Wales. *APC-V.19*, 428.

2) 9 August 1590. Cargo was confiscated by Captain Morgan, seeking restitution. *APC-V.19*, 369.

3) 10 September 1590. Mention of 25 tons of oats and 5 tons of sugar confiscated by Captain William Morgan. *APC-V.19*, 428.

Daniel. Poland.

1) 28 October 1590. Joseph Marchwart master of this ship filed a complaint against Captain William Morgan that took a cargo of oats and sugar taken at the Isles of St. Micheal. *APCV.20*, 57.

David. Ireland.

1) 14 June 1573. Letter to Ireland that this ship and Captain Butler were wanted as pirates. *APC-V.8,113*.

David. Prussia.

1) 24 August 1589. Requested permission to depart Plymouth laden with 'deal board, wainscot and clapboard to their countries, (Konigsberg, now Kaliningrad). *APC-V.18*, 68.

David.

This ship was captured in the Portugal voyage against Spain. I am unsure of its origin.

1) 23 March 1589. Orders to bring this ship into Portsmouth and of the sale of her furniture, tackle, and other provisions. *APC-V.18, 440.*

Dolphin. (Encuson)

Records indicate this was a flyboat.

1) 16 April 1592. Notice to officials that this ship was in Dartmouth harbor preparing to sail to Newfoundland for fishing. Notice that if any foreigner was to attempt to hire this ship, to arrest them. *APC-V.22, 401–402.*

Dove. Zeeland.

1) 5 October 1600. The Privy Council received a letter of assistance to recover items from this ship that wrecked in Sussex, England that local inhabitants took. *APC-V.30, 713.*

Dragon. Dutch.

1) 31 April 1587. Loaded with a cargo from England merchants, the ship was captured and taken to Portsmouth under the pretense that the cargo was Spanish. Requested that the ship be released. *APC-V.15, 59–60.*

Dudley. Possibly Spanish.

1) 19 July 1590. This galleon was captured with letters of reprisal originating from Spain or Portugal and taken to Falmouth England. "Mariners of that ship have made spoil and havoc of the goods and do offer to make sale of the same to any who will buy it." An inventory was made of the surviving goods that weren't plundered. Seeking restitution. *APC-V.19, 329.*

Eagle. Bremen, Germany.

Records suggest this was a hulk.

1) 10 March 1577. While from St. Lucars, Spain toward Zealand to discharge her cargo of oils, wines, sugar, ginger, and other merchandise, was driven into Plymouth England. On 23 February was lost because of a storm. Letter requesting the recovery of items. *APC-V.10, 183.*

Elephant. Sweden.

1) 11 March 1590. Complaint filed by Duke Charles, brother of the King of Sweden, sent two ships to Queen Elizabeth. One account is that the ship

was transporting a cargo of ship masts to Spain with a license from England. Off the coast of France it began to leak faster than they could bail and pump water out, and it wrecked on the western coast of England where the cargo was stolen. This is an inventory. This rare list includes the location of where each stolen mast was at the time.

- One mast lay at Osmington of 20 hands and 84 foot long.
- One mast was located at Wearham that was 17 handles about and 24 feet long.
- 4 masts were at Corse Castle of 25 hands long.
- At Bruncksey Castle, 1 mast of 18 hands about and 84 feet long.
- At Christ Church was one mast 18 hands thick and 92 feet long.
- At Limington there were 3 masts 18 hands thick and 80 feet long.
- At Cowes Castle in the Isle of Wight, there was 21 from 17 to 24 hands.
- At Hampton, Mr. Lambert had 4 masts of 23 hands long and 80 foot long.

APC-V.20, 350.

Experience. Venetian.

1) 12 January 1599. Controversy regarding the cargo ownership and if it was a legitimate prize. One side claimed the cargo was Spanish, the other claimed Italian. The ship was taken to Plymouth. *APC-V.29, 455.*

2) 17 January 1599. Additional claims by English merchants that loaded cargo in this ship to Venice and lost that merchandise. *APC-V.29, 473.*

3) 26 February 1599. Orders from the judge of the admiralty to hold the council and address this and other issues on a Sunday. *APC-V.29, 617.*

4) 25 March 1599. Orders to give full restitution to the merchants who sustained losses. *APC-V.29, 672.*

Flying Ghost. Portugal.

Records suggest this was a hulk.

1) 3 February 1576. This ship captured and took all merchandise from the English ship the *Black Raven*. A Spaniard, Andrew Ruiz, had laid claim to the salt. *APC-V.9, 279.*

Flying Hart. Amsterdam.

1) 30 October 1597. Complaints about English pirates and the cargo of Spanish wool, ginger and other goods taken from this ship. Orders to place locks on all decks where storage was. *APV-V.28, 68.*

Fortune. Aberdeen Scotland.

Records suggest this was a bark.

1) 3 August 1579. A storm drove this ship to Seton where it perished. Much of the cargo was recovered by people living nearby. *APC-V.11, 220.*

Fortune. German/Prussia. Danzig.

Records indicate 120 tons.

1) 24 August 1589. Requested permission to depart Plymouth laden with 'deal board, wainscot and clapboard to their countries, (Prussian city that is now Kaliningrad). *APC-V.18, 68.*

2) 29 September 1589. Request to allow this ship at Plymouth, to travel to Italy with its cargo. *APC-V.18, 150.*

3) 30 May 1590. Released from service. Derick Lamberston was master. *APC-V.19, 185.*

4) 18 December 1597. Permission to sell foreign wheat in English ports. *APC-V.28, 189–190.*

Four Sons of Ammon. Dutch.

1) 12 July 1597. Complaint for plundering from this ship by the *Moon*, while the ship was along the coast of Spain and the cargo sold in English ports. Seeking restitution. *APC-V.27, 286.*

Gift. Ireland?

1) 24 March 1597. Letter to authorities to conclude the matter of the recovery of this ship and the goods pirated from it taken at Falmouth.

Gold Noble. Barbary, North Africa.

1) 24 December 1590. Complaint filed by John Bird who was a merchant and was pirated by an English ship and was "by violence put into great danger of perishing" and lost their anchors, cables, masts other furniture of the ship, the ordnance, shot and victuals. Bird disagreed with a decision the court ruled but made repairs to the ship and completed its voyage to Barbary. *APCV.20, 164.*

Golden Faulcon. Netherlands.

1) 16 March 1585. Complaint this ship was plundered by English pirates while on her way from St. Malloes to Flushing. *APC-V.14, 31.*

Golden Lion. Denmark.

1) 18 October 1577. Letter describing actions against Robert Hix, the pirate who plundered the merchandise from this ship, was to be brought to London to stand charges. *APC-V.10, 58.*

2) 11 November 1577. Seeking permission to persue the pirate but lacked tackle. *APC-V.10, 83.*

3) 6 November 1579. Reported as plundered by an English pirate. Sought restitution. *APC-V.11, 300–301.*

George.
1) 14 April 1580. While returning from Flanders with merchandise, was driven by a tempest on the coast of Northumberland at Wodrington. *APC-V.11, 447.*

Good Fortune. Of Lieth, Scotland.
1) 14 November 1601. A request for assistance for the recovery of pirated cargo taken near Cork by Walter Bethell. Seeking restitution. *APC-V.32, 361.*

Grace of God.
1) 2 March 1590. Reminder for payment to this ship for its service time against the Spanish fleet. *APC-V.20, 319.*

2) 15 July 1590. An old claim remained unpaid. Requesting pay for serving Queen's Elizabeth's navy against the Spanish. *APC-V.19, 325.*

Greenwolf.
Described as 250 ton.
1) 1 February 1570. Held in Dartmouth, orders to Captain Cornelius Rosendale that the ship was permitted to travel to Spain. *APC-V.8, 10.*
Griffin. Dutch.
1) 7 April 1597. This ship was captured by an English ship and pinnace belonging to the Earl of Cumberland and Sir Thomas Gerrard, carrying 153 pipes of sweet wine, 750 frayles of raisins and other goods. The Englishmen took 26 pipes of wine and a part of the raisins and cast the master on shore in Plymouth. Sought restitution. *APC-V.27, 19.*

2) 24 February 1598. Complaint that payment has not been made regarding incident of 7 April 1597. *APC-V.28, 334.*

Gripe. Germany.
Described as 80 tons.
1) 29 September 1589. Orders to release this ship and restore its ordnance, sails and cables. *AC-V.18, 151–152.*

Half Moon. Denmark.
1) 12 October 1596. Warrant issued for the arrest of Thomas Webb, once captain of this ship. Order given to search any house or houses for him and any accomplices. *APC-V.26, 168–169.*

Hare. Belgium.

1) 2 November 1578. Letter of complaint about an English pirate Clerk, who plundered the cargo of oil, cochianello and other merchandise. *APC-V.10, 366.*

2) 29 September 1590. Vessel was searched for contraband of war and Spanish goods. *APC-V.19, 479*

Hope. Netherlands.

1) 6 March 1585. It would appear this ship was plundered by John Bird of London. The claimant required further investigation. *APC-V.14, 22.*

Hunter. Germany.

1) 20 February 1589. Request for release from the port of Plymouth to continue their voyage. *APC-V.17, 82.*

James. Ireland.

1) 5 November 1598. This ship was pirated while transporting 4400 cow hides toward Spain. The ship was in Plymouth and had paid customs and requested restitution. *APC-V.29, 266.*

Jedion. Dutch.

1) 6 April 1565. At Dartmouth. Orders to Peter Carew to return ship with tackle and apparel. *APC-V.7, 211.*

John Baptist. Holland.

1) 23 October 1590. Complaint filed after this ship was in Plymouth then John Bostock captain of the *Crane* in her majesty's service "hath very disorderly riffled and taken out of the said ship certain commodities, keeping the pilot prisoner aboard her majesty's ship". Orders to question the master and all the crew. *APC-V.20, 46.*

Jonas. Holland.

1) 2 July 1589. Complaints of plundering by English ships and their cargo taken of rye, wheat, and corn off the coast of Portugal. The English agreed to pay a reasonable sum for the surviving corn on board and promised not to sell the grain to an enemy. *APC-V.17, 339.*

2) 15 February 1590. Orders to release this ship with all its tackle, furniture, and munitions. *APC-V.18, 366.*

3) 18 January 1590. Orders to Sir John Hawkins to take possession of 3000 clapboard taken from this ship. *APC-V.18, 315.*

4) 24 February 1590. Orders to pay Joachim Persell, master and owner of this ship, for the 240 tons of corn taken from this ship and prepare this ship for sail. *APC-V.18, 385.*

5) 30 April 1592. Letter of restitution from Captain Cornelius Cornerison for the following items that were plundered: 20 tons of syrup in divers casks, 9 tons in several casks and 17 bags of almonds, 50 packs of buck skins, 77 hogsheads of alleles, 30 chests of sugar, 99 hogsheads and six barrels of sugar, 17 half chests of sugar, 685 skins full of anneal, one barrel of dates and other like goods. Those were pirated by William Batten captain of the *Prudence* and a pinnace called the *Amity*. *APC-V.22, 417.*

6) 25 March 1592. The two parties regarding the cargo appeared before the council and felt another meeting was required. *APC-V.22, 371.*

7) 12 April 1592. Orders that this ship be returned and restored by the council. *APC-V.22, 396.*

8) 30 April 1592. This ship with her furniture, tackle and goods are to be returned to Captain Cornelius Cornerison.

9) 28 March 1596. The council became aware of the plundering from this ship by Sir Thomas Norreys after the ship had left Mallago toward Middleborough. It appears that the master and other crew members were slain during the takeover of the ship. *APC-V.25, 318.*

10) 7 April 1596. Complaint that this ship was violently boarded and plundered of its cargo of sugar, wines, raisins, and other merchandise by an Irish ship while to Middleborough. *APC-V.25, 324.*

11) 18 April 1596. Inventory of the items plundered. 177 pipes of wine, 1020 frails of , 38 puncheons of raisins of the sun, 16 barrels of almonds and 16 barrels of throes silk, all violently taken while at sea. All the stolen items were taken to Ireland. Seeking restitution. *APC-V.25, 354–355.*

12) 13 May 1600. The Privy Council received a complaint from Urian Inglekin who complained of bad treatment from Sir John Gilbert. *APC-V.30, 320.*

Josua. Hamburg, Germany.
1) 15 September 1591. This was one of four of the Earl of Cumberland's prizes taken at sea during King Philip's attempted invasion of England. The owners were seeking restitution. *APC-V.21, 447–448.*

Lady of Conception. Spain.
1) 22 May 1576. Orders to apprehend John Callis and William Battes of this ship. *APC-V.9, 127–128.*

Lamb. Germany.
1) 12 November 1589. The ship was seized in a Portugal voyage and brought to Portsmouth. The cargo of two flats of nails and four small barrels

of steel would be sold if they were determined not to belong to Spain or Portugal. *APC-V.18, 216.*

2) 24 August 1589. Orders to release this ship with its merchandise of wax, steel, nails, and other merchandise that does not pertain to the Spanish King. *APC-V.18, 60.*

3) 16 October 1589. Orders to return the 2 flats of nails and locks that do belong to Jacques de Foy. *APC-V.18, 173–174.*

4) 12 November 1589. Continued request to return 2 flats of nails and 4 small barrels of steel taken during the Portugal voyage. *APC-V.18, 216.*

Lion. Germany.
Records indicate 120 tons.
1) 15 April 1590. Master Hans Opperson was released after all cargo was confiscated of tackle and furniture. Seeking restitution. *APC-V.19, 63.*

Lombardo. Italy.
1) 24 April 1586. This is the first of several entries regarding the salvage of this ship that was burned and everything that could be removed, was removed. A meeting between all parties was requested.

2) 4 May 1586. Further description of the cargo was wine, and other merchandise. Orders to pay the mariners of the ship. Restitution for the loss of the cargo and ship. *APC-V.14, 74, 85.*

3) 19 June 1586. Additional information indicates the cargo plundered by an English ship includes: 'butt of Cuitte, a butt of Muscadine, a bag of fennel seed and certain things' taken from this galleon. *APC-V.14, 153.*

4) 15 January 1587. Restitution regarding the salvage of this vessel had been settled in court. Payment made to the captain.

5) 20 September 1587. Partial compensation was to be paid. If not, subject to confinement in a prison. *APC, V.15, 244.*

Lyon. Of Dublin. Ireland.
1) 31 March 1572. Addressed the spoilage by the King of Spain to the ship belonging to Captain Malbye. *APC-V.8, 75.*

Madre de Dios. Portuguese.
There appears to be some wonderful and colorful embellishment of facts currently on the internet regarding the 'millions of dollars' of jewels, gold and silver taken from this ship, but none shared their sources. There are a few recorded events on which many of those stories are based. Some of these

are the facts I will share and none included vast treasure, but pepper a highly valued commodity.

1) 6 September 1592. This ship was captured at sea by English and taken to Dartmouth. The cargo was divided and placed in several small ships for transport. *APC-V.23, 181.*

2) 1 October 1592. Notice to withhold wages of mariners suspected of pilfering certain items of the cargo. *APC-V.23, 218–219.*

3) 25 October 1592. Captain John Marchaunt was ordered to appear before the Privy Council on this day. *APC-V.23, 266.*

4) 27 October 1592. Several small English barques were loaded with pepper from this ship to be unloaded at the house of the Friars at Greenwich. *APC-V.23, 269*

Maniceli, Gallian. Venice.
1) 6 September 1592. Warrant issued for the apprehension of Captain Edward Glemham for plundering this ship and for bringing the plundered cargo into England. Peter Houghton had made an offer to purchase the *Edward Constance* and should he do so, was required to pay the Venetian's restitution. *APC-V.23, 180.*

2) 17 September 1592. Enquiry to the 'certain goods to a great value' belonging to the Spanish king. It is clearly stated that the plundered prizes do not belong to Captain Glemham. *APC-V.23, 198.*

Maria de Scopo.
1) 24 March 1597. Letter to authorities to complete the matter of commodities brought into England. No other information given. *APC-V.28, 373.*

Marie. Spain.
1) 28 January 1582. Letter of complaint about the ship being plundered at Calais in her voyage to Biskay and by a tempest and foul weather was forced to cut her masts down and to repair at Falmouth where the ship was plundered. *APC-V.13, 315.*

Margaret. Scottish.
1) 24 April 1597. Complaint from Scottish merchants regarding the loss of their cargo being transported by this ship, plundered by English from the *Dolphin* of Plymouth. Required the captain to account for his actions. *APC-V.27, 67.*

Mary. Germany.
1) 22 March 1589. Orders to deliver all furniture and tackle that belong to the ship to Captain John Martins. *APC-V.18, 432.*

2) 15 September 1591. This was one of four of the Earl of Cumberland's prizes taken at sea during King Philip's attempted invasion of England. The owners sought restitution. *APC-V.21, 447–448.*

Maryann. Denmark.
1) 17 August 1589. Orders to return the ship captured by pirates with all that was on board before the plunder including tackle, cargo, and furniture. *APC-V.18, 44.*

Mary Gallant. Scotland.
1) 13 August 1601. French merchant complaints that this ship was captured by English pirates and taken into Dover by Captain Bredgate. Request to allow the ship to leave. *APC-V.32, 154.*

Mary Marerie. Venice.
1) 15 November 1590. Captured on the seas with the *Ugiera Salungina* under suspicion of working with Spain and brought into Plymouth for inspection and inventory of the cargo, but some had already been plundered. Complaint filed against Mr. Davies. *APC-V.20, 77–78.*
2) 18 January 1591. Ship was moved to Weymouth to inspect the cargo of pepper and other valuable merchandise. *APC-V.20, 223.*
3) 24 January 1591. Lawsuit filed by Venetian merchants regarding the owner of the goods confiscated on board this ship. *APC-V.20, 234.*
4) 5 July 1591. Additional information of the cargo taken; 36 bags and hogshead of pepper and 66 chests of sugar and other goods plundered by the English. Seeking restitution for loss. *APC-V.21, 259.*

Mermaid.
1) 6 January 1579. Plundered by pirates of a cargo of clothes and other merchandise. Promise was made to apprehend the pirates. *APC-V.11, 9.*
2) 15 October 1589. Taken with a cargo of corn on the coast of Portugal to be sold in England. The corn was sold and a request that the ship with her apparel, tackle, furniture, ordnance, and munitions be allowed to depart with the sum of the sale of the corn, with a favorable wind. *APC-V.18, 188.*
3) 13 February 1596. Merchants of Newcastle complained of plundering a cargo of rye and iron, while the ship was leaving Scotland to Newcastle. Seeking restitution. *APC-V.26, 489–499.*

Mercury. Amsterdam.
1) 24 October 1592. Letter to Sir Walter Raleigh regarding this ship and the *Crescent* that had been captured and brought into Dartmouth, to be released and their captors apprehended. *APC-V.23, 237.*

Michael. Hamburg.

1) 8 June 1600. Report that this ship was captured and taken into Plymouth by Sir Thomas Shirley. Orders to officials in Plymouth to restoring this ship. *APC-V.30, 358.*

Morians Head. Denmark.

1) 27 August 1587. Complaints of piracy by Englishmen. The ship was taken to Helford Haven and cargo unloaded and sold to local merchants. Seeking restitution. One individual was apprehended, the other could not be located. *APC-V.15, 212.*

Ostrich.

1) 29 September 1589. It was determined that this ship was to be used by the Spanish King to invade England and to be held. *APC-V.18, 160.*

2) 5 November 1589. An order to release this ship to its master and all ordnance, munitions, sails, tackle apparel and other furniture and to allow the ship to depart. *APC-V.18, 207.*

Our Lady. Of Aransusia.

I was unable to locate the home of this ship. The Privy Council of England addressed the issue since it involved an Engish captain.

1) 11 August 1577. This ship was laden with iron ore and taken off the coast of Galicia Spain by Captain Hix. In a letter is mentioned to arrest and search this ship when located. *APC-V.10, 14.*

Parrot.

1) 18 December 1597. This ship was captured on the seas by Lord Thomas Howard. The council requested "that there are divers English priests and some Jesuit in the army we would have you discover if any of them be disguised amongst those Spaniards." The cargo would be sold to defray costs. *APC-V.28, 192–193.*

Pawl. Scotland.

1) 18 June 1592. Complaint filed by Giullemettes de la Fargue, widow, who sent Stephene de la Fargue, her servant, into England with 60 tons of wine transported by the *Pawl* of Anstruther. She was seeking the apprehension and arrest of Stephene. *APC-V.22, 539.*

Pelican. Lubeck Germany.

Records suggest this was 160 tons.

1) 11 March 1579. Seeking restitution for the plundered cargo of hops. *APC-V.11, 414.*

2) 12 April 1590. A complaint that the ship was taken from Falmouth to Cork Ireland and all the cargo was sold without authorization. Seeking punishment to the pirates and safe return of cargo and ship. *APC-V.19, 45–46.*

3) 15 April 1590. Taken of its cargo of tackle, furniture everything but the ballast and Master Lucke Luers was released to their destination. *APC-V.19, 63.*

Peter. Dutch.

1) 14 January 1586. Seeking restitution for cargo plundered by English pirates and taken to North Wales. *APC-V.14, 300.*

Poppingay. Germany.

1) 6 January 1598. This ship was captured by Sir John Gilbert on the *Antelope* and the cargo deemed a lawful prize, inventoried and to be sold. *APC-V.28, 224.*

Popinjay. Holland.

1) The ship was laden with deal board, masts, and oars. The ship was taken by an English pirate. The master took his ship back and captured the pirate and seeks punishment. *APC-V.13, 175.*

Post Horse. Holland.

1) 21 August 1579. The council issued orders to return all tackle, apparel and munitions to this ship based on a previous inventory. *APC-V.27, 353–354.*

Primrose. Barry, Glamorgan, Wales.

1) 14 October 1590. Captain William Morgan had fulfilled his obligations with merchants in the Low Countries to the full value of 25 tons of oats and five tons of sugar and the owners of this ship received 13 tons of the oats, but refused to pay, and by violence, the oats were taken away. Request that Morgan be held accountable for his actions. *APC-V.20, 29–30.*

Prodigal Child. Rostock Germany.

Records indicate 120 tons.

1) 30 May 1590. Released from service. Adrian Brewer was master. *APC-V.19, 185.*

Red Cock. Sweden.

1) 3 November 1589. A brief description of the cargo that was taken when the ship was seized which included: "one flat of nails. One danske chest first opened with haberdasher wares in it. One other chest with some small

quantity of locks. Shoeing horns and mariners" knives. One pack of payes unfolded". *APC-V.18, 205.*

Red Heart. Sweden.
1) 20 February 1589. Request for release from the port of Plymouth to continue their voyage. *APC-V.17, 82.*
2) 2 November 1589. A request for an inventory of items not on the original inventory. *APC-V.18, 203.*
3) 3 November 1589. A brief description of the cargo that was taken when the ship was seized which included: "one pack of bayes." *APC-V.18, 205.*

Red Heart. German.
1) 29 September 1589. It was determined that this ship was used by the Spanish King to invade England and to be held. *APC-V.18, 160.*

Red Lion. Germany
1) 8 February 1589. Captain Mathew Jansen. Laden with Spanish cargo, this ship was forced into Foy Belgium by tempest before it could reach London. Request to release the ship from Foy to complete her voyage. *APC-V.17, 72.*
2) 7 August 1589. License to sell a cargo of corn brought into Cornwall from Portugal without fee of customs expense. *APC-V.18, 17.*
3) 29 September 1589. Request to allow this ship at Plymouth, to travel to Italy with its cargo. *APC-V.18, 150.*
4) 11 December 1591. Complaint filed regarding piracy committed against this ship in July belonging to Hans Ulderkins loaded with meal, malt, beer and other merchandise by Captain Henry Eile and Nicholas Lorraine 'notorious pirates'. Seeking restitution. *APC-V.22, 116.*
5) 25 February 1599. This ship was captured at sea and seeking restitution of her furniture, ordnance, victuals, and apparel belonging to the ship. *APC-V.29, 596.*

Reynold. Prussia.
1) 24 August 1589. Requested permission to depart Plymouth laden with 'deal board, wainscot and clapboard to their countries, (Prussian city that is now Kaliningrad). *APC-V.18, 68.*
2) 29 September 1589. Request to allow this ship at Plymouth, to travel to Italy with its cargo. *APC-V.18, 150.*

Rich Dollar. Holland.
1) 16 August 1590. Complaints of English pirates and of the goods stolen. *APC-V.19, 389.*

Rose. German.

1) 22 March 1589. A letter requiring the items removed from this ship that was taken in a Portugal voyage to be recovered when the ship perished in the port of Plymouth. *APC-V.18, 432.*

2) 8 May 1589. Controversy between London merchants and a Swedish merchant regarding a cargo of wine that was taken in London. Seeking restitution for payment of mariners. *APC-V.17, 166.*

3) 9 January 1598. This ship was captured and taken to Portsmouth. Orders to restore the ship and deliver it to the owner. *APC-V.29, 437.*

Salvator. German.

1) 4 August 1589. Orders to inventory the cargo brought into Portsmouth and make sale of some quantity of the corn taken with payment to be made to Captain Thomas Bainton. *APC-V.18, 11.*

2) 24 August 1589. Orders to release this ship with its merchandise of wax, steel and nails, and other merchandise that does not pertain to the Spanish King. *APC-V.18, 60.*

3) 12 November 1589. The ship was seized in a Portugal voyage and brought to Portsmouth. The cargo of two flats of nails and four small barrels of steel would be sold if they were determined not to belong to Spain or Portugal. *APC-V.18, 216.*

Sampson. German.

Records indicate 180 tons.

1) 7 August 1589. Orders to sell the cargo of 'deal and clove board' as long as it does not pertain to the king of Spain. *APC-V18, 18.*

2) 15 April 1590. Taken of its cargo of tackle, furniture everything but the ballast, Master Bonny Peterson was released to their destination. *APC-V.19, 63.*

3) 15 September 1591. This was one of four of the Earl of Cumberland's prizes taken at sea during King Phillip's attempted invasion of England. The owners were seeking restitution. *APC-V.21, 447–448.*

Sampson. Dutch.

Record indicates this was 300 tons.

1) 27 April 1600. English Captain Watson captured this ship while at sea and took it into Bristol. Controversy arose regarding items taken. *APC-V.30, 277–278.*

2) 29 July 1600. This ship was to be used for her majesty's service because of its size, to transport items to Ireland. *APC-V.30, 547–548.*

Sea Rider. German.

1) 6 April 1589. A request by Lawrence Swere, master of this ship, that the books of laden, bills, charter parties and other material taken from this ship be returned. *APC-V. 17, 122.*

2) 25 May 1589. Furthermore, Sir Francis Drake was responsible for the removal of the documents and goods. Seeking restitution. *APC-V.17, 205.*

Sourwater. Dutch.

1) 13 March 1576. This ship was to be released after a certain time of being detained. If they were not to be released soon, are subject to losing their tack. *APC-V.9, 307.*

Spars Juniper. Of Danzig, Germany.
Records indicate 160 tons.

1) 30 May 1590. Released from service. John Vet was master. *APC-V.19, 185.*

Spruce Maiden.

1) 18 December 1597. This ship was captured on the seas by Lord Thomas Howard. The council requested "that there are divers English priests and some Jesuit in the army we would have you discover if any of them be disguised amongst those Spaniards." The cargo will be sold to defray costs. *APC-V.28, 192–193.*

St. Agatha. Venice.

1) 16 March 1597. This ship entered Portsmouth with a load of corn. But there was a shortage of agreed amount and the ships ordnance, furniture and tackle was held for repayment. *APC-V.26, 550.*

2) 3 December 1597. Further complaint from Martin Frederico that the corn taken from him did not receive full value and sought restitution for the loss. *APC-V.28, 167.*

3) 14 May 1598. Orders to make full restitution to Martin Frederico for the balance due on the grain. *APC-V.28, 440.*

St. John. Hamburg.

1) 19 November 1598. This ship was reported as wrecking on the Goodwin Sands off the coast of England with a load of marble stone, dry flats, and other merchandise. All but one crew member died. Merchants requested that whatever could be recovered to be returned. *APC-V.29, 292–293.*

St. Petero Mayor. Possibly Spanish.

1) 9 November 1589. This ship ran onto ground and wrecked at Hope a bay near Salcomb in the county of Devon. All goods, tackle and furniture were saved, and inventory made. *APC-V.18, 213.*

St. Pancratius. Flemish.

1) 1563 (?). Found on the back of a requisition from the Spanish envoy requesting that Sir John Perrot, vice-admiral in Wales, to answer for capturing this ship. *CSP-D-Addenda, 546.*

St. Peter. Amsterdam.

1) 12 August 1593. The council addressed an issue from November and December 1592, regarding this ship loaded with packs of wax, linen cloth, sails, grogram's and other merchandise, that hit the sandbank in Goodwin Sands and its cargo was plundered by local inhabitants. Seeking restitution. *APC-V.24, 456–457.*

Star of Reape. Dutch.

1) 31 April 1587. Loaded with a cargo from England merchants, the ship was captured and taken to Portsmouth under the pretense that the cargo was Spanish. Requests that the ship be released. *APC-V.15, 59–60.*

Sumachia St. Mary Dascopo. Venice.

1) Passport granted to allow passage to Venice then return to London. *APC-V.21, 417.*

Sumachia St. Paul. Venice.

1) Passport granted to allow passage to Venice then return to London. These are recorded as two individual ships. *APC-V.21, 417.*

Swan. Dutch.

1) 13 March 1576. This ship was to be released after a certain time of being detained. If they were not to be released soon, are subject to losing their tack. *APC-V.9, 307.*

2) 6 January 1598. This ship was captured by Sir John Gilbert on the *Antelope* and cargo deemed a lawful prize, inventoried and to be sold. *APC-V.28, 224.*

St. John Baptist. Italy.

Records suggest this was 200 tons.

1) 29 May 1580. Julian Borraci of Genoa loaded with cargo of lead and tin at London for Italy, the ship was stolen while at anchor in the Thames River. One of the pirates was identified as English. *APC-V.12, 39.*

Swiftesure. Danish.

1) 24 December 1587. Complaints of piracy by an English ship seeking restitution. This vessel was described as a flyboat. *APC-V.15, 309.*

Three Kings. Holland.

1) 9 January 1598. Orders to return this ship, her ordnance, sails, anchors and other furniture to the owner Peter Jasperson, after it was determined this was not a lawful prize. *APC-V.29, 438.*

2) 4 March 1598. Orders to restore this ship and arrest those involved. *APC-V.29, 626.*

3) 6 January 1599. Contrary winds made this ship travel into Portsmouth loaded with salt. Orders for this ship to transport soldiers into Ireland. *APC-V.29, 431.*

Tobias. Sweden.

Records suggest this was 200 tons.

1) 7 September 1590. This ship was captured by Captain Whiddon with Martyn Simonson as master and taken to Plymouth with a cargo of 6 masts, 'five hundredth deal boards and two hundredth and fifty fur [sic] poles' all property of the King of Sweden. Furthermore, Whiddon had removed a brass cannon engraved with the King's army on it. Seeking restitution. *APC-V.19, 423–424.*

Treasurer. Denmark.

1) Complaints following a voyage out of Portugal with a cargo of salt, sugar and spices ran aground near the town of Lidd. The inhabitants of the town "under the color to lend assistance," removed the cargo. Had sought restitution. *APC-V.18, 107.*

Two Gossips. Unknown.

1) 9 May 1591. David Gwin captured this ship during the Spanish armada and turned the ship with all her ordnance, furniture and apparel to Peter Botilion, Gabriel Barry and John Artson. *APC-V.21, 103–104.*

Tyson. Italy.

1) 5 September 1589. Controversy between John Plademo master of the ship and Martin de Fredieringo regarding a cargo of wine. The master complained of the delay and was seeking a quick solution to the disagreement. *APC-V.18, 72.*

Ugiera Salvagina. Venice.

Records indicate this was an argosie.

1) 15 November 1590. Captured on the seas with the *Marie Margerie* under suspicion of working with Spain and brought into Plymouth for inspection and inventory of the cargo, but some had already been plundered. Complaint filed against Mr. Davies. *APC-V.20, 77–78.*

2) 18 January 1591. Ship was moved to Weymouth to inspect the cargo of pepper and other valuable merchandise. *APC-V.20, 223.*

3) 24 January 1591. Lawsuit filed by Venetian merchants regarding the owner of the goods confiscated on board this ship. *APC-V.20, 234.*

4) 6 April 1591. Englishman John Davies captured this ship and took 200 bags of pepper, a barrel of mace and 'certain jewels' and other things of great value. Seeking restitution including the prosecution of Davies. *APC-V.21, 39–40.*

5) 11 April 1591. 30 bags of pepper for Spain or Portugal were ordered to be removed. *APC-V.21, 50.*

6) 26 April 1591. Complaint filed against the crew of this ship for taking their apparel and other goods. *APC-V.21, 73.*

7) 2 May 1591. The crew filed a complaint to be relieved of 'their great losses, hindrances sustained by the spoil." Rejected an offer of purchase of remaining pepper. *APC-V.21, 82.*

8) 27 June 1591. Orders for the sequestration of the goods from this ship. APC-V21, 230–231.

9) 25 July 1591. Decision to sell pepper to Edward Palmer of London, haberdasher. *APC-V.21, 320–321.*

10) 15 December 1591. Complaints that the matter has not been settled to the Venetian's satisfaction and Philip Corsini merchant, filed an appeal. *APC-V.22, 125.*

11) 25 January 1592. Decision to bring John de Rivera and Philip Corsini together and solve the matter. *APC-V.22, 204–205.*

12) 25 April 1592. Further delay regarding a satisfactory decision of the Venetian cargo. *APC-V.22, 405–406.*

13) 30 April 1592. Charges brought against those who uncrated and placed new markings on the 25 bags of pepper in deposit at Dartmouth. *APC-V.22, 411.*

Cargoes; About Pepper

The incident just mentioned above illustrates that pepper was the most important spice of this era and was always shipped in bulk quantities. Pepper was followed in popularity by cinnamon, ginger, and cloves. Certainly, a prize cargo worthy of debate. As far as the documents indicate, this matter had not been settled. It was so important that the marks that individuals made to claim their portion(s) were recorded in the documents I reviewed. Recorded 16 May 1592. *APC-V.22, 465–467.*

Loaded by Jerome and Nicholas Stella --

95 bags   21 bags   25 chests and 10 butts of sugar
of pepper   of pepper   muscovado; 55 chests of sugar panels.

Loaded by Lewis Vezzato --
20 bags of pepper

32 bags of pepper.

   Lewis Vesato loaded 43 bags of pepper, leaving 29 bags of pepper held

Lewis Vesato loaded 19 chests of sugar; 10 chests of sugar panels and 9 chests of sugar muscovado held.

   Lewis Vesato loaded 49 chests of sugar; 20 chests of panels and 29 chests of sugar muscovado held.

Lewis Vesato loaded 11 chests of sugar. 11 chests of sugar muscovado held.

2 chests of muscovado.

5 chests of muscovado.

 79 elephants' teeth.

5 barrels of camphor.

Loaded by Raphael Fantoni

Raphael Fantoni loaded 57 bags
of pepper and 30 bags of pepper on hold.

11 chests of sugar muscovado
11 chests of sugar panels. .

14 chests 4 butts sugar muscovado.
20 chests of sugar panels.

Loaded by Christofer Manlique

44 bags of pepper.

Loaded by Frances da Corona.

7 chests of sugar muscovado.

The bags of pepper belonging to the Italians had been taken away with these marks.

25 bags of pepper at Dartmouth.

11 bags of pepper sent to London.

1) 12 July 1592. The council sat in session regarding the goods taken from this ship. *APC-V.23, 26.*

2) 15 August 1592. After the long debate this issue has been referred to arbitration. Each party was to leave a deposit in the value of the goods already received and placed in certain coffers and there will be two locks. Each party would have an interchangeable key in their possession until the council concluded this matter. *APC-V.23, 92–93.*

3) 17 July 1593. The council, lord treasurer and the lord admiral passed down a decision to distribute the pepper accordingly to those parties as

required. The individual who possessed the key to the lock on the warehouse would not give the key up. The council sent orders to have the lock opened or cut off. *APC-V.24, 388–390, 403–404*

Unicorn. Scotland.

1) 23 February 1597. This ship was held in Dover after leaving Dunkirk then brought up the Thames carrying a cargo of salmon and other fish. A determination as to whether this was lawfully seized. *APC-V.26, 509.*

Unicorn. Denmark.

1) 5 June 1598. This ship was plundered by the English ship the *Flying Dragon.* The *Unicorn* was hired to transport Spanish and Portuguese prisoners to Lisbon for an exchange of English prisoners. A warrant was issued for the crew of the *Flying Dragon. APC-V.28, 485–486.*

Young Froe. Pomeranian.

1) 24 August 1589. Request to the commissioners of the port of Portsmouth for the sale of corn, wheat and rye removed from this ship. *APC-V.18, 64–65.*

2) 5 September 1589. Concerns from the council at Southampton for pay to the soldiers that participated in the voyage to Portugal could be paid from the sale of corn from this ship. *APC-V.18, 73.*

3) 6 September 1589. It was determined that the quality of the corn was poor and that the sale of wheat and rye would be sufficient to help meet the debts. *APC-V.18, 76.*

4) 9 October 1590. Mention of the cargo removed from this ship including not stolen or spoiled. *APC-V.20, 31.*

5) 18 October 1590. A request to the English not to plunder the cargo of the ship including tackle and furniture aboard. But much was "purloined and was conveyed to London." Their lords wish to carefully 'enquire and examine' what was taken. *APC-V.20. 34.*

6) 11 September 1601. The council reviewed information from Joachim Coster, master of this ship, when the ship anchored in Cadiz Road and passed the Castle of Resilles but did not receive permission to enter the river, but he reported that he saw 300 sails of French, Dutch and Scottish ships that had come from Spain. *CSP-D, 1601–1603, 96.*

Whalefish. Denmark.

1) 18 July 1592. It was reported that this ship was captured by two English ships, the *Salamander* and *Mary Grace* and her cargo of salt and other merchandise was taken. *APC-V.23, 36–37.*

2) 8 April 1593. Request to the lord deputy of Ireland to release this ship with its cargo of planks for London shipyards. *APC-V.24, 166.*

3) 19 April 1593. Complaint filed against the mayor of Youghal, Ireland for removing many sails and tackle from this ship and a silk ensign belonging to the ship. Requests the return of the stolen items. *APC-V.24, 198.*

White Falcon. Netherlands.

1) 9 July 1579. Letter to London requesting assistance plundered by pirates during her voyage from Hamburg to London. *APC-V.11, 182–183.*

2) 28 April 1597. The council received a letter of complaint by Dutch merchants that the English ship the *Minion* had plundered a cargo of sugar from this ship. Her majesty indicated that the *White Falcon* should accept the losses as full value of sugar. *APC-V.27, 71.*

1–5. Recorded Storms that affected ships in shipping lanes

This list is based on events recorded in the thousands of documents reviewed. To my knowledge, this is the first list of this type ever compiled for the Tudor period of history.

1) 23 December 1553. Affected the French fleet on its way to Corsica (in the Mediterranean Sea).

2) 17 March 1555. 7 or 8 French galleys lost because of storm.

3) 17 December 1555. 4 galleys of Malta, Italy lost at sea.

4) 12 December 1559. Mention of 'foul weather' upon this part. (Newhaven). The French feared some of their ships were driven upon the English coast.

5) 21 December 1559, *CSP-F V.3, 467,* note 1 in the Affairs of Scotland mentions a tempest had driven some of the English fleet across to Holland and Zealand.

6) 13 January 1560. Known to have sunk 4 or 5 English and 4 French ships in the English Channel.

7) A tempest of late March to April 1576 affected: The *Peter* of Bristol, Bark *Allen* and 5 English ships.

8) 1 May 1576. Possible storm from north into Bristol Channel area. Affected the *Peter* of Bristol.

9) January 1582. A tempest that wrecked the *Dragon* and *Hunter* of Belgium on Yarmouth.

10) February 1589. A Danish ship forced into London by bad weather. Did not wreck.

11) 3–4 September 1591. This storm played havoc on the Spanish and English fleets after the attack off the Azores. The *Revenge* was one of the ships to perish.

12) 5 October 1600. The *Dove* of Zeeland was driven on shore at Sussex England from foul weather.

PART 2. CAPTAINS' LOGS

The life of a mariner could be very hazardous. Even daily routines possessed many hazards. Climbing the sometimes wet rigging to the yards with cold hands in a rough sea with high winds, a man could be blown to his death, whether he landed on deck or in the ocean. These ships could not readily turn around, and the cold sea would kill the man before the ship arrived anyhow.

Sleeping quarters were wherever a man could hang his hammock, usually below decks during bad weather or above when weather allowed it. Without a decent sleep, the sailor could not think clearly, endangering not only himself but his mates.

Among the other hazards of the life at sea was scurvy. Fresh vegetables, fruit and meats had to consumed before they spoiled, and that made the time until re-supply perilous, with the threat of a deficiency of vitamin C and other nutrients.

The dangers of life at sea are somewhat offset by rare rewards, such as when a prize is captured and divided among the crew, a windfall which could set a man up for life.

2–1. A Victorious English Sea Battle, 1593.

Captain Nicholas Downton recorded this event in 1594 while he was commanding the *Sampson*. This will be only the second time this incredible story has been published. Sea battle stories are common only from about 1680 onward; this is a very rare narrative of a Tudor-era sea battle for survival.

For the most part, this record is drawn from *A New General Collection of Voyages and Travels Consisting of the Most Esteemed Relations...* Volume 1, London, 1745.

The latter end of the year 1593, the right honorable the Earl of Cumberland, at the charges of himself and friends, prepared three ships of equal rate, each accommodated with the same quantity of victuals, and number of men, there being in all four hundred and twenty of all sorts. The Royal Exchange went as admiral, George Cave, captain; the Mayflower, vice-admiral under the conduct of William Anthony; and the Sampson commanded by the author, Nicholas Downton. The directions were sent to them at Plymouth and were to be opened at sea.

The first of April 1594, they set sail from the Sound, steering their course towards the coast of Spain. The twenty fourth, at the admiral's direction, they divided themselves east and west from each other, being then in the height of forty-three degrees, with orders to come together again at night.

The twenty-seventh, in the morning, the Mayflower and little pinnace took a prize, bound from Viana in Portugal for Angola in Africa. This bark, containing twenty-eight tons, had seventeen persons on board. There were in her twelve butts of Galicia wine, some rusk in chests and barrels, with five butts of blue coarse cloth; besides other coarse linen for Negro's shirts: which goods were equally divided among the fleet. The fourth of May, the Sampson had sight of the pinnace, and the admiral's shallop, which had taken three Portuguese caravels, whereof they had sent two away, and kept the third.

The second of June, they had sight of St. Michael: and next morning, sent their small pinnace, which was of twenty-four tons, with the small caravel, taken at the Burlings, to range the islands, and see if anything was to be gotten; appointing them to meet West South-West, twelve leagues from Fayal: but their going was to no purpose. They missed them when they had most need of them.

The thirteenth, they met with a mighty carrack from the East Indies, called Las Cinque Llaguas; or The Five Wounds. The Mayflower was in fight with her before night. The Sampson having fetched her up in the evening, the captain commanded to give her a broadside: but shield he stood very heedfully trying to discover her strength, and proper place to board her in the night, when the admiral came up, at the very first discharge she made, he was shot a little above the belly, which rendered him unserviceable for a good while after: yet by means of one Captain Grant, an honest, true hearted man, whom he had with him, nothing was neglected: so that the Mayflower and the Sampson never gave over, trying her by turns with their ordnance, till midnight, when the admiral joined them. It was intended then to have entered her; but Captain Cave desired it might be deferred till morning, at what time each ship should give her three broadsides, and then clap her aboard: yet, when morning came, by one delay or other, it was ten o'clock before they attempted it.

The admiral laid her aboard in the mid-ship; and the Mayflower advancing in the quarter, to lie at the admiral's stern, on the starboard side, the captain was slain at the first coming up: whereby the ship fell to the stern of the outlier of the carrack, which (which being a piece of timber) so damaged her fore-sail, that they said she could come no more to fight: however it was, it is certain they did not, but kept aloof. The Sampson boarded her on the bow, but not having room enough, her quarter lay on the Exchange's bow, and her bow on the Carrack's bow. The Exchange also, at the first onset, had her captain, Mr. Cave, shot in both the legs, on whereof he never recovered; and for that time, was not able to do his office: nor had he any, who would undertake to lead out his company, to enter upon the enemy.

Captain Grant led the Sampson's men on the carrack's side, but his forces being small, and not manfully backed by the Exchange's crew, it made the enemy bolder than they would have been; insomuch, that six men were presently slain, and many more hurt whereupon the rest returned aboard, and could never be prevailed on afterwards to give the assault. Some of the Exchange's men did very well, and many more (no doubt) would have followed their example, if there had been any principle man, who would have pushed them forward; and brought all the company to the fight, instead of running into corners to keep themselves out of harm's way. But Captain Downton acknowledges, that their ship was as well provided for defense, as any that he had ever seen' and the Portuguese, encouraged perhaps by the slack working of the English, placed their men, and had barricade made, where they might stand out of danger of the shot. They also annoyed the company very much with wildfire, so that most of them were burnt in some part or other; and all the while they were putting out the fire, the enemy were plying them with small shot, or darts. This unusual casting of fire did much dismay many of the men, and was the occasion of their drawing back.

The ships not having men to enter, plied her with their ordnance, as high up as they could be mounted, for otherwise they could do her little harm: at length, the Sampson, by shooting a piece out of the fore-castle, being close by her, fired a mat on her beakhead, (bulkhead?) and the flame more and more increasing, ran from thence to the mat on the bowsprit; and from the mat up to the wood of the bowsprit, and thence to the topsail yard: which fire made the Portuguese, who were abast, inclinable to yield, but they who had the charge before, encouraged them, pretending, that it might easily be extinguished: whereupon again they stood stiffly to their defense; but presently the fire grew so strong, that the author saw it beyond all help, although she had been already yielded to them. Then the Sampson's men desired to be off from her, but had little hope to obtain their desires nevertheless, they plied water very much to keep their own ship well.

The danger was so great, that Captain Downton expected nothing less, than that the ship, himself, and divers hurt men, would have ended there with the carrack, but most of the people might have saved themselves in boats. But when his apprehensions were greatest, she disengaged herself, by the burning of the spritsail yard, with the ropes and sail, and the ropes about the spritsail yard of the carrack, wherewith she was fast entangled. The Exchange also being farther from the fire, was afterward more easily cleared, and fell off from behind. As soon as the English ships were out of danger, the fire got into the forecastle of the carrack; where, catching hold of Benjamin, and such like combustible matter that lay there, it flamed out, and ran over all the vessel in an instant.

The Portuguese leaping overboard in great numbers, the author sent Captain Grant, with the boat, to sue his discretion in saving of them. He brought aboard two gentlemen, one an old man called Nuno Velio Pereira who had been governor of Mozambique, and Sosola (Sofala?) in the year 1582; and afterwards of another place of importance, in the East Indies. The ship, wherein he was returning home, having been cast away a little to the east of the Cape of Good Hope, he travelled over land to Mozambique. The other, called Bras Carrero, was captain of a carrack which was cast away near Mozambique, from whence both came, in this carrack, as passengers. The men, of the inferior sort, were likewise saved; only these two they clothed and brought into England: the rest, who were taken up by the other ship boats, were set on shore in the Isle of Flores: except two of three Negros, whereof one was born at Mozambique, and another in the East Indies.

This fight was six leagues southward of the Sound between Fayal and Pico. The people, who were saved, told them, that the reason why they would not yield, was, because this carrack was on the king's account, to whom all the goods, with which she was laden, belonged; and that the captain was much in the king's favor, expecting, at his return into the Indies, to have been appointed vice-roy. Besides, this ship was not at all encumbered either within or without, and was more like a ship of war, than otherwise. She was furnished with the ordnance and hands of a carrack that was cast away at Mozambique; together with the company of another that was wrecked a little to the east of Cape of Good Hope: yet, through sickness, which they caught at Angola, where they watered, they had not above one hundred and fifty white men left; but a great many Negros. They said, likewise, that there were three noblemen and three ladies onboard: but they varied much from one another in their reports.

She burned all that day and night; but next morning, her powder, which was lowest, consisting of sixty barrels, blowing up, she was torn in pieces, which swam upon the surface of the water. Some of them slain, she was bigger than the Madre de Dios; others, that she was less: but she was much under masted, and under sailed: yet she went well for a ship that was so foul. The Sampson bestowed on her, before she laid her aboard, about forty-nine great shot at seven discharges, six or seven at a time. She lay aboard about two hours, and during that interval, discharged upon her some twenty scars: and thus much may suffice concerning their dangerous conflict with that unfortunate carrack.

The last of June, after long traversing the seas, they had sight of another mighty carrack, which diverse of the Sampson's company, at first, took to be the great St. Philip, the admiral of Spain: but next day, fetching her up, they found her indeed to be a carrack; which, after some few shot bestowed upon her, they summoned to yield; but standing stoutly to their defense, utter refused: wherefore Captain Downton, seeing no good could be done without boarding her, consulted what course should be taken therein: but by reason the chief captains were either slain or wounded in the former conflict, and murmuring arose among some disorderly and cowardly companions, their valiant and resolute determinations were crossed. In short, to sum up the whole in few words, the carrack escaped their hands. After this, they attended about Corvo and Flores for some West India purchase: but being disappointed of their expectations, and victuals growing short, they returned for Portsmouth; where the Sampson arrived the twenty-eighth of August.

[*A New General Collection of Voyages and Travels Consisting of the Most Esteemed Relations*... Volume 1, London, 1745. 250–252.]

2–2. Spanish Quicksilver, 1592.

These are notes written by Captain Thomas White in July 1592.

The twenty-sixth of July 1592, Captain Thomas White returning from the Barbary, in the Amity of London, in the height of thirty-six degrees, at four in the morning, had sight of two ships, about three or four leagues distant. By seven of the clock he fetched up, and came within gunshot of them; whose boldness in displaying the King of Spain's arms, made him judge them rather ships of war, than laden with merchandise: and indeed, by their own confessions afterwards, they were so sure to have taken him, that they had debated among themselves, whether it was better to carry the ship to St. Lucar, or Lisbon. Having waved each other amain, the Spaniards placed themselves in order of battle, one a cable's length before the other; and then the fight began, both parties continuing to charge and discharge as fast as they were able, for the space of five hours, at the distance of a cable's length at most. During this interval, the Amity received in her hull, masts, and sails, thirty-two great shot; besides at least five hundred from muskets and harquebusses, which were reckoned after the fight.

Mr. White finding them so stout, attempted to board the Biscayne, which was foremost. After lying aboard about an hour, and plying his ordnance and small shot, at length he stowed all her men. The other, in the flyboat, thinking he had entered his men in the fellow, bear room with him; with intent to have laid him aboard, and so entrapped him betwixt them both. He perceiving the drift, fitted his ordnance in such short, as to get quit of her, so that she boarded her companion: by which means, they both fell from him. Hereupon Mr. White kept his loof [aloof?], hoisted his top-sails and weathering them, cam close aboard the flyboat, with his ordnance prepared and gave her a whole broadside; whereby several of the men were slain, as appeared by the blood which ran out the scupper holes. After this, he tacked about, and new charging all his ordnance, came upon the ships again, and ordered them to yield, threatening otherwise to sink them. One of them, which was shot between wind and water, would have complied, but the other called him traitor: upon which Mr. White told him, that if he would not yield presently also, he would sink him first. Not being willing to try the experiment, they presently put out a white flag and yielded; yet refused to strike their own sails, having been sworn never to strike to any Englishman.

He then commanded their captain and masters to come aboard, where they were examined by him; and then stowing them, he sent some of his own men aboard their ships to strike their sails and man them. They found in both one hundred and twenty-six persons living, and eight dead bodies, besides those which had been cast over-board. The victory was obtained by forty-two men, and a boy; whereof two were killed, and three wounded. The two prizes were laden with fourteen hundred chests of quicksilver, with the arms of Castile and Leon fastened upon them; besides the great quantity of bulls, or indulgences, and ten packs of gilded missals, and breviaries, sent on the king's account; also a hundred tons of excellent wines, designed for his fleets; all which the English brought shortly after into the River of Thames, up to Blackwall.

By taking of this quicksilver, the king of Spain lost, for every quintal of the same, a quintal of silver, that should have been delivered him by the masters of the mines [in Peru] which amounted to six hundred thousand pounds, and the two millions, and seventy-two thousand bulls for living and dead persons, (designed for the provinces of Nova Hispania, Yucatan, Guatemala, the Honduras, and the Philippines) taxed at two rials the piece, besides eighteen thousand bulls at four rials, amounted in all to one hundred and seven thousand, seven hundred pounds. So that the total loss to the king of Spain was seven hundred and seven thousand, seven hundred pounds; not reckoning the loss and disappointment sustained on account of the mass books and the wine.

[A New General Collection of Voyages and Travels Consisting of the Most Esteemed Relations... Volume 1, London, 1745. 249–250]

2–3. The capture of the *Madre de Dios*, a Spanish Ship.

The following account is from the pen of Sir John Hawkins.

This information, Sir John called a council of officers, among whom were the captains Norton, Dounton, and Abraham Cock, of the Earl of Cumberland's fleet; M. Tomson of Harwich, captain of the Dainty of Sir John Hawkins, one of Sir Walter Raleigh's fleet; and M. Christopher Newport, captain of the Golden Dragon, newly returned from the West Indies. This intelligence having been communicated to the assistants, and the attempt to take the other carracks, heartily recommended by Sir John they all agreed to the proposal; as did Sir Robert Cross, who next day joined them with the Foresight. Immediately departing thence, six or seven leagues to the west of Flores, then spread themselves from north to the south, each ship two leagues at the least distance from another: by which means, they were able to discover the space of two whole degrees at sea.

In this sort, they lay from the twenty-ninth of June, to the third of August; at what time captain Tomson in the Dainty, had sight of the huge carrack, called the Madre de Dios, one of the greatest bulk belonging to the Crown of Portugal. The *Dainty* being an excellent sailor, got the start of the rest, and began the conflict somewhat to her cost, with the slaughter and hurt of divers of her men. A while after, Sir John Borrough in the Roebuck, of Sir Walter Raleigh's, came up to second her; and continued the fight within musket-shot, assisted by Captain Tonson, and Captain Newport; till Sir Robert Cross, vice admiral of the fleet, who lay to leeward, advancing, Sir John asked his advice, what was best to be done? He answered that if the carrack was not boarded quickly, she would recover the shore, and fire herself as the other had done. Whereupon Sir John, and Sir Robert Cross, grappled her at the same time: but after a while, Sir John receiving a shot under water, and ready to sink, desired Sir Robert to fall off, that he might also clear himself, and save his ship; which was as much as either of them could do, they were so entangled.

The same evening, Sir Robert Cross finding the carrack draw near the island, persuaded his company to board her again, or else there was no hope of taking her. After many excuses and fears, being at last by him encouraged, they fell athwart her foreships all alone, and so hindered her sailing, that the rest had time to come up to his succor; yet the carrack recovered the land: but after her had fought with her single, three hours, towards evening, my lord Cumberland's two ships came up, and with very little loss, entered with Sir Robert Cross; who had by that time broken their courage, and made the assault easy for the rest.

The general having disarmed the Portuguese, and stowed them for better security on all sides, viewed the vast bulk of this carrack, which did then, and may still, justly provoke the admiration of all who had not seen the like before. But his attention was diverted by the dismal sight of many bodies slain and dismembered; or torn in a deplorable manner, with the violence of the shot, and groaning through the anguish of their wounds. In short, the decks were covered with blood and limbs; but especially about the helm: for the steerage requiring no more than twelve or fourteen men at once, and some of the ships raking her at the stern with their ordnance, oftentimes, one shot, slew four or five of them. Whereupon the general, moved with commiseration, sent his own surgeons to attend the wounded, denying them no relief that was in his power.

The commander of the carrack, was Don Fernando de Mendoza, descended of the house of Mendoza in Spain; but being married in Portugal, lived there. This gentleman was much in years, well spoken, of comely personage, and good stature, but hard fortune. In his several services against the Moors, he was twice taken prisoner, and both times ransomed by the king. In his return from the East indies, in a former voyage, he was driven upon the sands of Juda, near the coast of Sofala, being then also captain of a carrack, which was there lost; and though he escaped the sea himself, yet he fell into the hands of infidels on shore, who kept him under long and grievous servitude. The king still preserving a regard for the man, and desirous to better his condition, was content to let him try his fortune once more in this easterly navigation, committing to him the conduct of this carrack; wherein, he went from Lisbon, general of the whole fleet: and in that degree had returned; but that the late vice-roy of Goa, who had embarked for Portugal, in the Bon Jesus, by reason of his late office, was preferred. Sir John pitying the misfortunes of Mendoza, at length resolved to set him at liberty, with most of his people, putting them on board certain vessels, furnished with all kinds of necessary previsions for the purpose.

After this, the general, (to prevent the unprofitable spoil and pillage, whereunto he saw the minds of many inclined) seized upon the whole of the queen's use; and then taking a view of the cargo, upon a slender inspection, perceived, that the wealth of the prize would fully answer expectation, and be more than sufficient to content both the adventurer's desire, and the soldier's fatigue. Here the author observes, that by this ship falling into the hands of the English, they had discovered that secret trade and Indian wealth, which hitherto lay strangely hidden, and cunningly concealed from them; and that the small and imperfect glimpse [of that trade] which only some few of them had a view of before, was now turned into the broad light of full and perfect knowledge.

The carrack being, according to estimation, no less that one thousand six hundred tons, had full nine hundred of those stowed with merchandise: the rest of the tonnage being allowed party for the ordnance, which were thirty-two pieces of brass, of all sorts; party to the passenger, and victuals; which could not be any small quantity, considering there were betwixt six and seven hundred persons of board, and the length of the navigation. According to the catalogue of the commodities, taken at Leadenhall, the fifteenth of September 1592, the principal wares, after the jewels, (which were no doubt of great value, though they never came to light) consisted of spices, drugs, silks, calicoes, quilts, carpets, and colors.

1) The spices were pepper, cloves, maces, nutmegs, cinnamon, green ginger.
2) The drugs; Benjamin, frankincense, galingale, mirabolans, aloes, zocotrina, camphire.
3) The silks; damasks, tassatas, sarcenets, altobassos (that is counterfeit cloth of gold) unwrought China silk, sieaved silk, while twisted silk, curled cypress.
4) The calicos were, book calicos, calico lawns, broad white calicos, fine starched calicos, coarse white calicos, brown broad calicos, brown coarse calicos.
5) There were also canopies, and coarse diaper towels; quilts of coarse sarcent, and of calico; carpets like those of Turkey.

Whereunto to be added, the pearl, musk, civet, and ambergriece.

The rest of the wares were many in numbers, but less in value: as elephant teeth, porcelain vessels of China, coco-nuts, hides, ebony wood, as black as jet, bedspreads of the same; cloth of the rinds of trees, surprising both on the account of the matter, and artificial workmanship. All these commodities being valued by men of judgment, at a reasonable rate, amounted to no less than one hundred and fifty thousand Pound Sterling, which being divided among the adventurers, (whereof her majesty was the chief) was sufficient to content all parties.

The cargo being taken out, and the goods freighted in ten of the ships, the carrack was sent for London; to the end, that the dimensions thereof might be exactly taken, both for the satisfaction of posterity, as well as the present age. This was done by Mr. Robert Adams, who made a most particular and judicious description of it. He found the length from the beak to the stern, (where was erected a lonthorn one hundred and sixty-five foot. The breadth is the second close deck, (whereof she had three) where she was broadest, forty-six foot and ten inches. She drew in water thirty-one foot at their departure from Kochin in India; but not above twenty-six at her arrival in Dartmouth, being lightened in her voyage by divers means, some five foot. She carried in height seven several stories, one orlop, three close decks, one forecastle, and a spar-deck, of two floors a-piece. The length of the keel was one hundred foot; and of the main mast one hundred and twenty-one foot; whole circumference at the partners, was ten foot eleven seven inches. The main-yard was one hundred and six foot long: by which perfect commensuration of the parts, appears the hugeness of the whole, far beyond the mold of the biggest shipping used among us, either for war or trade.

Don Alonso de Basson, for suffering these two carracks to be lost, (the Santa Cruz being burnt, and the Madre de Dios taken) was disgraced by his prince for his negligence.

[A New and Complete Collection of Voyages and Travels. London, 1778. 247–249]

2–4. Sea Fight of Flores, 1591.

"'Tis not in mortals to command success,
But we'll do more, Sempronius, we'll
deserve it."
— Cato.

It was the last day of August, 1591. At anchor off Flores, one of the westerly islands of the Azores, lay at anchor an English fleet, under Lord Thomas Howard. It consisted of only six of her Majesty's ships: the Defiance, bearing the admiral's flag; the Revenge, vice-admiral Sir Richard Granville; the Bonaventure, commanded by Captain Crosse; the Lion, by George Fenner; the Foresight, by Sir Thomas Vavasour; and the Crane, by Duffield. Of these none were of large size; the Crane and Foresight were small; the bark Raleigh, commanded by Captain Thin, was also of small force.

Near the English men-of-war lay also six "victuallers of London," and two or three pinnaces. They had been six months at sea, and gladly availed themselves of the possibility of getting fresh water and provisions in the fertile Western Isle; consequently, at the moment when we commence our story, several of the ships' companies were on shore, bent on this needful business. And now, whilst the admiral was congratulating himself on being able to refit, and get comforts for the many seamen who were ill on board his fleet, a gallant little vessel hove in sight, and approaching the English admiral's ship, let down a boat, into which jumped her captain, who was speedily rowed to the Defiance, and brought on deck to the presence of the admiral, to whom he was well known.

"What news, Captain Middleton?" asked Lord Thomas Howard; "what news from England?" "In truth, my good lord, I have not a moment to speak of England now," was the blunt rejoinder. "My tidings are of pressing moment. For three days I have kept the Spanish fleet company, hovering about them, and I have now to tell you that it is close at hand fifty-three sail of the line, of as huge size as any of the invincible armada, as the Dons called it."

In those days of daring adventure and of hatred to Spain, the tidings of a Spanish fleet in sight generally sufficed to raise the spirits and delight the ears of the comrades of Drake and Raleigh; but it was with no pleasure that Lord Thomas Howard listened to the seaman's announcement of the coming foe. As we have said, several of the ship's companies were on shore; moreover, the ships were in all the confusion of refitting, and required fresh ballast; while deadly sickness had been rife on board them and rendered great numbers of seamen helpless. There were ninety cases of illness on board the Revenge alone, and the Bonaventure had not men enough on board to handle her mainsail.

The admiral was utterly unable to offer the Spaniards battle; therefore, the best preparations were made which the time permitted to save the Queen's fleet. Sir George Cary had a bark there, containing twenty men; the admiral ordered them to be transferred to the Bonaventure, and the bark to be sunk. Then in haste and confusion (many of the ships being unable to weigh anchor and obliged to let slip their cables) the English put to sea.

All, at least, but the Revenge, which lingered still at anchor to receive on board the men still on the island, who hurried, in obedience to her signals, to the shore. Not all came, however. Many were inland, and unable to obey in time, and when the Revenge at last weighed anchor, she had on board only one hundred fighting men.

Let me tell you, in the words of Sir Walter Raleigh, what chanced in consequence of this generous devotion to his absent comrades. "The Lord Thomas, with the rest, very hardily recovered the wind, which Sir Richard Granville, not being able to do, was persuaded by the master and others to cut his mainsail, and cast about, and trust to the sailing of the ship, for the squadron of Seville were on his weather-bow. But Sir Richard utterly refused to turn from the enemies, alleging that he would rather choose to die than to dishonor himself, his country, and her Majesty's ship; persuading his company that he would pass through the two squadrons in despite of them, and enforce those of Seville to give him way, which he performed upon divers of the foremost, who, as mariners term it, sprang their luff and fell under the lee of the Revenge. But the other course had been the better and might well have been answered in so great an impossibility of prevailing."

So says the brave and wise Raleigh; and no doubt it is both unwise and inhuman to sacrifice human life needlessly; but such a deed as Granville now undertook was not, could not be in vain.

To hold life as naught, compared with honor, is the creed which made England great, and which when her sons fail to recognize as a duty, will justly deprive her of her place amongst nations. I am writing for the boys of England, and I believe, indeed I should be ashamed to think otherwise, their hearts will glow at the story of Sir Richard Granville's grand, though hopeless action off Flores.

But let us return to the gallant Revenge.

While she was beating off the foes nearest to her, the San Philip, which was to windward, came sailing down on her, and so huge was the great Spanish ship, that she actually took the wind out of the sails of the Revenge, so that she lay unable to answer her helm.

While thus bereft of her sails, the ships under her lee luffed up and attacked her. And now our glorious admiral was fighting at the same time the San Philip, a regular three decker, carrying three tiers of ordnance on each side, and eleven guns in each tier, and the Admiral of Biscay's ship, of the same huge size, commanded by Brittandona. One would have thought the good ship already outnumbered, but while the two great men-of-war engaged her, four others boarded her, two on her larboard and two on her starboard side.

And now the Revenge was hailed by one of the small London victuallers, which well merits to have her name recorded in that day's proud story. The George Noble, of London, had already received several shots through her hull, but she came to crave the admiral's orders, and to ask how she might best aid him. Sir Richard bade the captain save himself, and leave the Revenge to her fortune: he would not sacrifice the heroic little vessel in a vain contest.

The fight began at three o'clock in the afternoon; it lasted long into the night. The great San Philip having received the lower broadside of the Revenge, which was of cross-bar shot, fell off, and it is reported, foundered shortly after. One of the great galleons of Spain and the admiral of the hulks were sunk; and the other ships suffered frightful losses.

Again and again the Spaniards tried to board the Revenge, and every time the dauntless English repulsed and drove them back. Thus, the hours sped on, and during that terrible conflict, one English ship fought "fifteen several armadas," as Sir Walter Raleigh calls the Spanish ships.

An hour before midnight a musket-shot hit the admiral in the side; he refused to leave the deck to have it dressed, and while the surgeon was in the act of attending to him there, he received another in the head, and the doctor was killed. But still the Revenge fought on till daylight began to dawn over the sea. The Spaniards, who had suffered greatly from her guns, now drew off, and the action languished, but as "the day increased the men of the Revenge decreased, and as the light grew more and more, by so much more grew our discomfort. For none appeared in sight but enemies, save one little ship called the Pilgrim, commanded by Jacob Whiddon, who hovered all night to see the success; but in the morning, bearing up with the Revenge, was hunted like a hare amongst many ravenous hounds; but escaped."

The sun rose. All the Revenge's powder to the last barrel was now spent; all her pikes broken; forty of her best men slain; and the greater part of the remainder wounded. At the beginning of the fight she had, as we have said, only one hundred hands free from sickness, the remaining ninety lying powerless on the ballast. Hope had fled, no friendly sail was to be detected on the horizon. The Revenge was dismasted, "her tackle cut asunder; her upper works altogether erased," nothing remained for flight or defense: she lay a mere wreck upon the waters, surrounded by the mighty fleet of Spain.

Then Sir Richard Granville called the master gunner to him, and bade him split and sink the ship, that England might see how, after so many hours fighting, and with so great a navy, the Spaniards had been unable to take the Revenge. "Yield yourselves," he said, addressing the seamen, who gathered round their dying admiral, "to the mercy of God, rather than to that of men, and sully not the glory of your nation in order to prolong your lives for a few miserable hours or days."

The master gunner grimly assented to his chief's will; but the captain and the master, who had perchance dear home ties, or at least took a wiser and more just view of their position, remonstrated; reminding Sir Richard that there were many brave men on board yet living who might do their country and their queen "acceptable service hereafter." Moreover, they assured him that the Spaniard would never possess his glorious ship for she had six feet of water in her hold already, and three shot holes under water, so weakly stopped that with her first roll in the sea she would assuredly sink. Still Sir Richard persisted in his despairing wish. But the master of the Revenge had in the meantime gone on board the General, to negotiate with Don Alfonso Bazan, to arrange the terms of surrender. And there on the deck of the Spanish flag-ship the blunt Englishman told, how Sir Richard would fain die and all with him rather than surrender; but at the same time declared that the crew would yield on condition that their lives should be spared, and that they should be sent back to England, the mariners free, and the officers on payment of such a ransom as they could afford; they were also to be assured of not suffering imprisonment, or being doomed to the galleys.

The chivalrous Spaniard at once assented. Even their foes had been won to boundless admiration and amazement by the marvelous valor of the English, and Don Alfonso Bazan was anxious to save the life of the wounded Granville.

When the master returned with these favorable terms, the whole crew accepted them, except the master gunner, who, seizing a sword, would have slain himself if he had not been overmastered by his comrades and locked into his cabin.

In a short time, therefore, the Spanish boats surrounded the Revenge, to take off the crew, many of whom, still fearing Sir Richard's resolution to sink the ship, stole away to the General and the other ships of the Armada.

Don Alfonso then sent a courteous message to the wounded commander, beseeching him to leave the Revenge, which was a mere slaughterhouse, the decks dyed with blood and covered with the slain. Sir Richard, feeling that he was dying, replied that the Spanish Admiral might do with his body as he would, he esteemed it not; and the captors tenderly bore him from his cabin to their boat. As he was carried out of the ship he fainted, and when he revived again he besought the few grieving followers who still surrounded him to pray for him.

Nothing could exceed the humanity and courtesy with which the noble Spaniard treated his wounded foe. He left nothing unattempted for his recovery, assuring Sir Richard repeatedly of his respect and admiration.

But every effort was in vain; Sir Richard Granville died on board the General three days afterwards, and his body was committed to the deep which had been his "field of fame." Thus, in the words of Raleigh, "being dead, he outlived not his own honor." In this extraordinary fight the Spaniards lost nearly a thousand men.

The Admiral of the Hulks (Luis Continho) and the Ascension of Seville were both sunk by the side of the Revenge; one ship went down in the Road of St Michael after leaving the scene of contest; another ran herself on shore to save her men.

The reasons assigned for the singular abandonment of the Revenge by her consorts are said to have been these: the impossibility of reaching the Revenge through the surrounding squadrons; the small number of Howard's ships; and the dangerous vicinity of the island of Flores.

These reasons appear quite insufficient to account for Howard leaving an English admiral to his fate and escaping at his expense; and it has indeed been proved that Lord Thomas did wish to enter between the squadrons and risk all for his gallant comrade, but the crews refused to obey his commands and peril the queen's ships and subjects in an utterly hopeless contest.

The Foresight, however, commanded by Mr. Thomas Vavasour (we cannot bear to omit a single name of those who were willing to aid the noble Granville), stayed for two hours as near the Revenge as the weather would permit; not forsaking the fight till he was about to be encompassed by the Spanish squadrons, from which he cleared his ship with difficulty. The other English ships poured occasionally volleys into the Spaniards, and entered amongst them as far as they could while keeping the weather gauge of the enemy, until parted from them by the night.

Our story is not told yet. A few days after the fight was ended, and the brave "Revenges" dispersed among the Spanish ships, a fearful storm arose from the west and north-west, which dispersed the whole fleet; fourteen sail of which, together with the Revenge (on board of which two hundred Spaniards had been put), were cast away upon the Isle of St. Michael.

"And thus," says Raleigh, quaintly, "it pleased them to honor the burial of that renowned ship the Revenge, not suffering her to perish alone, for the great honor she achieved in her lifetime."

The story of this gallant fight was told in England, not only by the survivors from the Revenge, but by one of the Spanish captains who had fought in it, and who, being severed from the Armada by a storm, was shortly after taken by a small English ship called the Lion of London and brought prisoner to England. We have, therefore, the unprejudiced and reluctant testimony of our enemies to the truth of the story which records how Englishmen kept the seas "In the brave days of old."

[*Sea fights and Land Battles from Alfred to Victoria*. London, 1869. 27–35]

2–5. Lost Treasure, 1596.

The unfortunate voyage of Captain Benjamin Wood, toward the East Indies in 1596:

In 1596, three ships, the Bear, the Bearwhelp, and the Benjamin, equipped principally at the expense of Sir Robert Dudley, were put under the command of Captain Benjamin Wood. The merchants employed in this voyage, were mess. Richard Allot and Thomas Bromfield, of the city of London: who intending to pierce as far as China, obtained Queen Elizabeth's letter to the king of that country in their behalf; which letter is inserted in Hakluyt's collection, vol. 3 p. 853; but of the voyage there is scarce any account to be met with: for the fleet miserably perished, and the relation, if any there was, of the misfortune is lost. All the account we find of it, is in a letter to the king of Spain, and his council of the Indies, from the licentiate Alcazar de Villa Senor; who was auditor of the royal court of St. Domingo, judge of commission in Puerto Rico, and captain-general at New Andalusia. This letter, dated October 2, 1601, was intercepted in its passage, and found among Mr. Hakluyt's papers by Purchas, who has given extract (as he calls it) so far as concerns the business, very tedious, and scarce intelligible, from whence the following account is gathered. This letter however gives no light into the voyage itself, nor by what accident the ships, which set out for the East Indies, came into the West Indies; not what became of them; nor the nature of the sickness which reduced the men to four: but wholly relates to what passed, after those sailors had quitted the ship they came in, and landed at Utias.

By this letter then it appears, that three English ships, bound to some of the Portuguese parts in the East Indies, in their passage, took three Portuguese vessels, one of them from Goa, whose captain had in his charge a large rich stone, which was for the king of Spain: also money for paying the soldiers of a frontier garrison, a great quantity of gold and silver plate, jewels, and rich merchandise; all which the

English took. After this, all the men died of sickness, except four whose names were, Richard, Daniel, Thomas, and George. These in a boat with what goods they could load, put into a river in the Island of Utias, three leagues from that of Puerto Rico. Here, after landing the goods, their boat sunk, and they remained with only a small boat, made of boards, which they had taken from some fisherman at St. John's Head in Puerto Rico: where, coming for water, George was left behind; who, being found by Don Rodrigo de Fuentes, and five others, gave them an account of all that happened, and where his three comrades and the goods were to be found. Upon this, they passed over to Utias, with a letter from George to his companions, advising them to deliver up themselves, with their weapons and goods. Being near the place, they set up a white flag, and the English another, who, upon the promises of Don Rodrigo, and his consorts, yielded themselves, with the arms and effects.

The Spaniards divided the money, and hid the stones, gold, and other things, except a small quantity of silks, and plate in bars, which they kept to give color to their story. After they had eaten, drank, slept, and lived sociably with the Englishmen awhile, they agreed to murder them. Accordingly, they killed Richard and Daniel; but Thomas escaped to a mountain. Going back to Puerto Rico, they poisoned George, and sent to Utias to seek Thomas, but missed of him; and he, to every body's surprise, floated over to Puerto Rico on a piece of timber: which they hearing of, sought many ways to murder him. Meanwhile, Don Rodrigo, and two others of the accomplices, informed the governor of the city of St. Juan de Puerto Rico, that they had brought a small quantity of goods from Utias; and were forced to fight with three Englishmen, whom they had killed before they could get them. They made oath of the affair, and suborned others to attest the truth of what they asserted: But, not agreeing in their story, they were at length all sent to prison; from whence afterwards some of them broke out, with their ring leader Don Rodrigo: who, though he was bolted and chained, and had two soldiers to guard him, filed off his irons by night, and carried off with him two black Moors of his.

From thence he went to the River Toa, but two leagues distant, where he continued a long time in sight of the city, with a horse and arms, being favored by many of his wife's relations: so that he could not be taken. Although the accomplices, upon their examination, confessed the fact; yet they concealed most of the things that were hidden by them, but laid the whole contrivance upon Don Rodrigo; who also confessed the matter but in part, though confronted by evidence, and denied the having several goods, though proved to have been his custody: as the great precious stone, two gold chains, with several bracelets and rings set with small stones; three bags of testones of eight and four rials; a quantity of broken silver, weighing fifty pound: two sacks of plate in bars, two hundred pound weight each; of all which, he delivered up but ten pound and an half, and confessed to about forty pound more; twenty-six of which he gave to bribe Christoval de Mercado, employed to take examinations in the affair. He denied that George told him the great stone was laid up in a sort of little press, between two boards, and where it was to be found; though it was proved, that the first time he went to Utias, he brought from thence a velvet purse, without telling his companions what was in it, at the mouth whereof appeared certain boards, as large as two hands joined together; which, by testimony of Thomas, was the same that contained the stone. He owned he had such a purse, but said it was stolen from him. The said Mercado, besides the twenty-six pound of plate, which he had of Rodrigo, got also from him and his accomplices a hundred and twenty-two crowns of gold, four hundred and fifty rials of four, with some of the other goods.

After Rodrigo's escape, the rest confessed the whole affair; but either through favor or fear, no one would assist the licentiate to bring the villainous Don to justice. Afterwards Juan Ruiz broke prison, and fled to the cathedral church, from whence the licentiate took him: whereupon a suit commenced before the ecclesiastical judge; who gave sentence, that he ought not to be protected. After this, the licentiate pronounced sentence of death against Juan Ruiz, Juan Martinez, Pedro Camacho, and one Juan Lopez de Alceda, a constable, who was assisting to them in secreting the goods; which sentence he resolved to put in execution, unless in five days they delivered up the goods.

How this affair ended, does not appear, the letter having been written before the five days expired; Nor is it of much use farther than to shew the end of that unfortunate voyage, the villainy of the Spanish cut-throats, and that the licentiate's concern in the prosecution of those assassins was wholly on account of their defrauding the king of Spain, without the least regard to the murder of the Englishmen: who, in his letter, are treated as robbers and thieves; though England, at the time, was at war with Spain: which justified their taking of the three ships, and made them lawful prizes.

[*A New General Collection of Voyages and Travels.* Volume 4. London, 1747. 252–254]

2–6. The Wrecking of the *Delight*, 1583.

A relation of Richard Clark of Weymouth, master of the ship called the Delight, going for the discovery of Norembega [a mythical city of immeasurable wealth, in the vicinity of today's New England], with Sir Humphrey Gilbert 1583. Written in excuse of that fault of casting away the ship and men imputed to his oversight.

Departing out of St. John's harbor in the Newfoundland the 20 of August unto Cape Raz, from thence we directed our course unto the Isle of Sablon or the Isle of Sand, which the general Sir Humphrey Gilbert would willing have seen. But when we came within twenty leagues of the Isle of Sablon, we fell to controversy of our course. The general came up in his frigate and demanded of me Richard Clark master of the Delight what course was best to keep. I said that west southwest was best: because the wind was at south and night at hand and unknown sands lay off a great way from the land. The general commanded me to go west northwest. I told him again that the Isle of Sablon was west northwest and but 15 leagues off, and that he should be upon the island before day, if he went that course.

The general said, my reckoning was untrue and charged me in her majesty's name, and as I could shew myself in her country to follow him that night. I, fearing his threatening's, because he presented her majesty's person, did follow his commandment, and about seven of the clock in the morning the ship stroke on ground, where she was cast away. Then the general went off to sea, the course that I would have had them gone before, and saw the ship cast away men and all, and was not able to save a man, for there was not water upon the same for either of them much less for the admiral, that drew fourteen feet. Now as God would the day before it was very calm, and a soldier of the ship had killed some fowl with his piece, and some of the company desired me that they might hoist out the boat to recover the fowl, which I granted them. And when they came aboard, they did not hoist it in again that night. And when the ship was cast away the boat was astern being in burthen one ton and a half: there was left in the boat one oar and nothing else. Some of the company could swim, and recovered the boat and did haul in out of the water as many men as they could. Among the rest they had a care to watch for the captain or the master.

They happened on myself being the master, but could never see the captain. Then they hauled into the boat as many men as they could in number, 16, whose names hereafter I will rehearse. And when the 16 were in the boat, some had small remembrance, and some had none: for they did not make account to live, but to prolong their lives as long as it pleased god, and looked every moment of an hour when the sea would eat them up, the boat being so little and so many men in her, and so foul weather, that it was not possible for a ship to break half a coarse of sail. Thus, while we remained two days and two nights, and that we saw it pleased god our boat lived in the sea, (although we had nothing to help us withal but one oar, which we kept up the boat withal upon the sea, and some went even as the sea would drive us) there was in our company one master Hedly that put forth this question to me, the master.

I do see that it does please god, that our boat lies in the sea, and it may please god that some of us may come to the land if our boat were not overladen. Let us make sixteen lots, and those four that have the four shortest lots we will cast overboard preserving the master among us all. I replied unto him, saying, no, we will live and die together. Master Hedly asked me if my remembrance were good: I answered I gave God praise it was good, and knew how far I was off the land, and was in hope to come to the land within two or three days, and said they were but threescore leagues from the land, (when they were seventy) all to put them in comfort. Thus, we continued the third and fourth day without any substance, save only the weeds that swam in the sea, and salt water to drink. The fifth day Hedly died and another moreover; then we desired all to die: for in all these five days and five nights we saw the sun but once and the star but one night, it was so foul weather. Thus we did remain the sixth day: then we were very weak and wished all to die saving only myself which did comfort them, and promised they should come soon to land by the help of God: but the company were very importunate, and were in doubt they should never come to land, but I promised them that the seventh day they should come to shore, or else they should cast me overboard: which did happen true the seventh day, for at eleven of the clock we had sight of the land, and at 3 of the clock at afternoon we come on land. All these seven days and seven nights, the wind kept continually south. If the wind had in the meantime shifted upon any other point, we had never come to land: we were no sooner come to land, but the wind came clean contrary at north within half an hour after our arrival.

But we were so weak that one could scarcely help another of us out of the boat, yet with much ado being come all on shore we kneeled down upon our knees and gave god praise that he had dealt so mercifully with us. Afterwards those which were strongest helped their fellows unto a fresh brook, where we satisfied ourselves with water and berries very well. There were of all sorts of berries plenty, and as goodly a country as ever I saw: we found a very fair plain, champion ground that a man might see very far away: by the seaside was there a little wood and goodly trees as good as I ever saw any in Norway, able to mast any ship, of pine trees, spruce trees, fir, and very great birch trees. Where we came on land we made a little house with boughs, where we rested all that night.

In the morning I divided the company three and three to go every way to see what food they could find to sustain themselves, and appointed them to meet there all again at noon with such food as they could get. As we went abroad we found great store of pease, as good as any we have in England: a man would think they had been sowed there. We rested there three days and three nights and lived very well with pease and berries; we named the place St. Lawrence, because it was a very goodly river like the river of St. Lawrence in Canada, and we found it very full of salmons. When we had well rested ourselves we rowed our boat along the shore, thinking to have gone to the Grand Bay to have come home with some Spaniards, which are yearly there to kill the whale: and when we were hungry or a thirst we put our boat on land and gathered pease and berries. Thus we rowed our boat along the shore five days: about which time we came to a very goodly river that ran far up into the country and saw very goodly grown trees of all sorts. There we happened upon a ship of Saint John de Luz, which ship brought us into Biskay to a harbor called the passage.

The master of the ship was our great friend, or else we had been put to death if he had not kept our council. For when the visitors came on board, as it is the order to do in Spain, they demanded what we were, we said we were poor fisherman that had cast away our ship in Newfoundland, and so the visitors inquired no more of the matter at that time. As soon as night was come he put us on land and had us shift for ourselves. Then had we but ten or twelve miles into France, which we went that night, and then cared not for the Spaniard. And so shortly after we came into England toward the end of the year 1583.

A true report of the late discoveries, and possession taken in the right of the crown of England of the Newfoundland, by that valiant and worthy gentleman, Sir Humphry Gilbert, knight.

Wherein is also briefly set down, her highness lawful title thereunto, and the great and manifold commodities, that are likely to grow thereby, to the whole realm in general, and to the adventurers in particular: together with the easiness and shortness of the voyage.

[*The Third and Last Volume of the Voyages, Navigation, Traffics, Discoveries, of the English Nation.* London, 1600. 206–208]

PART 3. SHIPWRECKS

3-1. Four English Wrecks at Flamborough Head

Tensions between France (while they occupied Scotland) and England had escalated to a point that any ships of war that could sail, did; and just as many were being prepared to sail as soon as possible. During the English Reformation, a deeper division occurred since England converted to Protestantism when Elizabeth ascended the throne, while France remained Catholic. Furthermore, Mary Queen of Scots challenged Elizabeth's claim to the throne because Elizabeth I and Mary I were both labeled bastards by an act of Parliament when John Dudley, the Duke of Northumberland, manipulated the young and dying King Edward VI to alter the line of succession to place Lady Jane Grey on the throne. Lady Jane was then to marry the duke's son, who would then be poised to become the father of the King of England.

During the month of December 1559, records show both France and England had sent their merchant and war ships to sea. Meanwhile, both navies were preparing to sail any able ship as soon as possible.

The French ambassador Noailles reported to the Queen Dowager in a letter "affairs of Scotland". A sturdy description of the character of Admiral Winter of the English fleet was shared as 'brave, venturous and resolute' on 21 December 1559 as Mary, Queen of Scots began to work with Scottish lords, also Protestant, in preparation to expel France from Scotland.

Thirty additional English ships were being rigged and ready to sail on 21 December 1559, not paid for by Queen Elizabeth, but by the individual captains who were given permission to plunder whatever they could to fund the cost of maintaining a ship, crew, and officers.

An additional record indicates that 'the arming of the navy has been pushed on with redoubled vigor.' Fourteen vessels were waiting for a favorable wind to set out for Berwick in northern England under the command of Admiral Winter who was to serve as Vice-Admiral. The remaining ships would guard from the mouth of the Thames River to the North Sea.

Across the channel, France was preparing merchant and ships of war for Scotland to support their preparations for the war campaign. Among the cargo to be carried was men, horses, wine, wheat, gunpowder, hand tools, shot, iron and brass cannons; sometimes up to 30 cannons per ship would be transported to Scotland. The smaller French ships carried hogs, wine, ordnance and powder, men, and horses. These ships were about 60 tons. At Dieppe, a carrack was being readied to sail and the *Flower de Lyde* was only waiting for a favorable wind to sail.

15 December 1559 — two row barges, one of 120 tons and the other 90 tons, had been readied to sail from Newhaven to the Castle de Mino to transport gold from the castle to possibly fund their war efforts. The castle was built by the Portuguese in 1482 in present-day Elmina, Ghana, (Formerly the Gold Coast). At the height of the gold trade in the early 1500s, some 24,000 ounces, or 1500 pounds of gold were exported annually from the Gold Coast, accounting for approximately one tenth of the world's supply. In a curious note regarding the voyage to the castle, it was mentioned that the profits would be split four ways: for the admiral, for the ships, the merchants, and victuallers. Perhaps someone thought the ship would not arrive back? Records suggest that a small row barge attempted to sail but returned because of a storm in the channel. There are conflicting records of the fate of this ship that will be reviewed in another chapter.

23 December 1559 — 900 plates of copper, 708 corslets (a piece of defensive armor covering the body), 1045 corries and hagbutts (a firearm with a long barrel), and 13, 971 pounds of fine powder left Zealand, Denmark for England. Denmark was the leading miner of copper in the area at the time. Copper was primarily used for lining ship's hulls or mixing with tin to produce bronze for cannons.

Wednesday, 27 December 1559 — at about 9:00 AM with a favorable wind from S.S.E., the admiral lifted anchor and sailed, then between 3 and 4 o'clock he dropped anchor at Goldemore Gate, next to the Nase, off Harwich.

Thursday, 28 December 1559 — about 10:00 in the morning, they lifted anchor and sailed to Nase with a S.S.E wind. At 4:00 the wind direction changed to W.S.W., which brought them to anchor at Yarmouth Road.

30 December 1559. The Marquis d'Elbeuf was still sitting in Calais waiting for a favorable wind to sail with 'treasure and certain ships.'

> "Yesterday morning the Marquis du Boeuff had not left Calais. He has treasure and certain ships, but not of any great strength. Knows not what he will do now, knowing the departure of the English Ships."

> [Calendar of State Papers, Foreign Series, of the Reign of Elizabeth, 1559–1560. Pg. 256, Document 529. London, 1865.]

4 January 1560 — They encountered strong winds that were NE and had to cut their anchors and cables and were forced to return to 'Orwellwards afore Harwich'. The strong winds damaged several ships and a couple broke masts.

With a favorable wind from the south on 11 January, the admiral lifted their anchor then sailed to Flamborough Head. Flamborough Head is a promontory, 13 km or about 8 miles long on the Yorkshire coast of England, between the Filey and Bridlington Bays of the North Sea, and about 385 km, or about 240 miles, north of the Thames River. It is a chalk headland, with sheer white cliffs.

The following day at 4:00 am a strong N.N.W. wind forced them to turn around and sail south and seek safety in the Humber River that flows into Leeds and Sheffield, Yorkshire.

13 January 1560 — The Marquis d'Elbeuf and other French lords had departed Calais with 17 merchant and war ships carrying men, horses, wheat, wine, cannons, and powder. Furthermore, one or possibly two of those ships were carrying 'the treasure' that would accompany the Marquis d'Elbef on a trip to Scotland. Unfortunately, no records could be found regarding a description of the treasure mentioned. At one time, a record would have occurred. Perhaps somewhere in a dark French archival basement, that record still exists.

16 January 1560 — Anchors were lifted at 11:00 with a favorable S.E. wind and headed north toward Flamborough Head again.

The following is an extract from a log that Admiral Winter kept.

16 January 1560, Tuesday, weighed at 11 o'clock a.m., wind S.E. and by S. and came to Flamborough Head. There "the traverse of the weather" was such that they lost all their boats; and there were dispersed, being in number twelve; viz.

The *Lion*, Mr. Winter.

Admiral; the *Philip and Mary*.

Mr. Rob. Constable, Vice-Admiral; the *Hart*.

Mr. William Gorge; the *Antelope*.

Mr. Southwick; the *Jennet*.

Mr. Malyne; the *New Bark*.

Mr. Byston; the *Greyhound*,

Mr. Lock; the *Swallow*.

Mr. Holstock; the *Tiger*.

Mr. Croker; the *Willoughby*.

Mr. Spencer; the *Jarfalcon*.

Mr. Stoneher; the *Falcon*.

The following vessels were left in Yarmouth road, for the
safety of the victuals and munitions:

The *Bull*, Mr. Winchester.

The *Saker*, Giles Graye.

Mr. *Hare*.

[Calendar of State Papers, Foreign Series, of the Reign of Elizabeth, 1559–1560. Pg. 295, Document 601. London, 1865.]

A violent tempest coming from the English Channel turned north as they arrived back at Flamborough Head. The storm affected 12 English and 17 French ships, mostly war ships of 200 to 500 tons with multiple decks of heavy iron cannons.

Thursday 18 January 1560 — with a N.W. wind, they sailed north then anchored at Bamburgh Castle, Farne Island at 4:00pm. That evening the weather flared up again and "wind vyring (veering) out," they had to return to sea after cutting anchors and cables.

Saturday, 20 January 1560 — 'came to anchor before Eymouthe (Weymouth). Wind S.W. and by W'. This is the last entry Admiral Winter made in the rare log that has survived history.

If we are to take literally the admiral's log entry of the loss of 12 ships, then I would assume the log entry for the day after would have included some mention of the loss of 12 ships and not just cutting of anchors and cable.

Where this becomes difficult is when I reviewed the ships records of the 12 lost ships, I was able to review all but 4. Two of those 12 ships that the admiral reported as lost, had been disassembled for use in or as other ships 2 years before the storm of 13 January 1560. The *Greyhound*, built in 1544, was rebuilt in 1557, then rebuilt in 1609. This gives an example of the problems encountered following the lives of ships 460 years ago.

What is clear is that a violent tempest hit and affected 29 ships. Did the admiral lose any of them?

It was reported on 20 January 1560 in a letter from Berwick that several English lords indicated that all "their hope was on the ships that had not yet arrived". As a P.S. in the same letter, "the proportion of the treasure now coming will not last long if the whole garrisons as well old and new, be therewith defrayed." Money in some form was shipped in one or two of the 12 ships under the command of Admiral Winter.

On the same day, a letter from the Earl of Arran expressing an urgency for supplies. The ships contained materials required to maintain a navy and army that had not been replenished in twenty days. Within the same letter there is mention of 2 Scottish ships that overtook the ship of M. de Martigues and killed fifty to sixty men.

21 January 1560 at about 10:00, the *Antelope* with Willian George and the *New Bark* with Mr. Malyre in command, straggled into Berwick. They had letters from the admiral describing the tempest and their lost boats. The admiral describes that they were unable to spot survivors.

"Other requisites are wanted, as well for these seven ships, as for the rest, which he thinks to be as ill-furnished as the others." From a letter from Berwick, 21 January 1560. There are 4 ships that are unaccounted for at that point.

"Thirteen French ships are in company and fourteen are to follow," a French ambassador reported to the Queen Regent of Scotland. He reported that no more copper would be transported to England for fear, "we would make too much ordnance, so he bought 100,000 weight more which cost 53s 4d Sterling per count." Just at this point alone, there were 1,125 plates of copper on one ship.

In correspondence on 22 January from Newcastle, the Duke of Norfolk indicated that he had "heard nothing of the ships with grain of which there will be a great lack if it does not arrive shortly."

From Inchkeith [an island in the Firth of Forth, Scotland] the following day, 8 ships were spotted opposite Dunbar steering toward the Isle of May. The Queen was informed that a boat was sent to ascertain who they were but were not allowed to approach.

This account supports the supposition that at least 7 or 8 ships had survived the tempest.

Beyond 24 January 1560, there are no additional accounts or information about the remainder of the 12 ships. Based on that, it is safe to speculate that at least 4 or 5 were wrecked off the coast at Flamborough Head.

The only names mentioned in correspondence that are known to have survived that violent tempest that rolled up the English Channel, affecting all ships at sea, were the *Antelope*, built in 1546 at 300 tons, and the *New Bark*, at 200 or 300 tons.

This is what is available:

The *Lion*, Mr. Winter. The Lion was launched in 1536 with a weight of 160 tons. It fell into the category of 'Fourth Rate', but the type is unknown. From 1539 to about 1547, it had an armament of 34 to 36 iron cannons, 4 brass guns, and 8–14 handguns. Between 1544 and 1547, it saw service in Scotland. Records indicate it was condemned in 1559. It was suggested that it captured a Portuguese merchant ship near the Isle of Wright on 1 January, 1560. Unknown. The later entry could easily be another ship with the same name, or a variation of the name.

Admiral; the *Philip and Mary*. Records suggest it was launched in 1556 as a Third Rate, 500-ton galleon. In 1584, it was rebuilt in 1584 as the *Nonpareli*.

Mr. Rob. Constable, Vice-Admiral; the *Hart*. Unknown.

Mr. William George, the *Antelope*. Was known to have arrived in Berwick, 21 January 1560.

Mr. Southwick; the *Jennet*. Unknown.

Mr. Malyne, the *New Bark*. Was known to have arrived in Berwick, 21 January 1560.

Mr. Byston; the *Greyhound*. This vessel was launched 1544 as a 200-ton galleon. In 1546, it had 21 iron guns with 8 brass guns. It was rebuilt in 1558 as the *Greyhound*. Unknown.

Mr. Lock. The *Swallow*. This ship was acquired in 1544 as a Third-Rate galleon of 300 tons. During its first trip to Scotland in 1544, it had 47 iron and 6 brass guns. In 1560, it most likely had 29 iron and 8 brass cannons with a crew of about 160 men. It has a recorded history off the coast of Scotland in 1569. In correspondence from Newcastle on 22 January, a report indicated that Mr. Holstock brought the *Swallow* into Tynemouth.

Mr. Holstock; the *Tiger*. The *Tiger* was launched in 1546 as a Fourth Rate 200-ton galleon with 16 iron and 3 brass guns. It was broken up for scrap or rebuild in 1570.

Mr. Croker; the *Willoughby*. The *Mary Willoughby* was a Scottish Fourth Rate galleon that was captured in 1547. It had 35 iron and 6 brass guns with a crew of 120 to 160 as of 1555. It was sold in 1573.

Mr. Spencer; the *Jarfalcon*. In correspondence from Newcastle on 22 January, a report indicated that the *Jarfalcon* was brought into Tynemouth.

Mr. Stoneher; the *Falcon*. This vessel was launched in 1558 as a 100-tons pinnace with 22 iron and 4 brass guns and a crew size of 80, at about 1560. It was sold in 1575. In correspondence from Newcastle on 22 January, a report indicated that the *Falcon* was brought into Tynemouth.

The *Bull* and the *Saker* remained in safety at Yarmouth Rd on the Thames.

Thus, the fate of 4 ships is unknown. The *Lion*, *Hart*, *Jennet*, and the *Greyhound* may be the ships lost because of the tempest on 13 January 1560.

Of course, the records of the 12 ships covered in this part are by no means of any great certainty. Records from the time certainly do not compare to the information-keeping habits of the last couple hundred years. Still, it seems safe to speculate that there are 4 to 5 English ships lying off the coast of Flamborough Head within a couple miles of land. Whenever possible, a captain will try not to lose sight of land during a storm or lose sight of the sun or stars to steer by.

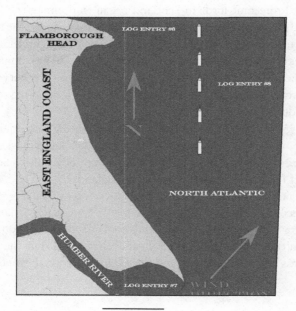

3–2. Four French Wrecks Off Amsterdam

Scotland and France had long been allies under the "Auld Alliance" first established in 1295. Basically, it was an alliance between Scotland and France to control England's invasions. However, during the 16th century, divisions appeared between a pro-French faction at court and Protestant reformers.

The Protestants saw the French as a Catholic threat and when conflict broke out between the two factions, they called on English Protestants for assistance in expelling the French from Scotland.

In 1542, King James V of Scotland died, leaving only a week-old daughter who was proclaimed Mary, Queen of Scots. James Hamilton, Earl of Arran, was appointed Regent and agreed to the demand of King Henry VIII of England that the infant Queen should marry his son Edward. This policy was soon reversed, however, through the influence of Mary's mother Mary of Guise and Cardinal Beaton, and Regent Arran, rejected the English marriage offer. He then successfully negotiated a marriage between the young Mary and François II, Dauphin of France.

The Siege of Leith ended a twelve-year encampment of French troops at Leith, a port near Edinburgh, Scotland. The French troops arrived by invitation in 1548 and left in 1560 after an English force arrived to attempt to assist in removing French troops from Scotland. Leith was not taken by force and the French troops finally left peacefully under the terms of a treaty signed by Scotland, England, and France.

In 1557, Protestant lords in Scotland began to promote the Protestant religion and had hoped for support when Elizabeth ascended the throne.

Mary Queen of Scots married Francis II of France at a tender age, but he died and Mary returned to Scotland to find that those in the realm were tired of having the French in their country. Further divisions grew between them. The new Protestant queen in England and the French, adhering to Catholic beliefs, produced further tensions.

In late 1559, France had already been transporting large quantities of ordnance, powder, shot, hand tools like shovels and pickaxes, baskets, wheat, wine, men, and horses assembled and shipped out of Calais to Scotland to supply their forces to prepare for war with England.

The French navy during the middle 1500s is a bit of an enigma because very few records of their ships are available. It appears that many of their vessels were captured from Spain and England, only compounding the difficulty in tracking not only the routes of their ships, but the life of the ship. Records of the French navy and their ships improved beyond 1600.

A rating classification was adopted to classify ships into first, second, third, fourth, fifth and sixth rates based on the complement of crew, then later according to their number of carriage mounted cannons. That system can also be used to classify French navy ships.

An English spy in France reported on 19 December that five or six ships laden with wheat had departed Calais for Scotland. From various locations near to Calais, wine, hogs, and many pieces of ordnance would be on twenty or twenty-two ships, including the Marquis d'Elbeuf who would voyage to Scotland. At that time, the marquis was traveling with his wife to Calais.

René, Marquis d'Elbeuf (1536–1566), youngest son of Claude of Lorraine, Duke of Guise, served as a French ambassador to Scotland. Mary Queen of Scots was his niece.

On the same day, Captain Rose had departed from Dieppe (a port on the English Channel in the Normandy region of northern France) in his own ship of 60 tons pretending to have the Marquis on board, possibly as a diversion.

Francis Edwards, the English spy in France, informed England that the French King would reassign all merchant ships to best serve his affairs in Scotland.

There were only two of the king's ships being prepared to sail. A carrack and the *Flower de Lyce* were soon rigged and ready to sail from Dieppe.

Furthermore, 2 row barges at Newhaven were ready to travel to Guinea. Guinea is a coastal country in West Africa, formerly known as French Guinea. A row barge is a flat-bottomed boat mainly used for transporting bulk material on rivers or in canals. The two barges had received their stores and were ready to travel to Castle de Mino, a castle built by the Portuguese in 1482, in present-day Elmina, Ghana (formerly the Gold Coast). The barge was to pick up gold to possibly fund the war effort.

An interesting note is included in the correspondence that "the profit of the same shall be divided in four parts; for the admiral, for the ships, the merchants, the victuallers and captain Sore with his 150 men". This is a unique story and will be covered in greater detail in another part.

The carrack was reported to be undergoing maintenance: "had aground to be caulked and tallowed, she will not be ready before the 14th of next month (January)."

By Christmas, twenty French ships had arrived with supplies and men in Scotland. Among them were 4 'great ships' perhaps at 500 tons. The pink that the Marquis was reported as being on, was driven out of the firth by a storm. No word of his safe arrival was known by the 28th. But further research revealed that the Marquis had not yet left Calais and there appears to be a reason for the deception; "he has treasure and certain ships, but not of any great strength," the spy reported to England.

By 31 December, the admiral with the great carrack of 700 tons, Captain Sorres with the *Le Claude* at 500 tons, Guilliame de Sannes with the *La Venteureuse* at 300 tons and the *Le St. Jehan* at 300 tons, departed Calais for Scotland.

The same violent tempest that swept along the English Channel affecting the 12 English ships on 13 January 1560, also affected 17 French ships. The Marquis d'Elbeuf, M. d'Andelot and other French lords were on some of those ships and because of the violent storm, 4 of those 17 were driven into the coast of the Netherlands.

It was reported to England that the 4 ships wrecked close to "Egmond, four leagues on this side of Amsterdam". One ship of 500 tons lost eighty horses and the others were able to swim to land.

"Divers men saved, 800 by count drowned cast on land, an evident argument that more are lost not yet extant."

One of the four ships was the *Jennet* and of 700 men, 400 had survived and the horses that had survived were at the Hague.

There are no further reports on the ships beyond that.

There are four ships that can be located to within a 20 square mile radius off the coast of Amsterdam.

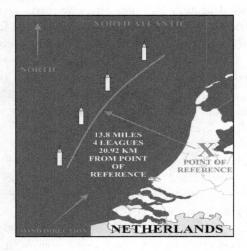

3–3. Castle de Mino Voyage, 1559/60.

This incident appears to be more than just a missing ship. Certainly, this could blossom into a series of events that could warrant a movie. Intrigue, deception, and the theft or plundering of a very large shipment of gold, coupled with a few odd notations in documents, could fulfill that, but I will attempt to only share the facts, which are more interesting than a story.

Francis Edward was a spy, or ambassador, it depends on which reference is reviewed. He wrote to Secretary Cecil 26 November 1559 with events from France. He noted that ships were preparing for a voyage, possibly to Scotland, at Newhaven. 4 merchant ships of 6 or 7 tons each were rigged as were 2 row barges that possibly at one time belonged to the French king. One was 120 tons, the other was 90 tons.

The row barge morphed many times since it was first built, but during this period, it was a single main mast with a flat bottom that required no ballast. This type of ship hugs the coast and is not a deep-water vessel.

The 2 barges were made ready to sail to Calais in 4 or 5 days and would carry the Marquis D'Elbeuf and accompany the other 12 ships at Newhaven to Calais, but they were unsure of a destination at that point in time.

During the night of 28 November 1559, a favorable wind came about to the S.E. to S.W., and 16 ships departed Newhaven for Calais. The 4 large ships stayed off the coast by Calais.

12 December, the marquis departed Rue with his wife after dinner, toward Calais, about a 12-to-15-hour ride by horse. It was believed that Termes and Andelot would accompany him and were already at Calais.

On 13 December, the two row barges finally received orders to sail to Castle de Mino in present-day Ghana for gold and had taken on supplies for that voyage. The following is a very curious mention in the same letter by Edwards.

> The profit of the same shall be divided in four parts; for the lord admiral, for the ships, the merchants, the victuallers, and the Captain Sore and his mariners in both ships, about 150 men. Some men think that if they meet with a good purchase, they will not refuse the same. They are bravely rigged and have three tops apiece; they lack no cordage, great or small, crow's feet nor merlin. By the rigging they may be known, if they go any other ways.

[Calendar of State Papers, Foreign Series, Elizabeth. V–3, 183–185]

The two barges would have departed Calais 13 December 1559 to the Castle de Mino. This type of ship could be rated at about 11 miles an hour, or 264 miles covered in a single day with a good wind, to travel about 4800 miles in about 18 days, again with a good wind. That could place them at the castle about 31 December, but many factors could affect that estimate.

If the wife of the marquis did accompany him on the voyage, I would assume they may have stayed for a day or two to experience the castle. Many such castles were built no the :Gold Coast" as a safe means to protect and store gold for foreigners. At the height of the gold trade in the mid–1500s, approximately 25,000 ounces of gold were exported from the gold coast.

The two row barges loaded their cargo from the castle and could have departed on 1 January 1560 for the 18-day voyage to Newhaven. Based upon those calculations, the two barges would have arrived outside the English Channel on 13 January 1560 when a violent tempest hit the channel. I have already shared 2 separate incidents that resulted in the devastation that tempests caused when 4 French ships wrecked off the coast of

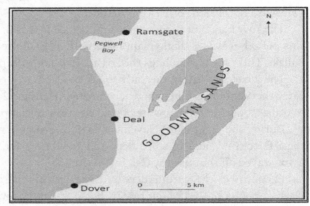

Amsterdam, and English ships wrecked off the Northern Coast of England.

We learn from a letter from Francis Edward to Secretary Cecil on 2 February 1560, that the marquis was with him at Dieppe. Edward is quoted, "I shall answer him as ye know, and gratify him with the same, if he asks any news. He intends to take passage tonight, as there has been no wind before." Edward writes in his letter that a ship arrived from Ghana having lost her captain and 14 men on the coast which allowed only 5 to bring her home. The ship had one ton of grain, 500 elephant teeth and five ounces of gold, "they could bring no more on account of the death of their men."

Coincidence that they would have arrived back at the time of the 2 February letter? One last piece of the puzzle is from a letter 6 June 1560 to Secretary Cecil. While examining any ties to the marquis or Andelot through documents and or correspondence, the index refers me to page 100, letter 163, number 2 for an 'Andelot' reference. But, when I read the entire letter, there is no name Andelot in the letter at all, only a curious reference to "Touching the treasure" and mentions a letter from Sackville regarding that comment.

I am unable to locate that referenced letter from Sir Richard Sackville in the index or manuscript collection.

Several pieces of information that were reviewed for this incident were not learned from the index of the *Calendar of State Papers* covering three volumes from this time, but only from within correspondence. For example, there is no mention of Guinea in the index for the 2 February 1560 letter from Francis Edwards. What else is missing or omitted?

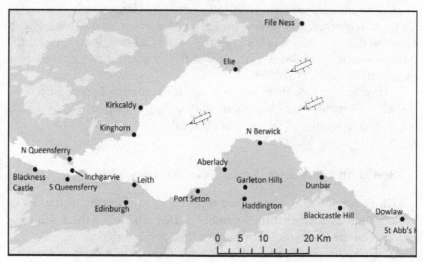

On 13 January 1560, Challoner reported to Secretary Cecil of the great loss of ships from the storm. Furthermore, he wrote "And fear lest the Marquis himself is perished. This is not the shipwreck which he made mention of a month passed."

Based on recorded sightings and correspondence, the marquis and Andelot lived well beyond this incident. In an early account of the two row barges, a single obscure reference is made that the Marquis D'Elboef would take one of the barges, perhaps the 120 ton, and Andelot would possibly take the 90 ton.

So, if the Marquis and Andelot arrived back in Newhaven in one ship, where is the other? Does the 90-ton lost before the entrance to the English Channel remain? If so, would it be safe to assume that the wrecked or scuttled ship could have been recovered of all that could be, including the gold from the castle de Mino, regardless of the loss of the captain and crew? Then, if that is the case, this shipment of gold could be written as lost at sea due to the tempest on 13 January 1560. But if not at the shipwreck, perhaps to pad someone's coffer? This is where great storytelling could come into play. If the marquis took the other ship carrying gold, killed the captain and all those who were not part of the plot, then sailed home to Newhaven under the pretense that all but 5 ounces of gold were lost, he would do so much richer.

So, all that would remain in present times, would be possibly a bare 90-ton row barge.

Unless the ship was truly lost and sunk with a large supply of the gold and not recovered. An 18-day voyage to Newhaven would have placed them on day 13 somewhere between the coast of Lisbon, Portugal, and the Northwestern tip of Spain in the Bay of Biscay when the violent tempest slammed the English Channel.

Many "ifs" in this incident, so I will leave that to fiction writers to embellish. But there is a chance that a 90-ton ship stripped of — or loaded with — gold is lying off the coast of Portugal.

3–4. Three Goodwin Sands Wrecks. 1593.

On 12 August 1593, the council received a complaint by merchants of Holland and Zealand that in November or December 1592, three ships ran aground on the Goodwin Sands and lost their goods.

The Goodwin Sands is a large sand bank about 10 miles long and located about 6 miles off Deal Point in Kent, England. The sand bar is about 85 feet of sand that lies between 18" to 20" above the water level to about 10' under the water level depending on tides.

The *St. Peter* of Amsterdam, the *Red Lion* of London, and the *Golden Lion* of Middleborough, were loaded with "many packs of wax, linen cloth, sails, grograms and other diver's merchandise of value and pertaining to the merchants of Holland and Zealand."

It was reported by towns along the coast that the same cargos were spotted floating on the sea or washed ashore along the coast from the Isle of Thanet in Kent to the town of Rye in Sussex, about a 48 mile stretch of coastline littered with items from these ships, now added to the hundreds of other ships that have run onto this treacherous sand bar over the span of hundreds of years.

Authorities from local coastal towns reported that local residents had "taken up, spoiled, embezzled, concealed and carried away without regard of the misery and affliction of the poor mariners and owners of the ships and goods". Orders were issued for the restitution with an emphasis placed on the fate of the poor men's losses.

Based on the debris trail along the coast, perhaps it would be safe to assume the ships were travelling north from the English Channel towards perhaps London when they hit the sand bar.

The single document tied to the council notification of 12 August 1593 is a letter from Challoner to Secretary Cecil on 13 January 1594 regarding the council, that was distressed with the news of the loss and that the Marquis had perished, (he did not, by-the-way) and "this is not the shipwreck which he, Marquis (?) made mention of a month passed", placing it in November and December 1592.

These three ships made the ultimate sacrifice for their service for the Crown of Queen Elizabeth. Though among the many wrecks from this location, the names of those that ran onto the sandbar in this early period of English naval history, makes this perhaps a treasure not in gold or silver but in facts.

3-5. Three French Wrecks, 1560.

Nicholas Wotton, Dean of Canterbury and York, sent the Queen updates on 18 October 1560 including news that he had not heard about the two barques from Guinea (Ghana). This could be a reference to the "Castle de Mino Voyage" from early in 1560, covered earlier.

Within the second week of September 1559, complaints had been received from merchants against Sieur de Citeville for redress for the cargo on the three ships that was lost. "Citeville was a naughty man and kept to himself in his castle so that justice could not well be administered to him", wrote Cotton.

Furthermore, Wotton informed the queen that the French King Francis II had prepared three ships of war to send against those responsible for sinking three French ships from Rouen.

A single reference document to those three ships is on 20 January 1560. "The Credence of Mr. Spenser" mentioned 3 ships loaded with victuals and about 60 Frenchmen had been driven on ground. The Frenchmen had been killed and the ships plundered by the Laird of Grange and his company. Sir William Kirkcaldy of Grange was a Scottish politician and soldier who fought for the Scottish Reformation. His career ended holding Edinburgh castle on behalf of Mary, Queen of Scots and he was hanged at the conclusion of a long siege.

It was reported on 16 January 1560, that the Laird of Grange defeated 300 Frenchmen, and many were killed in battle. Furthermore, a ship of Count Martiguess was taken with six horses, many harness and culverins and a little French barque named the *Farnade*.

Grange had 1000 horse soldiers under his command at that time, but that did not prevent the French from lighting his house on fire, but "it only damaged the corners", but the houses "before the gate" were all destroyed.

The Laird of Grange was in defense at his home of Hallyards castle northwest of Auchterool and about 4 miles west of Kirkcaldy. There is a reference to French being spotted at Burtisland at the time of the wrecks. That could place them in the Firth of Forth, between Earlsferry and North Berwick inside of what is now the Isle of May National Reserve, a small island at the east of the Firth of Forth. The Firth of Forth is the estuary or firth of several Scottish rivers including the River Forth and is a broad funnel-shaped fjord. Beneath the estuary and its sediments lies a rock floor that locally extends well below sea level.

The possibility that three French ships of war lie on the bottom of the Firth of Forth is very possible following the only documents discovered.

3-6. Zealand Wreck, 1560.

22 January 1560, Thomas Gresham wrote to Secretary Cecil and informed him of current events. Included is an observation that the ships of war must depart soon, because the victuals were used up.

> "As he was writing, news has arrived that Clayshe (Clays) Johnson, a hoy of Antwerp, was sunk in Zealand by a great bark, wherein the queen had laden thirteen puncheons of brimstone, weighing 13,000 weight; which being perceived by the queen's ships of war, they manned out the boats and ships and saved the most of goods."

[*Calendar of State papers, Foreign Series*, Elizabeth, V.3. 617 #7.]

There are no further leads resulting from this tidbit. It is clear that an English hoy sank in Zealand. There is no correspondence relating to this incident prior to the letter. There are no references to this incident after 22 January 1560. Records are only of this incident.

3-7. Dover Wreck, 1558.

15 January 1558, Christian III, King of Denmark, wrote to Queen Mary.

"He knows that the piratical incursions made on Norway and other portions of his domain do not meet with her majesty's approval, but it is necessary to the sake of peace, that such should be repressed."

[Calendar of State Papers, 1553–1558.]

The king was tired of receiving information that his ships had been pirated and sent a kind notification to Mary. Enclosed with the letter was a copy of a petition to the king dated 27 September 1557 from Lawrence Johnston, citizen of Copenhagen. Johnston complained that on 22 July 1557, he was sailing to Fla, Norway when his ship was captured by French from Dieppe and ordered to steer to Dieppe to sell his cargo. They stated that they should take from him whatever Dutch goods they found aboard, paying him, however, for their carriage. He indicated he could not resist.

26 December 1557, the ship was retaken by a Belgian who transferred him aboard the ship, and he was taken to Dieppe. The letter indicates that he walked to Calais, that is about 120 miles, which at 3 mph is about a 40-hour walk.

When Lawrence Johnston arrived at Calais, he was informed that his ship had been captured again, from the Belgian who originally took it from him; this time by William Gryn, a Blacnoul (Blackwall?) captain of the Queen of England's ship Grenehunt (*Greyhound*) and taken to Davern (Dover?) where the ship was stripped of its cargo, furniture, anchor, ropes and sails, which were sold and the ship "knocked to pieces on the rocks."

Lawrence applied for restitution while he was at Dover, but being unsuccessful, he traveled to London and applied to the Privy Council who detained him for six weeks. I was unable to determine a reason other than suspicion.

2 August 1558. Queen Mary acknowledged the petition submitted by Lawrence Johnston. The matter was submitted to the council, but Johnston "refused to abide the question of law". Furthermore, Mary indicated to the King of Denmark that Lawrence should address the French on the matter, not English.

3 July 1558. A letter was sent to Johnston that required him to consider a true value of the ship alleged to have been taken by the *Greyhound* and of the goods in her, and what became of the ship.

No other records are known to exist at this point.

It would be safe to speculate that a ship of unknown size ran aground about Dover, perhaps between Folkstone and Ramsgate, perhaps at the strait of Dover. Everything worth removing was taken and all that would be there now would be an empty, stripped ship from 1558.

3–8. Three French ships, 1560.

Contained within a letter titled "The Credence of Mr. Spenser" of 20 January 1560, he mentioned that 3 ships laden with victuals and 60 Frenchmen was driven on ground, the men were slain, and the ships spoiled by the Laird of Grange and his company.

That is the extent of the snippet in the letter. But we can learn more because I was able to determine the location of Laird of Grange.

16 January 1560, the letter indicated that the Laird of Grange was at Kircaldy. "Last Friday, Grange defeated a band of Frenchmen of 300 and had the charge of 1000 horse soldiers".

20 January 1560, the letter mentions that the Laird of Grange's "house was not cast down, but the corners burnt and the houses before the gate were destroyed. Coffers and "balhusses" were missing after being opened, then taken in the ships." Grange, the Scottish politician and soldier held lands at Hallyards Castle in Fife, located to the north-west of Auchtertool.

The council mentioned in their letter that the ships were spoiled by Grange's company. A letter of 16 January 1560 mentions that William Kirkcaldy was at Kirkcaldy and 4 days later when a report was made regarding his home being set on fire, but it only sustained minor damage. That most likely is Hallyards Castle which is regarded as his home at that point in time.

Perhaps a storm blew the 3 ships into the safety of the harbor area of Edinburgh, but they ran aground or sank off the coast for the Laird of Grange's men to have killed everyone.

These 3 ships could be lying just offshore, perhaps between Wormiston and Kinghorn, about 20 miles of coast.

3–9. Seven or Eight French Galleys Lost, 1555

In a letter Peter Vannes wrote to the council on 17 March 1555, he indicated that the siege of San Fiorenzo in Corsica had ended because of the lack of provisions and aid from French galleys, but that 7 or 8 galleys had been lost because of a tempest.

That is the extent of the document.

French and Ottoman forces joined in the Mediterranean to disrupt coastal regions under the influence or control of the Holy Roman emperor. The French were a driving force as they raided the coasts of Corsica, Elba, Naples, and Sicily.

By winter, the French left behind only a few ships and troops and the Genoese launched a counter-invasion and retook Corsica completely in 1555. The signing of a treaty in 1559 brought the war to an end.

No additional information relating to this incident could be found in conventional records. 7 or 8 French galleys were lost. Perhaps they were from a port in southern France toward the Island of Corsica, off the west of Italy from Rome in the Mediterranean Sea.

Unless an obscure hidden document surfaces from a dark archive, those are all the facts for this incident.

3-10. Four Italian Galleys Lost, 1555

Sir John Mason wrote to the Privy Council on 17 December 1555. Among the updates he reported to the council was that 4 galleys of Malta, Italy, were lost at sea and "the bodies have been recovered, but the ordnance and rest are lost."

Within the letter is a mention of 'navigation to the Guineas (Ghana). The 4 ships that were lost are only mentioned in a snippet of the original document, but that no longer exists in the British Library.

No preliminary related documents could be located. The only safe conclusion could be these ships could have been caught in a tempest in the Mediterranean Sea or overtaken by French ships.

The only weather/storm recorded in a document was 17 March 1555 in which 7 or 8 French galleys were lost because of a violent tempest. That same tempest may very well have destroyed these 4 Italian ships. That storm can add 11 or 12 now known accounts of ships that lost their lives in the line of duty.

3-11. Lost Cargo of 1.4 Million Spanish Reals.

This interesting incident may not fit under the literal definition of a shipwreck, but under 'missing'. No conclusion could be arrived at based on limited historical records other than a single mention in a letter Thomas Gresham, the queen's agent in Flanders, who wrote to the Privy Council on 30 November 1554 while in Seville Spain.

Thomas Gresham traveled from Medina de Campo to Puerto Real, Spain. He departed on 23 November 1554 on his 400-mile journey and arrived in Seville 26 November to find his servant had completed the task of preparing

100,000 ducats (gold or silver coin) for transport. "All packed, sealed, matted and corded and the mules hired to transport them."

Recorded comments from the 'commons of the town' had expressed the concern that so much money would leave their realm and the "scarcity now throughout all of Spain."

Merchant ships departed Puerto Real carrying 1.4 million Spanish reals, reported on 30 November 1554. These ships carried a cargo of 50 containers. Each container was marked with a broad arrow sign and numbered from 1 to 50. Each box contained 22,000 silver Spanish reals.

110,000 ducats were transported on English ships.

No additional documents that even remotely relate to this incident were found. I would assume that much treasure would attract other documents to record its arrival. No recorded storms, but weather can be unpredictable in November.

1.4 million Spanish reals had departed Puerto Real, Spain. This one is particularly frustrating without closure of some type.

3–12. The *Clement* Wreck, 1547.

The lord protector to King Edward VI received information regarding a shipment of gunpowder to New Castle on 5 April 1547. Humphrey Wilson departed London through the Thames into the North Sea, then steered the *Clement* Northeast. He passed Great Yarmouth then steered her Northeast past the Humber River along the coast toward Tynemouth carrying 8 casks of superfine gunpowder.

The weather was described as fair in the letter as the *Clement* continued to Middlesbrough toward Tynemouth then finally arriving in Newcastle after what should have been an easy voyage.

The protector was informed that Humphrey Wilson had mistaken a church steeple five miles from Tynemouth and ran the ship on ground.

It is safe to speculate that the captain saw a church steeple in Whitburn. If he was hugging the coastline which is often done for the ease of navigation, then the ship may have run aground north of North Beacon to Souter Point.

There are records mentioning a church in town at that time and a rectory on the south side of the town, perhaps a mile from shoreline.

A quote from the original letter remains, "by the diligence of the country, the greater part of the munitions has been saved, only some powder is wet, and half a cask lost. If you will send some sulphur and saltpeter, and a man that understands it, it can be made to serve."

It has been suggested that in 1588, two Spanish galleons ran aground on Whitburn rocks in what has been described as rough seas, then the ships were plundered and a bell from one of the ships was placed in the church. History indicates that oak beams removed from one of the ships could be viewed in a shop into the 1950s prior to the building's demolition. The disposition of the Spanish ships is not covered in this book.

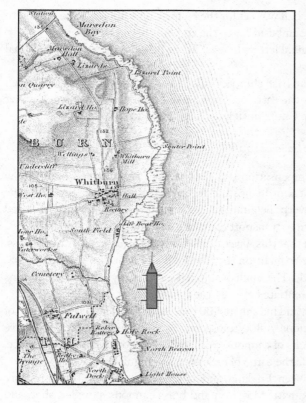

Early 1800s map of Whitburn with possible location that the ship ran aground.

3–13. Irish Ship Sunk, 1552.

The available documents are only fragments of the missing original letters and are scattered among a single volume of documents.

10 June 1552, the Privy Council first addressed Philip Chute, captain of Camber Castle, an artillery fort built by King Henry VIII to defend and guard the port of Rye, to determine how the Flemish prisoners in Rye were to be handled.

10 August 1552, the council requested one of the Flemish mariners to appear before them.

Additional information is learned from a letter to the master of the rolls to certify whether the Flemish pirates that sank the Irish ship had been sentenced or not on 1 September 1552.

Two very fragmented letters follow the matter into October, but nothing new is learned.

24 October 1552, bail was set for the Flemish on sufficient sureties and to be set free unless the ambassador to the emperor had concerns.

There are no original letters housed in the British Library. No additional resources located.

The Dutch sank an Irish ship, perhaps in May to early June 1552, between Ireland and perhaps the east coast of England. The pirates remained under the custody of Philip Chute until late October 1552.

3–14. The *Anne Galland,* 1556.

A request for compensation was filed to the Privy Council by Anthony Antonie surveyor of the ordnance and recorded on 10 July 1556 regarding the *Anne Galland* of Antwerp, Belgium, that belonged to Anthony Lincoln hired by the English crown to transport ordnance and munitions to Ireland.

Records indicate that this *Anne Galland* was a 400-ton second rate galleass. Perhaps a good time to mention that the English *Anne Galland* was recorded at 300 tons in records. The English ship led me in many different directions enabling me to differentiate between the two ships.

Anthony Lincoln and his ship of 400 tons sailed to Ireland with a cargo of ordnance and munitions. A 400-ton second rate ship at this time could have had two to three decks of cannons, perhaps 75–95 iron and brass ordnance. This does not include the cargo of ordnance and munitions.

Somewhere between England and Ireland lies the 400-ton ship *Anne Galland* with approximately 150 iron and brass cannons, powder, shot, and other munitions included with her tackle and furniture that was lost in service to her crown and country.

A petition was drafted by the council for compensation to Anthony Lincoln. There are no additional related documents located in contemporary sources.

3–15. A Hoy of Newcastle.

Among the topics discussed by the council and recorded on 27 May 1558, was a letter to the Earl of Westmorland lieutenant of the North (England), requesting his assistance to search for a hoy from Newcastle, transporting munitions to Berwick, about a 70-mile journey, that was lost.

There is only a solitary related document found from the vast collections of contemporary material available, a letter of 5 June 1558 of Westmoreland to the mayor of Rye for the arrest of Thomas Wayte of Rye and a man named Pope because of their "heinous disorder at sea, believed to be in the north." Rye is near East Sussex on the southern coast of England on the channel.

Based on that last documented evidence, there is a possibility the ship that belonged to Wayte and Pope was sailing south along the coast to Rye from Scotland and encountered this prize between New Castle and Berwick, plundered and sank it, or it was sunk.

No additional related documents could be found in contemporary records.

There is a ship of perhaps 100–400 tons, large enough to transport iron and brass ordnance, shot and powder, lying near the coast between New Castle and Berwick that may contain 50 to 100 iron and brass ordnance in addition to other related items of the ship. Though to edge on the safe side, most if not all the ordnance, tackle, rope, and sails could have been removed before the ship slipped under the waves. I am sure the ship did not give up willingly and a battle may have occurred.

3–16. The *Black Raven*, 1573.

A warrant for assistance was issued on behalf of John van Hove, Joes van der Plancke and Roger van Hull by the council on 13 December 1573 regarding the loss of the *Black Raven*.

The *Black Raven* was driven on the coast of South Wales loaded with Spanish wines and figs and much of the cargo was saved because of the diligent work by 9 mariners of the crew.

The letter by the council did not address specific individuals of a specific town as is often the case in most of these letters. Contemporary sources reveal two ships of that name from that period. First is the English *Black Raven* with correspondence and documents from December 1575 and February 1576. Furthermore, additional documents can be located beyond that point. Second, is the Danish *Black Raven* with a document from April 1587. If these documents are accurate, then the *Black Raven* of this event is not English or Danish.

Contemporary sources share no additional ship names that could furnish this ship with a home port. Germany, Portugal, France, or Spain could be home, though there is a stronger possibility of Germany. There is no listing of this ship in *Steel's Original and Correct List of the Royal Navy* published in 1782, in the numerous accounts from the period.

Is it possible that the account in which it was driven on land then later rescued by high tide to return to the ocean plausible? Or are the rare records containing the same name making the ship English or Danish not accurate?

There is not much to nibble on with this event. All that remains is a ship of unknown size that was driven on the coast of South Wales and the cargo was recovered. If the ship was headed north, a logical deduction could place the ship between west of Swansea, Wales, to possibly Milford Haven, approximately 60 miles off shoreline in total. A favorable wind from the south could have pushed the ship on shore.

3–17. The *Popingay* Wreck, 1574.

The Privy Council dispatched a letter to Anthony Russhe to appear before them and address a complaint filed by Ferdinand Points and a man named Godard, who were both London merchants. The admiralty court addressed the issue on 19 December 1574. The London merchants claimed that Anthony Russhe, gentleman, had undisciplined "dealings about certain goods" of the cargo carried on this ship.

The *Popingay*, (gaie?) called Emden, Germany home port. It apparently perished at Orford, Suffolk, northeast of London about 90 miles north of the River Thames. The trip, assuming that the ship departed Emden to Orford, would have been on a voyage of approximately 350 miles.

A wind from the east could have blown the ship to perish between what is now Felixstowe and Lowestoft. It is also possible to take the description at a literal value and safely speculate that the ship may have made it into the River Alde toward Orford castle. The castle was built in approximately 1170 by Henry II to strengthen his defenses. This would be at the top of a list of destinations for this ship at the time.

The River Alde that leads to the castle is of varying widths, perhaps 100' to 300'. Of course, it may have been wider then. The distance between Emden and Orford could eliminate a very small ship. But any size ship would clog the river if it sank. If that is correct, then the ship could have perished on the shore between Felixstowe and Lowestoft to the north.

Two members of the commission of the court of the admiralty complained of not receiving the complaint and that the matter was handled incorrectly and recommended a new commission to address the complaint.

3–18. Goodwin Wreck, 1577.

The council sent a letter to Lord Warden on 22 December 1577 to inform him of a ship laden with spices and a diverse collection of other wares and merchandise by Alderman Pullison, that the ship wrecked on the Goodwin Sands.

It has been estimated that up to the present day about 1800 ships have hit this sand bar because it may not have been seen by someone not following a chart or without a pilot on board. Statistics from the era this book covers are very rare. I hope this book will help historians place early wrecks there.

The letter requested that the lord admiral give orders to officers of the five major ports for assistance and aid in recovering the goods without plundering and stealing the cargo and return them to their owners.

Polison Pullison was alderman of London. That could place the ship in London to be loaded with spices and other items, then departed the Thames then turned south to wreck on the sand bar. It is possible that the ship and captain were not from the area, as local mariners would have known the sand bar was there and was to be avoided.

3–19. Five Sussex Wrecks, 1576.

A petition was written and recorded by divers gentleman of the west parts of England to Queen Elizabeth seeking her blessing for an enterprise for the discovery of "sundry rich and unknown lands" and endorsed by Sir Humphry Gilbert on 22 March 1574.

The privy council received a request on 22 March 1576 for assistance from Doctor David Lewis, judge of the admiralty court, for the recovery of the goods of 5 English ships wrecked on the coast of Sussex "richly laden with merchandise from the south parts."

John Roche Dasent, editor of *The Acts of the Privy Council of England*, included this note immediately preceding the last paragraph. "Possibly the return voyage of Sir Humphrey Gilbert," of the office of general surveyor of all horses, armor, weapons, munitions, and artillery throughout England and was working on a seven-year grant from the queen.

A letter recorded 22 March 1574 is a short letter from the gentlemen of the west parts to wish Sir Gilbert a safe upcoming voyage.

The council addressed a letter of assistance to Lord Cobham, Justice Manhood, Doctor Lewis and Doctor Forth that they were required to assist the bearers in the search and recovery of certain wrecked goods on 19 June 1577. That is the end of the trail.

Five of an unknown quantity of other ships were wrecked along approximately 90 miles of shoreline from Camber in the east to Chichester harbor area. Based on that, returning from the south parts could place the ships on a return voyage to London east through the English Channel. If the ships were hugging the coast, an unknown sudden storm may have driven the five English ships onto the shore between Brighton and Eastbourne, about 13 miles of shoreline. "Richly laden" from prizes taken in the south, possibly French, Spanish, or Portuguese, could imply many things including gold, silver, pepper, or other valuable cargo not mentioned in correspondence, not including the ship's tackle, ordnance and other munitions that could not be salvaged at the time of the wreck.

It is a shame to leave the wrecks of 5 possible 'ships of the line' at 200 to 500 tons at that, but that is where the trail ends.

3–20. Sandwich Wreck, 1576.

Lord Cobham was informed 16 October 1576 by Acerbo Veluteli that a certain ship from Marsila (Marseilles? Marsala?) was cast away near Sandwich, England. Certain pieces of ordnance and munitions were recovered and a request was made to have the items restored and transported to their original destination.

That is the extent of the letter.

The only possible link is a reference to a small bark from Marseilles named the *Catherine* with Peron Alhand as master, loaded with "merchandise of Province belonging to certain subjects of the French King," to be transported to London, "Quietly and safely without hurt."

This was a letter addressed by the council 28 December 1576 after the wreck taking into consideration the long time it takes correspondence to arrive and be addressed, a month to even two. This could be the request for a safe conduct of this ship to London when it wrecked on Sandwich.

A ship, perhaps 80 to 200 tons, departed Marseilles, on the Mediterranean side of France, and sailed around Spain through the English Channel. It is possible the ship hit a cross wind as it passed the Strait of Dover traveling east. If the ship was following a wind from south to east, it could have been hit by a wind from the north or east along the North Sea, slamming the ship onto the coast at Sandwich, thus ending its life.

That part of England along the Sandwich coast presents about 10 miles of land on which to wreck. With a mention of recovery of ordnance and munitions, it is safe to speculate that only a bare ship remains.

3–21. The *Angel Gabriel*, 1575.

On 3 January 1575, the Privy Council reviewed a letter to John Rathermaker seeking assistance for the recovery of the *Angel Gabriel* of Antwerp, laden with spices that was captured and sank on her way home from a northern port beside the Isle of Sillye (Scilly).

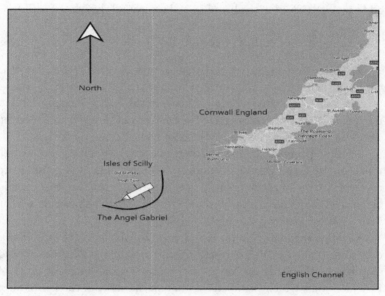

The approximate location of the resting place of the Angel Gabriel of Antwerp.

That is the only reference found that relates to this incident.

The year 1575 saw an increase in pirate activity in the waters around England, mostly in the channel. Queen Elizabeth was closely monitoring the Spaniards and the number of fighting men was 182,929 of which 62,462 were armed, and the royal navy consisted of 24 ships.

The *Angel Gabriel* most likely departed a northern port, perhaps in Ireland, Scotland, or England, sailed south in the Celtic Sea toward Antwerp, and as the ship passed the Isles of Scilly, they encountered pirates, most likely English, or French, Spanish, or Portuguese and the cargo of spices was taken. It would be safe to speculate all the ship's tackle, anchors, sails, furniture, and anything useful was taken. Then the ship was either sunk as target practice or burned and set adrift to sink off the coast.

The Isles of Scilly are about 25 miles off the south-western tip of Cornwall. The inner waters are described in old charts as shallow during spring tides.

Many hazards are recorded, even in early maritime books, about the Scilly islands. The Seven Stones are regarded as a very dangerous 2-mile section as they are mostly below the water level. The islands are small with many rocks above water and just as many below, which are hazardous to those without charts and can be treacherous to pass between.

I believe the *Angel Gabriel* lay within 10 miles on the south side of the isles. There would only be a skeleton remaining, and a ballast pile. It seems safe to add the *Angel Gabriel* to the list of ships lost around the Isles of Scilly.

3-22. The *St. Catherine*, French, 1577.

The Privy Council dispatched a letter on 14 March 1577 to Bishop Thomas Godwin, the Dean of Canterbury, stating that the *St. Catherine* of Marseilles, a French ship, was driven onto the coast of the Isle of Sheppey, land it was presumed at the time belonged to the Church of Canterbury. The letter was a request to consider the case of the poor men affected by the loss.

A follow-up to the Dean of Canterbury on 23 March 1577 indicated that much of the cargo that was removed from the ship was returned to the owner, but the inhabitants of the isle had plundered the ship's goods and furniture. The request indicated to return as much as possible to Captain Peter Ayllan, master of the ship.

Based on the limited information, it is probable that the *St. Catherine* had departed Marseilles, sailed round Spain through the Channel and as, the ship passed the Strait of Dover, hit a tempest, as an incident of 23 March 1577 mentions, which slammed the ship on the shore of the Isle of Sheppey, northeast of Canterbury. That would suggest she hit the shoreline about 8 miles from what is now the Swale National Nature Reserve to Sheerness on the northern tip of the Isle. The Dean of Canterbury was within 4 to 12 miles of the wreck site.

The ship may have survived and been recovered. High tide may have freed the ship from its coastal confines, but I was unable to locate any additional references to this incident. Somewhere in a dark basement of a French archive may lie additional information.

3-23. The *Peter* of Bristol, 1576.

The Privy Council was notified and requested assistance from Bristol merchants on 1 May 1576 that a ship called the *Peter* of Bristol, "being very richly laden with certain merchandise" of Bristol merchants was cast away by tempest. Only 4 mariners survived. The goods, or part of, were retrieved by "sundry of inhabitants upon the sea coast of Somerset, Cornwall and South Wales".

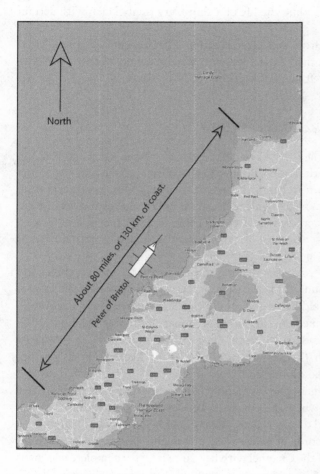

No additional references found. The Bristol merchants were not recorded in other transactions and could not be found in the archives searched.

The *Peter* of Bristol was perhaps a merchant ship of 50 to 100 tons and a crew of perhaps 60 to 100. The ship departed Bristol with very valuable merchandise headed west to what is now Lundy Heritage Coast (Lundy Island then), turned perhaps S.S.W. into the Channel to eventually pass the Scilly Islands, but encountered a violent tempest blowing from the north between Ireland and England. The storm would have pushed the ship towards the coast, which is littered with blind sand bars and shallow, jagged rocks that are sometimes below the water level at higher tides.

All the experience of a seasoned captain and master and crew could not overcome the force of a tempest or prevent it from violently killing perhaps 60 to 100 men and ending the life of a ship "very richly laden with certain merchandise".

Further details from the letter mention what can be interpreted as a debris trail from South Wales to Somerset, about 80 miles of coast. The *Peter* of Bristol certainly left its mark on the coast of England.

3–24. The *Eagle* of Bremen, 1577.

10 March 1577, the Privy Council addressed an issue regarding Harmon Allastson, master of the *Eagle* of Bremen (a Hanseatic German port) regarding a complaint filed by merchants of Antwerp that this ship was transporting a cargo of oils, wines, sugar, ginger, and other merchandise and was driven into Plymouth by contrary winds. On 23 February 1577, the *Eagle* of Bremen was lost in a tempest and most of the merchandise had fallen into the hands of inhabitants of Plymouth and Storehouse.

That is the only reference relating to this wreck found in archives. No records could be found of the London or Antwerp merchants. The task of recovery fell on Arnold Beard and no additional information was uncovered.

The *Eagle* of Bremen was loaded in St. Lucars (Sanlucar de Barrameda), Spain, with cargo and sailed north along the coast of Spain and Portugal toward the English Channel to proceed toward Zeeland. Foul weather forced her into Plymouth England.

There just is not enough information that can be extracted from the letter to pinpoint exactly where the ship sank. Perhaps it was outside of Plymouth while she attempted to sail to Zeeland, or possibly in Plymouth Harbor.

There are no records of recovery, so one might speculate that the *Eagle* lies at the bottom of the Channel with her cargo intact, a complete merchant ship of perhaps 20–50 tons.

3–25. The *Tobie*, 1593.

The following is a rare account given by a surviving member of the crew. The story the mariner shares is so heart-wrenching and traumatic, it deserves mention here.

> The casting away of the Tobie near Cape Esparel (Cape Spartel, Morocco?) corruptly called Cape Sprat without the Strait of Gibraltar, on the coast of Barbary, 1593.

The Tobie of London, a ship of 250 tons manned with fifty men, the owner whereof was the worshipful M. Richard Staper, being bound for Liuorno, Zante and Patras in Morea [southern Greece], being laden with merchandise to the value of 11 or 12 thousand pounds Sterling, set sail from Blackwall the 16 day of August 1593, and we went thence to Portsmouth where we took in great quantity of wheat, and set sail forth of Stokes Bay in the Isle of Wight, the 6 day of October, the wind being fair, and the 16 of the same month we were in the height of Cape St. Vincent, where on the next morning we described a sail which lay in try right a head off us, to which we gave chase with very much wind, the sail being a Spaniard, which we found in fine so good of sail that we were fainne to leave her and give her over.

Two days after this we had sight of Mount Chiego, which is the first highland which we describe on the Spanish coast at the entrance of the Straight [sic] of Gibraltar, where we had very foul weather and the wind scant two days together. Here we lay off to the sea. The master, whose name was George Goodley, being a young man, and one which never took charge before for those parts, was very proud of that charge which he was little able to discharge, neither would take any counsel of any of his company, but did as he thought best himself, and in the end of the two days of foul weather cast about, and the wind being fair, bare in the straights mouth.

The 19 days at night he was thinking that he was farther off the land that he was, bare sail all that night, and an hour and a half before day had run our ship upon the ground on the coast of Barbary without the straight four leagues to the south of Cape Espartel [presumably Spartel, Morocco] Whereupon being all not a little astonished, the master said unto us, I pray you forgive me: for this is my fault and no man's else. The company asked him whether they should cut off the mainmast: no said the master we will hoist out our boat. But one of our men coming speedily up said, sirs, the ship is full of water, well said the master, then cut the main mast overboard: which thing we did with all speed. But the after part suddenly split a sunder in which sort that no man was able to stand upon it, but all fled upon the foremast up into the shrouds thereof; and hung there for a time: but seeing nothing but present death approach (being so suddenly taken that we could not make a raft which we had determined) we committed ourselves unto the lord and began with doleful tune and heavy hearts to sing the 12 psalm. Help lord for good and godly men. Howbeit before we had finished four verses the waves of the sea had stopped the breaths of most of our men. For the foremast with the weight of our men and the force of the sea fell down into the water, and upon the fall thereof there were 38 drowned, and only 12 by God's providence partly by swimming and other means of chests got on shore, which was about a quarter of a mile from the wreck of the ship. The master, called George Goodley, and William Palmer his mate, both perished. M. Caesar being captain and owner was likewise drowned: none of the officers were saved but the carpenter.

We twelve which the lord had delivered from extreme danger of the sea, at our coming ashore fell in a manner into great distress. At our first coming on shore we all fell down on our knees, praying the lord most humbly for his merciful goodness. Our prayers being done, we consulted together what course to taken seeing we were fallen into a desert place, and well-traveled all that day until night, sometimes one way and sometimes another, and could find no kind of inhabitants; only we say where wild beasts had been, and placed where there had been houses, which after we perceived to have been burnt by the Portuguese. So at night falling into certain groups of olive trees, we climbed up and safe in them to avoid the danger of lions and other wild beasts, where we saw many the next morning.

The next day we travelled until three of the clock in the afternoon without any food but water and wild date roots: then going over a mountain, we had sight of Cape Espartel, whereby we knew somewhat better which way to travel, and then we sent forward until we came to an hedgerow made with great canes; we spied and looked over it, and beheld a number of men as well horsemen as footmen, to the number of some five thousand in skirmish together with small shot and other weapons. And after consultation what we were best to do, we concluded to yield ourselves unto them, being destitute of all means of resistance. So, rising up we marched toward them, who espying us, forthwith some hundred of them with their javelins in their hands came running towards us as though they would have run us through, howbeit they only stood us flatting with their weapons, and said they we were Spaniards: and we told them that we were Englishmen; which they would not believe yet. By and by the conflict ended, and night approaching, the captain of the Moors, a man of some 56 years old, came himself unto us, and by his interpreter which spoke Italian, asked what we were and from whence we came.

One Thomas Henmore of our company which could speak Italian, declared unto him that we were merchants, and how by great misfortune our ship, merchandise and the greatest part of our company were pitifully cast away upon the coast. But he void of humanity and all manhood, for all this, caused his men to strip us out of our apparel even to our shirts to see what money and jewels we had about us: which when they had found to the value of some 200 pounds in gold and pearls then gave us some of our apparel again, and bread and water only to comfort us. The next morning they carried us down to the shore where our ship was cast away, which was some sixteen miles from that place. In which journey they used us like their slaves, making us (being extremely weak) to carry their stuff, and offering to beat us if we went not so fast as they. We asked them why they used us so, and they replied, that we were their captures: we said we're their friends, and that there was never Englishman capture to the king of Morocco. So, we came down to the ship, and lay there with them seven days, while they had gotten all the goods they could, and then they parted it amongst them.

After the end of these seven days the captain appointed twenty of his men well-armed, to bring us up into the country: and the first night we came to the side of a river called Alarach, where we lay on the grass all that night: so the next day we went over the river in a frigate of nine oars on a side, the river being in that place above a quarter of a mile wide: and that day we went to a town of thirty houses, called Totteon: there we lay four days having nothing to feed on but bread and water: and then we went to a town called Cassuri, and there we were delivered by those twenty soldiers unto the Alcaide, which examined us what we were: and we told him.

He gave us a good answer, and sent us to the lewes house, where we lay seven days. In the meanwhile that we lay here, there were brought thither twenty Spaniards and twenty Frenchmen, which Spaniards were taken in a conflict on land, but the Frenchmen were by foul weather cast on land within the straights about Cape de Gate, and so made capture. Thus at the seven days end we twelve Englishmen, the twelve French, and the twenty Spaniards were all conducted toward Morocco with nine hundred soldiers, horsemen and footmen, and in two days journey we came to the river of Fez, where we lodged all night, being provided of tents. The next day we went to a town called Salle, and lay without the town in tents. From thence we travelled almost a hundred miles without finding any town, but every night we came to fresh water, which was partly running water and sometime rainwater. So we came at last within three miles of the city of Morocco, where we pitched our tents: and there we met with a carried which did travel in the country for the English merchants: and by him we sent word unto them of our estate: and they returned the next day unto us a Moor, which brought us victuals, being at that instant very feeble and hungry: and withal sent us a letter with pen, ink and paper, willing us to write unto them what ship it was that was cast away, and how many and what men there were alive. For said they we would know with speed, for tomorrow is the king's court: and therefore, we would know, for that you should come into the city like captives. But for all that we were carried in as captures and with ropes about our necks as well English as the French and Spaniards.

And so we were carried before the king: and when we came before him he did commit us all toward, where we lay 15 days in close prison: and in the end we were cleared by the English merchants to their great charges: for our deliverance cost them 700 ounces, every ounce in that country conveying two shillings. And when we came out of prison, we went to the Alfandies, where we continued eight weeks with the English merchants. At the end of which time being well appareled by the bounty of our merchants we were conveyed down by the space of eight days journey to St. Cruz, where the English ships road: where we took shipping about the 20 of March, two in the Anne Francis of London, and five more of us five days after the expedition of London, and two more in a Flemish fly boat, and one in the Mary Edward also of London, other two of our number died in the country of the blood-flux: the one at our first imprisonment at Morocco, whose name was George Hancock, and the other at St. Cruz, whose name was Robert Swancon, whose death was hastened by eating roots and other unnatural things to slack their raging hunger in our travels, and by our hard and cold lodging in the open fields without tents.

Thus if fifty persons through the rashness of an unskillful master ten only survived of us, and after a thousand miseries returned home poor, sick, and feeble into our country.

Richard Johnson.
William Williams, carpenter.
John Durham.
Abraham Rouse.
John Mattews.
Thomas Henmore.
John Silvester.
Thomas Whitting.
William Church.
John Fox.

[*The Third and Last Volume of the Voyages, Navigation, Traffics, Discoveries, of the English Nation.* London, 1600. 17–19]

Forty men perished because of a bad decision by the master of the ship as he passed the entrance to the Straits of Gibraltar. Apparently the *Toby* wrecked on the coast about 14 miles south of Cape Spartel at about Asilah, Morocco.

3–26. The *Dragon* and *Hunter*, 1582.

The council addressed a request from William Harbrown "having both (ships) upon the seas and otherwise, sustained great losses and indebted to person sundry sums of money," for protection from debtors. The council recommended that all who were affected by the loss to appear before them, including Harbrown.

The third referenced letter of 5 June 1582 indicated that 5–6 months passed since the ships wrecked. The first letter, although it does not mention the ships or wrecks, is related nonetheless through Nathaniel Bacon.

The second reference letter of 15 May 1582 the editor noted in the margin: "Wrecking in Norfolk". The letter was a request for assistance for Jacob de Luegas and Adrain de Groot who purchased goods from Spanish and Dutch merchants laden in the two ships the *Dragon* and *Hunter* of Flushing, Antwerp, Belgium, cast away by tempest. The goods from the ships were taken by inhabitants in the county of Norfolk. The request was to recover as much of the goods belonging to Luegas and de Groot as possible.

The final reference is a notification to officials in Yarmouth on 5 June 1582, that inhabitants of Yarmouth were in possession of goods saved out of the *Dragon* and *Hunter*, "cast away by tempest upon the coast of this realm." No one else had come forward to claim the goods other than Jacob de Luegas who produced a bill of lading from Antwerp of the goods loaded on the two ships.

The *Dragon* and *Hunter* were loaded at Flushing, Antwerp, Belgium then departed into the North Sea; in January weather, which can be unpredictable, where the ships were headed is only speculation. Regardless where they were heaed, the *Dragon* and *Hunter* were driven onto the coast near Great Yarmouth. The debris could have extended from Lowestoft to perhaps Winterton-on-Sea. They were most likely merchant ships, perhaps 20 to 60 tons. A ship named the *Dragon*, a Dutch ship, has a single recorded event from 1587. The *Hunter* is a German ship from 1589 and they are most likely different ships.

If Mr. Dasent, editor of *The Acts of the Privy Council*, is correct with his note in the margin of the second document, then these are in fact wrecks. The mention of other ships with the same name is very common at this time and I can only rely on recorded documents or references.

I believe the *Dragon* and *Hunter* of Belgium lie off the coast of Yarmouth as complete ships, perhaps damaged from the storm, with much of their cargos.

3–27. The Bark *Allen*, 1576.

April 1576, the bark *Allen* of 90 tons was loaded in Burges, West Flanders, Belgium with wool. She put to sea and headed into the English Channel when a tempest overtook them. The skill of the crew and master allowed them to run aground to save the lives of the crew and save the cargo. The bark *Allen* ran aground while seeking the safety of Dunkirk Harbor.

The tempest that wrecked this ship is the same that affected the *Peter* of Bristol that wrecked on the coast between South Wales and Somerset. The same storm affected 5 English ships that were "richly laden" from prizes taken in the south and wrecked them on about 13 miles of coast between Brighton and East Bourne.

The bark *Allen* was cut up and completely lost perhaps on rocks, though there is mention that the ship's apparel and some tackle was recovered. Furthermore, all the goods and merchandise were recovered at no loss to the merchants, but not delivered according to an agreement between Thomas Allen, her majesty's merchant for the east countries, and the staplers in Flanders.

Thus, 14 June 1581, the staplers of Flanders filed a complaint with the council seeking restitution. The Privy Council did not take up the complaint because Thomas Allen's loss was understandable.

No additional documents relating to the wreck of April 1576 were located in archives, nor the 14 June 1581 complaint to the council.

At the entrance to Dunkirk Harbor, very little would remain of the 90-ton bark *Allen*. Perhaps a lonely ballast pile and some timber.

3–28. Hurst Castle Incident, 1579.

A request came from the council for the assistance of John Huff, Walter Cade and Phippe Grimes, owners of merchandise on the *Jesus* of London, that had 'cast away' near Hurst Castle in Hampshire.

The council requested assistance from the local authorities to preserve all cargo for restitution of the ship and crew. Bags of money (Spanish reales?) had been on board when the ship was 'wrecked', and it was speculated that the money was embezzled. Furthermore, orders were given that if anyone found the money being used, to notify authorities.

That is the extent of the primary letter.

Interesting fact: the *Jesus* of London was in ship inventory of 5 January 1548 and of 25 May 1557, but not the inventory of 1578.

John Dasent, editor of *The Acts of the Privy Council of England*, noted in the margin of the document he reviewed with this label; "Wrecking in Hants" of 4 November 1579. Did he feel this was literally a wreck, or was wrecked?

The ship or one of the same name has an established history with several recorded events (8 in this book), even preceding the "wreck" with documents from 1581 and 1585. It is very possible that either this ship did wreck, or another *Jesus* continued to serve and is seen in these documents. After all, it is a common name.

3–29. Wrecked barque, 1579.

On 13 December 1579, the Privy Council sent a request to individuals, "to be made throughout that county". This snippet of the original letter does not indicate the county of origin. The Council requested a collection be made to assist Robert and Thomas Coventries for the loss of their ship while returning from Ireland. The council requested that care be taken regarding the collected money and not to let it fall into the hands of those not deserving it.

The only leads are through the recipients of the council's letter. No additional information could be located regarding the Coventries brothers.

The only possible related document is through Chomly and Smith on 17 August 1579 regarding the 'lodging, victualling and transporting" soldiers into Ireland.

This bark had perhaps unloaded soldiers and related items in Ireland and was returning when the ship was lost.

3–30. Bristol Wreck, 1579.

The Privy Council addressed the mayor of Bristol "for taking up of the ship that sunk in the haven of Bristol."

That is the complete record: perhaps the shortest of the wrecks this book will cover. Beginning in June or July 1579, many records exist regarding transporting soldiers and supplies to Ireland to support English troops. This ship may have functioned in that capacity.

3–31. The *George*, 1580.

The Privy Council required Henry Woodrington to make restitution to David Endach, Burgess of Aberdeen Scotland, on 14 April 1580.

The Burgesses of the Guild of Aberdeen is among the oldest civic institutions in Scotland. Documents from 1124 mention them in what is accepted as the first known record. A letter from 1319 signed by King Robert the Bruce is addressed to them also. Bruce sent grants to the Burgh.

David Endach filed a complaint with the Scottish king recommending Queen Elizabeth address the issue that the crayer *George* while returning from Flanders laden with merchandise, encountered a tempest which drove her on the coast of Northumberland at Widdrington.

The *George* left Antwerp, then turned north to northwest along the English coast when a tempest blew in sending her onto the coast of Widdrington, Northumberland, a very small town about a mile from the coast. It is safe to speculate the *George* could be between Low Hauxley and Newbiggin-by-the-sea, about 10 miles of coast.

The lack of a cargo list or mention of what she was laden with, could indicate less valuable merchandise.

3-32. The *Fortune*, 1577.

The council addressed the Bishop of Dunelm on or about November 1577 regarding the barque *Fortune* of Aberdeen of Scotland, belonging to Henry Endiacht, that was driven on the coast near Seton, "where she perished, and yet no wreck." The goods she was carrying had been taken by local inhabitants.

Orders were given to the Bishop of Dunelm to ensure the taken items were restored to Endiacht. Some goods had turned up including anchors in communities. The bishop was told that if any additional items turned up, to turn them over to Endiacht.

That is the entire original letter. No additional references were located in archives.

It is possible the *Fortune* had departed Aberdeen, Scotland and travelled south most likely to Edinburgh or London, and was driven near the coast of Seton, where Seton Palace once stood as a popular retreat for Mary Queen of Scots and where she had her honeymoon when she married Lord Darnley. Though the date the palace was built is only estimated, it is thought to be early 1500s and was demolished in 1789 and Seton Castle was built.

Regardless of the departure location, the *Fortune* of Aberdeen could lie off the coast perhaps between Aberlady and Musselburgh, or about 10 miles of coastline east of Edinburgh.

Everything suggests the *Fortune* wrecked, including local inhabitants retrieving goods from the ship, except for 'yet no wreck" in the letter. Did it sink?

3–33. Newhaven Wreck, 1578.

The council sent a letter on 28 September 1578 to officials, including Sir Thomas Sherley, sheriff of Sussex, who had served on the board of commissioners against piracy, advising that a small flyboat had wrecked near Newhaven, Sussex, laden with wines and books, some of which were saved by Jasper Swift.

The remainder of the cargo was taken by local inhabitants. One gentleman, John Harr, returned "one butt of secke, (silk?), a chest of books and all the sails for the boat", but he refused to make full restitution.

Orders to Sir Thomas Sherley were to search the house of John Harris and anyone else that was suspected to have items from the ship and confiscate them.

On 16 November 1578, the council issued a warrant for additional individuals suspected of possessing items stolen from the ship.

No additional documents could be located in the archives. No outcome could be determined based on the surviving documents.

This flyboat, perhaps 60 to 120 tons, laden with divers types of merchandise, wrecked near Newhaven after a storm possibly sank her off the coast, but close enough to allow the recovery, or stealing, of the wine, books, and other items. All that possibly would remain would be a skeleton and a ballast pile. It would appear all her tackle, sails and furniture were taken, leaving a bare ship behind. But it would be safe to assume that much of the usable timber was also taken.

3–34. Thames Wreck, 1577.

The council dispatched a letter in October 1576 for assistance regarding Thomas Russel, a London merchant, who had goods and merchandise, pitch, tar, and clapboard, loaded into a vessel that had wrecked in the mouth of the Thames; local inhabitants from the counties of Essex and Kent plundered the ship.

That is the entire source letter. An editor's note in the margin specifies, "recovery of wrecked goods."

The only referenced document, the sole lead in this investigation, is dated 1 April 1578. It required Thomas Russel to show proof of ownership.

3–35. The *Hospital*, 1588.

I stated that I would not include the wrecks of the Spanish armada of 1588, but here I'd make an exception, as this was not necessarily a ship of war. There were many pieces of this puzzle to put together and it required a considerable amount of research.

The first reference is a letter of 1 November 1588 from the Privy Council to officials in Devonshire indicating that they were informed that a Spanish ship was cast on that coast by bad weather, being one of the fleet for the invasion of England.

The council sent an official to ensure that an inventory was made of all ordnance, munitions, armor, weapons, goods, and furniture on the ship. Additional orders were that of the 200 men reported on the ship, Anthony Asheley who was sent by the council, would separate the men of quality from the others, with the commoners and soldiers "to be executed, destroyed and dealt with by martial law as the most pernicious enemy of her majesty's realm."

17 November 1588. The council sent orders for the release of Flemish and French prisoners taken among the Spaniards in a ship, the *Hospital*, that was cast away by tempest on the Western coast of England. The letter, though ambiguous, mentions that the ship belonged to Don Pedroe.

The council sent a letter on 10 December 1588 to the same officials in Devonshire regarding the Spaniards captured when the *Hospital* (or St. Peters) wrecked in Devonshire, who were reported as "greatly diseased," and it was feared that the inhabitants of the area could also become ill. Furthermore, orders included the removal of all Spaniards who "should be conveyed into certain barns and out houses standing apart from other tenements and dwellings."

The final letter of this incident of 30 January 1590 was from the council to officials in Cockington to continue to keep Lopee Ruisse, "a subject of the king of Spain" from the *Hospital*, in custody.

That is the bulk of information contained in the letters of archives and no additional information could be located.

One helpful, unusual piece of information was found in the index of volume 16 *APC*, "*San Pedro Mayor*, (also called the *St. Peter* and the *Hospital*, a Spanish ship wrecked in Devonshire, she was one of two hospital ships for the Armada).

Based on the number of Spanish wrecks from the same storm that were scattered along the coast of Ireland, Wales and England, we can speculate

that this ship likely ended its days on the north side of Devon towards the
Celtic Sea.

3–36. The *Esperance*, French, 1589

The council dispatched a letter to authorities in Norfolk on 22 January
1589 informing them of a French Ship the *Esperance* of Dieppe, of which the
master and mariners were Scottish, was laden with Scottish merchant's
goods and bound for Scotland.

A storm drove the ship on the coast between Cromer and Boston in the
county of Norfolk on 1 January 1589 and wrecked her.

A great quantity of the cargo was stolen by local inhabitants. Despite
efforts by local authorities, they were unable to recover those items. A
request for a search was made by the council to the same authorities and to
aid in full restitution.

That is all the source information and no additional information was
located in archives.

Though there is not much else associated with this incident, it contains
all the ingredients I look for; name of the ship, date and most important, the
location of the wreck, and perhaps the conditions that caused the wreck to
happen is a plus. Unfortunately, there are not enough pieces of the puzzle to
help determine what she was carrying.

The *Esperance* of Dieppe was loaded and departed possibly for Aberdeen,
or another large port in Scotland, and was caught in a January storm in the
North Sea sending the ship on the coast between Cromer and Boston based
on the accounts from the letter. The *Esperance* had sailed around southeast
England and steered north towards Scotland when a storm, blowing from
the north, had wrecked her on about 35 miles of coastline on New Year's Day.
Bad way to begin a new year.

3–37. *St. Petero Maior*, 1589.

The council wrote to Sir William Courtenay on 9 November 1589 that
all the items recovered when a hulk called the *St. Petero Maior* ran aground at
Hope, a bay near Salcombe in Devon, would be under his charge.

That is the sum of the letter.

There is not enough information to add more to this incident. The letter,
as all letters reviewed in this series, is not the original letter but a paraphrase
and often information was lost when it was re-written. We do know the

ship's name, date, and location. Perhaps the *St. Petero Maior* wrecked in the mouth of the Salcombe Harbor, Devon. All that may remain is a skeleton of a ship and ballast pile.

3–38. The *Revenge*, 1591.

The wrecking of the *Revenge* cannot be shared without a brief account of the events that lead to it. There are many stories about her fate with the most important, at least to me, being a reference by Sir Walter Raleigh in 1591. Not a surprise that it differs from several colorful accounts on various websites. The full account is shared in Part 2–4.

31 August 1591, an English fleet was anchored off the coast of Flores, an island off the Azores, consisting of six of her majesty's ships. Near the six were victuallers from London and 2 or 3 pinnaces.

After 6 months at sea, the fleet was replenishing themselves when Lord Thomas Howard received news that fifty-three Spanish ships were quickly approaching. It was reported that illnesses were terrible within the fleet; 90 cases of illness on the *Revenge* alone and the *Bonaventure* did not have enough able-bodied seamen to handle her mainsail and the admiral became very concerned of their possible fate.

The *Revenge* still had men on shore when the decision was made to raise anchor with only about 100 men on board. Sir Walter Raleigh shared that Sir Richard Granville refused to turn from his enemies and the *Revenge* attacked any Spanish ship that came upon her until the *San Philip* with 3 decks and 3 tiers of ordnance with 11 guns per tier, came on her. The *San Philip* was so large, of 1500 tons, that she took the wind from the *Revenge's* sails so that she was unable to respond to the helm.

A small victualler, the *George Noble* of London, which had already received several shots through her hull, came to assist the *Revenge*. The battle between the *Revenge* and the *San Philip* began about 3:00 in the afternoon and lasted well into the night. Every time the Spaniards attempted to board the *Revenge*; the English drove them away.

At about 11:00 that night, a musket shot hit the admiral in his side and while the surgeon was attending him, he received a shot in the head and the surgeon was killed.

The *Revenge* continued to fight until the light of a new day was seen on the horizon. By the time the sun rose, the *Revenge's* powder was spent, her pikes broken, and forty mariners killed, and a great number wounded. "No friendly sail was to be detected on the horizon".

It was a difficult decision to make, but the order was given to dismast her, her tackle cut, "her upper works altogether erased." She lay a mere wreck surrounded by the Spanish fleet. The decks of the *Revenge* were described as looking like a slaughterhouse because the decks were "dyed with blood and covered with the slain."

Sir Richard Granville ordered the master gunner to "split and sink the ship." The master told Granville there were yet men willing and able to defend the ship and their honor regardless that there was 6 feet of water in her and 3 shot holes under the water line that was barely repaired.

The master of the *Revenge* had boarded the general to arrange the terms of surrender which included sparing the lives of the crew and a reasonable ransom paid for the officers. The Spaniard agreed. As the master returned to inform the crew, all but the master gunner agreed with the terms as the Spanish boats surrounded the *Revenge* to take the crew off the ship. It would be safe to assume the colors had been struck.

Three days later, Sir Richard Granville died from his injuries while on the general and his body committed to the sea. Sir Walter Raleigh is quoted, "being dead, he outlived not his own honor." A few very early accounts describe her story as "a stag among hounds at bay."

This sea battle also took its toll on the Spanish with a report that indicated they lost about a thousand men. The admiral of the hulks, Luis Continho and the *Ascension* of Seville were both sunk by the side of the *Revenge*; one ship went down in the Road of St. Michael; another ran herself on shore to save her men.

A couple days later, a tempest came from the west and northwest breaking up and dispersing the fleet of 14 ships including the *Revenge* with 200 Spaniards on board and blew the *Revenge* onto the coast of the Isle of St. Michael.

The Privy Council dispatched a letter on 20 January 1590 for assistance in recovering the *Revenge*. "One of her majesty's ships overthrown and drowned by the late tempest."

This entry is the source I located in archives that led me to the wreck. The date appears to be incorrect. This is the only reference located in archives about this wreck.

WAIST, QUARTER-DECK, AND POOP OF THE "REVENGE."
(Elisabethan period.)

"And the sun went down and the stars came out far over the summer sea,
But never a moment ceased the fight of the one and the fifty-three.
Ship after ship the whole night long their high-built galleons came,
Ship after ship the whole night long with her battle thunder and flame;
Ship after ship the whole night long drew back with her dead and her
   shame."

[Tennyson]

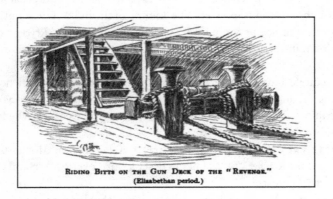

RIDING BITTS ON THE GUN DECK OF THE "REVENGE."
(Elisabethan period.)

3–39. The *Treasurer*, 1589.

On 15 September 1589, the council addressed Lord Cobham the lord warden of the Cinque ports, ensuring he understood and followed through with a complaint by Paul Riverson, citizen of Denmark, regarding an incident in January when he served as master of the ship the *Treasurer* of Aalborg, Denmark. After loading her with salt, sugar, and spices in Portugal, ran aground near the town of Lydd where the inhabitants took whatever they could. The council indicated that the bailiff of Lydd and the minister of Gilford near Rye, were charged as the "principal instruments" of the looting.

The council sent additional orders that restitution will be made to Riverson and those caught in possession of items from the ship would be placed in prison.

That is the context of the letter.

The *Treasurer* of Aalborg had loaded in Portugal with a cargo of salt, sugar, and spices, all very valuable cargo then, and sailed north, then into the English Channel possibly toward Aalborg Denmark, when a storm possibly blew down from the North Sea driving the ship on the coast of England. I suspect between Folkstone west along about 14 miles of coast, to Dungeness, a few miles from the letter reference of Lydd.

3–40. The *Rose*, 1589.

The Privy Council wrote the commissioners on 22 March 1589 that were responsible for the sale of goods in Plymouth and that those goods should be delivered to John Martins, skipper from Hambrough, England, regarding the ship *Marie* of Hambrough, England. The Privy Council ordered the commissioners that the items taken from the *Rose* of Hambrough that wrecked in the port of Plymouth were to be turned over to John Martins.

That is the context of the letter. No additional references could be located in the archives.

3–41. The *Dudley*, 1590.

The council addressed a complaint on 24 December 1590 from William and Martin Bond and widow Smith, filed against Captain John Clark of the galleon *Dudley*, that surprised a ship named the *White Horse* laden with salt, money, and other merchandise. A letter was sent to Lord Buckhurst, lord lieutenant of Sussex, and John Fortescu, Master of the Great Wardrobe and Under Treasurer of the Exchequer.

About 10 months had passed since the *White Horse* returned from Spain when the *Dudley* 'very dangerously shot and hurt the said ship and men, took away and rifled the said money and victuals." Furthermore, the cables, anchors and other furniture belonging to the ship were also taken. "And afterwards suffered the ship and salt to sink." The letter mentions that John Clark was outraged and a clerk complained of his actions, perhaps because of the possibility that the cargo was taken by local inhabitants.

The letter closes with legal action against those who did not return the items. For the council to have addressed this complaint suggests the *Dudley* was an English ship. I have a log entry for the *Dudley* dated 6 September 1592 mentioning that she had returned from Brazil with a load of sugar, very possibly another ship.

Either the ship referred to as sinking in reference to the letter of 24 December 1590 is a different *Dudley*, or the 1592 entry is of a different *Dudley*. If she was returning from Spain, it is possible she sank along the English coast in the region of Sussex before the Straits of Dover.

3–42. The *Elephant*, 1590.

The council sent orders on 11 March 1590 to the vice admirals, mayors, and sheriffs (The letter, though copied from an original, does not mention the location of those officials) that the Duke Charels, brother of the king of Sweden, sent two ships to her majesty, one called the *Elephant* laden with masts with a license to travel to Spain. Off the coast of France, she developed a very bad leak that could not be repaired and she wrecked on the western coast of England.

The masts were removed from the wrecked ship and taken to 'divers places.' The council ordered the officials that Theophilus Homodei or Severine John were to receive full restitution of the masts. Anyone who failed to comply with those orders, were subject to punishment of the law.

Following is a very rare inventory of the 37 masts.

- There lies at Portland Castle a mast of 22 hands about 84 foot long.
- At Osmynton, one mast about 20 hands and 84 foot long.
- At Wareham, one mast 17 hands about and 24 foot long.
- At Corse Castle at Newton House, lies 4 masts of 25 hands.
- At Bruncksey Castle lies one mast 18 hands about and 84 foot long.
- At Christ Church lies one mast 18 hands thick and 92 foot long.
- At Lymington lies three masts 18 hands thick and 80 foot long.
- At Cowes Castle in the Isle of Wight, 21 from 17 hands to 24 thereabouts of divers lengths.
- At Hampton, Mr. Lambert had 4 masts of 23 hands about 80 foot long.

The inventory list of masts is a valuable source of information not because of the items mentioned, but because it supplied the general location where the masts ended up and helps to narrow the wreck site to within about 50 miles of coast between the Isle of Wight to Portland Castle. No mast 80 feet in length is going to be carried far from the wreck site

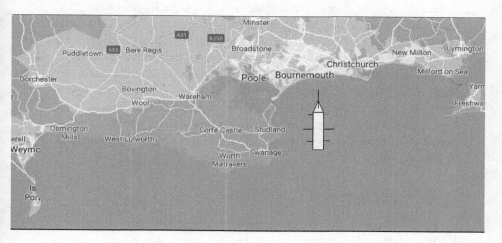

Based upon that, the *Elephant* could be lying off the coast about Bournemouth; the *Elephant* may have tried to reach that port. No doubt the *Elephant* was picked clean of anything salvageable.

3–43. Scottish Ships, 1559.

14 November 1559, the council addressed letters from the Earl of Northumberland received on the 9 November regarding 2 Scottish ships "lately driven on land" there (Northumberland?) and sent instructions to Sir James Crofts, captain of Berwick, that the ships wrecked near Berwick.

25 November 1559. Secretary Cecil had received a letter from the queen for the restitution of the 2 ships driven on land near Berwick, "Which the queen, in justice, must permit."

That is the extent of the reference to the event of 14 November letter.

The French ambassador Gilles de Noailles wrote to the queen dowager and reported on 20 December 1559, "One part of the fleet shall be stationed off the mouth of the Thames to intercept stores sent from France to Scotland; thus, the French already in Scotland would soon be starved out. A ship on its way to Scotland, laden with wheat, had been already captured at Dover."

My belief at this point is that the two Scottish ships were captured by the English, plundered, stripped of their tackle, sails, and anything else, and then run aground near Berwick; in lieu of the second postulation which is they wrecked because of a storm.

Following the rather interesting life of Sir Ralph Sadler who wrote in his letters following the French activity in Scotland on 10 December 1559, Sadler reported that on Thursday and Friday, 15 or 16 French and Scottish ships had been seen passing along the coast (Berwick area) with about 300 soldiers.

Through all correspondence of John Abingdon, Ambrose Cave and Richard Sacville, all in charge of victuals at the port of Berwick, no new or additional information could be located in archives. If any of these 3 men kept records at the time that could yield additional useful information, then perhaps they currently reside in a dark and cool library basement waiting to be discovered.

3–44. The *Katherine* of Calais, 1601

On 24 May 1601, the council sent a letter of assistance to authorities on behalf of Mathew de Questour and John Le Clerk, merchants in London, for the recovery of wine, oil, wool, and other goods lost when the *Katherine* of Calais wrecked in the entrance to the port of Shoreham, now Shoreham-by-sea.

Based on previously reviewed and recorded documents inclusive of French ships, this ship served for about five decades before her life ended on the coast of England.

Her voyage from Calais, France to Shoreham, England, was about 100 miles. Based on this record, she wrecked within a mile to two mile stretch of coastline centered by the River Adur, the entrance to Shoreham, England.

Shoreham-by-Sea (often shortened to Shoreham) is a seaside town and port in West Sussex, England that dates to pre-Roman times. The town is bordered to its north by the South Downs, to its west by the Adur Valley and to its south by the River Adur and Shoreham Beach on the English Channel.

Perhaps all that remains of this ship is a keel, timber, and a ballast field. Additionally, there may be glass containers that held wine and barrels used to transport the oil and wine. Tackle, ordnance, or other munitions may also have remained in addition to personal items.

I find no references to the possibility of a storm that drove her on the coast. Pilot error?

3–45. The *Exchange*, 1592.

The Privy Council dispatched a letter on 4 June 1592 to Peter Houghton regarding items taken from the *Exchange* of Chester possibly when she returned from Bordeaux and La Rochelle, France, and was wrecked, then plundered.

It would appear that because the *Exchange* had wrecked, the council determined that the ship was exempt from the Bordeaux convoy tax.

That is the full context of the vague letter.

The Council met at Richmond Court and released the articles and agreements made between the merchants that trade to Bordeaux and La Rochelle for this "first vintage and the admiral of the fleet"; basically, a tax was imposed on shipping of wine from France.

The letter is vague and possibly indicates that the *Exchange* "return thence before the fleet of London." It may be safe to speculate the *Exchange* wrecked along the coast of Wales, before it reached Chester laden with wine from France.

3–46. The *Symond*, 1579.

On 26 July 1579, Thomas Standley petitioned the council for assistance in recovering goods stolen from him when the *Symond* of Colborough, Pomerland, wrecked off the coast of Norfolk.

The *Symond* presumably departed Kolberg, Pomerania (now Kołobrzeg, Poland) into the Baltic Sea, steered through Denmark, possibly stopped at Copenhagen, then sailed north, then west into the North Sea, then south toward the English Channel where a storm blew her onto the coast near Norfolk, north of London and the Thames.

3–47. The *Nightingale* wreck, 1593.

The council reviewed information submitted to them in a letter of 19 June 1593 by 4 widows of mariners that died when the *Nightingale* caught fire in the Bordeaux River in France and the owners of the *Nightingale* had not yet paid for their husbands' service. If the letter is to be taken literally, before 19 June 1593, the *Nightingale*, perhaps while at anchor in the waterway or river leading to Bordeaux, caught fire, and burned until she sank. The river varies in width from about a couple of miles to 5 miles at different points.

The council requested that the owners and widows appear before them. A follow-up letter of 25 June 1593 contained basically the same information but was addressed to different individuals. I was unable to determine if the widows received compensation from the ship owners.

3–48. The *Fortune*, 1595.

The high court of the admiralty informed local authorities on 21 December 1595 of restitution that would be made to Gorkin, master of the *Fortune* of Emden, Germany, who "lately sustained shipwreck in Essex."

That is all.

Gorkin possibly departed Emden into the North Sea in late November to early December, then turned southwest and possibly encountered a storm coming through the English Channel sending the *Fortune* on the coast, perhaps between Harwich and Southend-on-sea, about 30 miles of coast.

The editor of the *Acts of the Privy Council* included a note in the margin next to the letter, "Wrecks and wrecking."

Four log entries are available for a *Fortune* of Germany; they have been shared in this book. Three are from 1589 to 1590; then there is a 7-year gap to 1597 when permission was requested to sell wheat in English ports. Each of the 4 log entries specifies the *Fortune* of Emden, Germany as does the letter of 21 December 1595. Possibly this ship the *Fortune* did not sink, or the last log entry was not labeled correctly.

I am more inclined to believe there is a ship lying off the coast of Sussex, England that had the name *Fortune*.

3–49. Goodwin Sands, 1568.

The only reference to this incident is a 2-line snippet of the original letter dated 29 March 1568, regarding correspondence from Lord Cobham to Secretary Cecil about a vessel lost on the Goodwin Sands on 22 March.

The Goodwin Sands claimed another unsuspecting ship.

3–50. The *Grey Fawlcon*, 1596.

The first reference is 3 June 1597. The council wrote to Thomas Middleton to inform him of James Bagg who had acquired oils and was paid for the sale of some of the oils because it was determined to be a lawful prize. But the high court of the admiralty determined it was an unlawful prize. No mention is made of a wreck.

The next reference of 25 June 1597 will supply some missing information.

The council dispatched letters notifying certain public officers that London merchants had proven the ownership of 85 tons of wine laden in the *Grey Fawlcon* of Camphire, Ireland, taken last year by the English (1596).

The merchandise belonged to Middleburg, Zeeland merchants and was brought to Plymouth by the *Grey Fawlcon*, "whereby by their negligence and default cast away on the coast near unto Plymouth".

Orders were sent by the council to confiscate any oil sold and to arrest anyone caught selling oil taken from the *Grey Fawlcon* wreck.

It may be possible that the *Grey Fawlcon* departed Camphire, Ireland laden with oils, wines, and other merchandise, headed south toward Calais France into the Celtic Sea, then turned east after about 250 miles. Perhaps as the ship passed Old Grimsby, an island off the eastern tip of England, that is where they encountered a ship of the English navy and were captured. If so, the ship was plundered of everything including anchors and left to the tide, eventfully being pushed on shore between Falmouth and east of Plymouth, about 20–25 miles of coastline.

The letter mentions that a great amount of the cargo was saved, but local inhabitants had helped themselves and it was well noted in the letter requesting authorities to make anyone in possession of any amount of the plundered cargo turn it over to an agent acting on behalf of the owners of the 85 tons of oil.

There is not enough information to determine if she was driven onto the coast because of a storm or released after she was stripped while at sea, then drifted onto shore.

The note "by their negligence and default" could suggest the crew did not or could not react in a way to save the ship during a storm.

The *Grey Fawlcon* of Camphire, Ireland wrecked on the coast of Plymouth in 1596. That is all the information located in archives.

3–51. Barbary wreck, 1597.

The Privy Council sent a letter to the lord chief justice of her majesty's bench on 10 April 1597 regarding a complaint by Michael Leeman and merchants of Holland and Zeeland, that William Holiday had "in a very contemptuous manner" displayed towards the court and he was placed in prison for a while.

In 1593, the *Tiger*, owned by Holiday with other ships in their company had plundered several ships of Holland and Zeeland, sinking one of the ships and throwing the mariners overboard.

Orders were sent to bring the *Tiger* into Plymouth, "a Spanish carvel laden with ginger, sugar, hides and some pearls" and the cargo seized then sold to partially satisfy Leeman. Holiday was ordered to pay 6000 Sterling in damages.

Holiday and "some of his malefactors" stood indicted for piracy, their prizes also seized and returned to Leeman and the merchants.

Though the letter is longer than those I am accustomed to, the location in which the ship sank can only be narrowed to a location in the Barbary. Though the term Barbary is slightly ambiguous, it refers to the Northern Coast of Africa, specifically the areas of Tripoli, Algiers and Tunis.

3–52. Goodwin Sands, 1567.

2 February 1567, Lord Cobham wrote to Secretary Cecil. The snippet of the original letter gives an account that the mariners of the recent Goodwin Sands wreck were not turning over everything from the wrecked ship.

8 March 1567, the council requested assistance for the collection of the goods off a ship of Middleborough that had wrecked on the Goodwin Sands.

No further information could be learned from either snippet to supply additional information.

3–53. Goodwin wreck, 1598.

The Privy Council sent letters on 19 November 1598 requesting assistance for Nicholas Rippet, merchant and owner of the *St. John* of Hamburg, laden with marble blocks, ffatts (flats) and other merchandise, in her course towards the Isle of Terceras, that wrecked on the Goodwin Sands and killed all but one person on board — a loss of approximately 60 to 120 crew. Perhaps a tempest blew south through the North Sea, wrecking her on the notorious sand bar off the south-east tip of England.

This ship would be found with large blocks of perhaps Italian marble, and thinner sheets of marble, the other merchandise may be there also if it was too heavy to salvage on the north-east side of the Goodwin Sands.

The *St. John* of Hamburg would be a merchant ship, perhaps 100 to 500 ton, large enough to carry heavy marble. The crew could be about 60 to 120. Possibly a tempest blew them south over the North Sea, sending her to the Goodwin Sands on the east side.

I would think, that if the wreck is located and determined by the cargo to be this ship, then to please treat it as a grave site and show respect.

3–54. The *Reindeer*.

On 31 December 1598, the council dispatched a letter to the vice admiral of Devon, regarding a ship of his, the *Reindeer*, victualled by him for the Straits, and which sailed in August transporting soldiers into Drogheda, Ireland.

The council requested Devon authorities to verify if the ship belonged to George Wadham.

No additional information could be located in archives.

The English ship the *Reindeer* had completed transporting soldiers to Drogheda, Ireland, above Dublin. The letter indicated it was difficult to unload the soldiers, and after the soldiers and crew left the ship, it was allowed to drift and possibly sank. The ship may have developed a bad leak causing it list to one side. There was no reason for the soldiers and crew to dispose of their only way home. The *Reindeer* could be lying between Dublin and Dundalk, on about 30 miles of coast.

3–55. The *Sea Cock*.

The Privy Council issued warrants to public officials informing them of Peter Danielson, late master and part owner of the *Sea Cock* of Vlissingen (Flushing, Netherlands) "had made pitiful complaint in the court of the admiralty" that this ship while in her course from St. Lucar Spain toward Middlebourough (Middleburg) Zeeland carrying goods and merchandise valued at twenty thousand Pounds Sterling belonging to the merchants of Middlebourough, had wrecked on the coast of Cardigan Wales. Blame was placed on the pilot.

Local inhabitants had pilfered "utensils, apparel, munitions, sails and other furniture of the ship" that had spread along the coast.

The warrants ordered all individuals who possessed those items to return them or suffer the full penalty of the law from the court of the admiralty.

The course from St. Lucar, southern Spain, to Middleburg Zeeland is about 1800 miles. The pilot certainly made a great error to be off course almost a thousand miles to wreck on the coast of Wales at about the inlet to Cardigan, or the voyage was affected by a storm.

Perhaps somewhere between Cwm-yr-Eglwys to Aberporth Wales lie the remains of a 20 to 60 ton ship called the *Sea Cock*. All that would perhaps remain is a keel and ballast pile.

Bibliography

Primary

A Collection of Voyages and Travels. Volume 2. London, 1744.

A New and Complete Collection of Voyages and Travels. London, 1778.

A New Universal Collection of Authentic and Entertaining Voyages and Travels. London, 1768.

A Report of the Truth of the Fight about the Isles of Agores, This Last Summer. London, 1591. (Source reference for the battle involving the *Revenge* in 1591).

Acts of the Privy Council of England. 32 Volumes. 1542-1604. London.

Barrow, John. *The Naval History of Great Britain. With the Lives of the Most Illustrious Admirals and Commanders*. Four volumes. London, 1761.

Calendar of State Papers, Colonial Series, East Indies, China, and Japan, 1513-1616. London, 1862.

Calendar of State Papers, Domestic Series, of the Reigns of Edward VI, Mary, Elizabeth. Multi-volumes. London.

Calendar of State Papers, Domestic Series, of the Reign of Elizabeth, 1601-1603; with Addenda, 1547-1585. London, 1870.

Calendar of State Papers, Foreign Series, of the Reign of Mary, 1553-1558. London, 1861.

Calendar of State Papers Relating to England, Foreign Series.

Derrick, Charles. *Memoirs of the Rise and Progress of the Royal Navy*. London, 1806.

Hakluyt, Richard. *The Third and Last Volume of the Voyages, Navigation, Traffics, Discoveries, of the English Nation*. London, 1600.

New General Collection of Voyages and Travels" Consisting of the Most Esteemed Relations... Volume 1, London, 1745.

Steel, D. *Original and Correct List of the Royal Navy*. London, 1782.

The Third and Last Volume of the Voyages, Navigation, Traffics, Discoveries, of the English Nation. London, 1600.

Valentine, Mrs. R. *Sea fights and Land Battles from Alfred to Victoria*. London, 1869.

Yorston's Popular History of the World, Ancient, Mediaeval and Modern. Yorston and Co., New York. 8 volumes in total. 1884. This is a wonderful multi-volume work encompassing portraits over a millennium.

Secondary

Archaeologia Cantiana. Vol.17 1887. Kent Archaeological Society. Information on the History of the Corporation of New Romney.

Campbell, John. *Lives of the British Admirals, Containing a New and Accurate Naval History*. London, 1779.

Cases, The, of Some Ships taken by the Spaniards. London, 1731.

Collection of Voyages and Travels, A. Volume 2. London, 1745.

Collection of Voyages and Travels, Now First Printed from Original Manuscript, A. 6 Volumes. London, 1740.

Colliber, Samuel. *Columna Rostrata" or a Critical History of the English Sea-Affairs*. London, 1727.

Duncan, Archibald. *The British Trident; or Register of Naval Actions. Volume 1*. London, 1804.

Falconer, William. *An Universal Dictionary of the Marine, or A Copious Explanation of the Technical Terms and Phrases*. London, 1784.

General History of Sieges and Battles by Sea and Land. London, 1762.

Glory of Her Sacred Majesty Queen Anne, in the Royal Navy, The. London, 1703.

Hervey, Frederic. *The Naval History of Great Britain; from the Earliest Times*. 5 Volumes. London, 1759.

History, and Lives of all the Notorious Pirates and Their Crews, The. Third Edition. London, 1729.

Instructions to Masters of Ships being a Digest of the Provisions, Penalties, &c. London, 1809.

Kent, John. *A Collection of Memoirs of Those Illustrious Seamen...*London, 1777.

Linschoten, John Huighen Van. *His Discours of Voyages Into Ye Easte & West Indies*. London, 1598.

Lindsay, W. S. *History of Merchant Shipping and Ancient Commerce*. London, 1874.

Lodge, Edmund. *Illustrations of British History, Biography and Manners in the Reigns of Henry VIII, Edward VI, Mary, Elizabeth, and James I*. London, 1791.

Mason, George. *The History of the Pirates, Free-Booters or Buccaneers of America*. London, 1807.

Memoirs of Samuel Pepys, Esq. London, 1889.

McMasters, Rev. S. Y. *A biographical index to the History of England.* Alton, 1854.

Naval History of Great Britain. London, 1794.

New Collection of Voyages, Discoveries, and Travels, A. Volume 1. London, 1767.

New General Collection of Voyages and Travels, A. Volume 4. London, 1747.

Notable and Wonderful Sea-Fight, Between..., A (Spanish and English Ship) Amsterdam, 1621.

Oxford, Earl of. *A Collection of Voyages and Travels consisting of Authentic Writers...* London, 1747.

Present Condition of the English Navy, The. London, 1702.

Steel, D. *Original and Correct List of the Royal Navy.* London, 1782.

------ *Complete Collection of all the Marine Treaties.* London, 1779.

Stephenson, Captain John. *The New British Channel Pilot, Containing Sailing Directions from London-Bridge to Liverpool.* London, 1799. Great harbor data.

Theobald, Lewis. *Memoirs of Sir Walter Raleigh.* London, 1719.

Tutchin, John. *An Historical and Political Treatise of the Navy.* London, 1704.

Walker, T. P. Commander. *Seamanship: Including Names of Principal Parts of a Ship...* London, 1897.

Manuscript collection consulted

Augmentation Office, Harleian and Cottonian Manuscripts.

Picture Sources

Baring-Gould, S. *The Western Antiquary, or Devon and Cornwall Note-book.* London, 1889. The Desire.

Derrick, Charles. Memoirs of the Rise and Progress of the Royal Navy. London, 1806. The Henry Grace de Dieu at the time of King Edward VI-1547.

INDEX

A

Admiralty Court 186, 187, 212, 215
Africa 119, 142, 214
  Angola 142, 145
  French Guinea 171
  Ghana 171
  Guinea 171
Alhand, Captain Peron 105
almonds 88, 122
anneal 88, 122
Anthony, Captain William 142
Antwerp 178, 184, 192, 197, 200
armor 53, 88, 102, 202
Asshe, Captain John 70
Aucher, Sir Anthony Aucher 36
Azores 116, 151
  Corvo and Flores 145
  Fayal and Pico 144
  Flores 144, 147, 151, 153, 156
  Isle of St. Michael 156

B

Baltic Sea 211
Banks, Edward, Captain 22, 78
Barbary 68, 114, 119, 146, 192, 193,
    213, 214
barque(s) 11, 111
Barret, Captain Robert 99
Basson, Don Alonso de 151

Basurto, Alonso de 63
Batten, Captain William, pirate 88
Bayning, Paul 62
Bazan, Don Alfonso, Admiral 155
beans 69
Bedford, Captain Richard 23, 90
Belgian/Belgium 121, 128, 179, 184,
    197, 198
Bertrand, Clay. See Shaw, Clay
Berwick 164, 185
Biskay, Bay of 162
Biston, Captain George 48, 49, 63
Biston, Captain William 63
Blewell, Peter 52
Boite, Captain Philip 88, 93
Bonner, Jonas 53
Bordeaux 64, 110, 211
Borrough, Sir John, Captain 148
Bosque, Juan Almeida. See Almeida,
    Juan
Bostock, Captain John 20, 98, 121
Bremen 117, 192
Bremen, Nicholas 113
Brest 105, 112
Bridgeway, John 51
Bristol 23, 48, 50, 53, 55, 57, 61, 62,
    65, 68, 70, 79, 92, 99, 100,
    115, 129, 198, 199
Brittany 60, 94, 110, 112
Brown, Thomas, Master 69
buck skins 88, 122

C

Cadiz 48, 66
Calais 36, 54, 67, 89, 92, 96, 106,
    108, 109, 110, 111, 113, 124,
    170, 171, 179, 213
Calles, Captain 61
camphor/camphire 150
cannon-perer 27
cannons 9, 13, 103, 171, 184
canvas 49, 58, 97, 101
Cape St. Vincent, Portugal 193
caps 49, 97
caravel(s) 11
Carew, Peter 121
cargo
    aqua vitae 47
    bulls 147
    carpets 150
    See also: cloth
    clothes 125
    cognac 109
    dates 88, 122
    figs 185
    fish 53, 68, 71
    See also: fragrances
    gold 9, 10, 91, 100, 123, 150, 157,
        158, 159, 171, 194
    gilt/guilt items
    See also: grain
    hides 47
    ivory 150
    jewels 62, 123, 149, 157, 159, 194
    lead, 79
    malt 128
    nails 122, 123, 127, 129
    pearls 194, 213
    porcelain 150
    salt 47
    seeds, 47
    silver 10, 123, 147, 157, 159
    spices 99, 115, 150, 187
    sugar 49, 53, 56, 59, 67, 70, 88, 94,
        112, 116, 117, 122, 125, 127,
        192, 213

syrup 88, 122
tin 79
wine 123
Carlingford, Ireland 57, 65, 67, 91
carpets 150
carrack(s) 11, 56, 58, 91, 101, 143
Carrero, Captain Bras 144
Carriles, Louis Posada. *See* Posada,
    Louis
Cartwright, a minister 47, 60
Cary, Sir George 152
Castle de Mino (Ghana) 171
Catell, Pierre 105
Catholics 163, 170, 173
Cave, Captain George 142, 143
Cavendishe, Thomas 46
Caverly, William 66
Cecil, William, 1st Baron Burghley,
    Secretary of State 173, 175,
    177, 209, 213, 214
Chatham 90
Chester, John 22, 35
China 47, 51, 57, 60, 70, 150, 157
Clifford, Alexander 20
cloth 51, 58, 79, 90, 91, 97, 101, 106,
    142, 150
    calico 150
    cotton 49, 97, 109
    grogram 61, 90
    linen 58, 61, 90, 97, 101, 106, 142
    silk 122, 150, 158, 201
Cock, Captain Abraham 147
Cock, Captain John 91
cognac 109
convoy tax 211
Cook, Captain Edward 50
copper 10, 11, 70, 110
Cork, Ireland 120, 127
Cornelius, Daniel, shipmaster 96
Cornwall 106, 128
cotton 49, 97, 109
court of the admiralty 186, 215
Crayer (type of ship) 11
Crocker, Captain, pirate 90
Cross, Captain Robert 66

Cross, Sir Robert 147, 148
Cross, Sir Robert, Vice Admiral 148
culverin 27, 79
Cumberland, Earl of 20, 111, 115, 120, 122, 125, 129, 142, 147

D

Dartmouth 21, 23, 36, 46, 54, 106, 108, 111, 112, 114, 117, 120, 121, 124, 125, 150
dates 88, 122
Davis, Master John 65
De la Moth, Mr., Gov of Graveling 67
demi-cannon 27
demi-culverin 27
Demundes, Captain Michael 93
Denmark 36, 55, 119, 120, 125, 126, 178, 179, 211
Devon 203, 204, 215
Dieppe 55, 69, 104, 105, 106, 107, 108, 110, 111, 112, 113, 171, 179, 203
discovery of Norembega 160
Dover 24, 55, 56, 62, 68, 91, 110, 125, 178, 179
Downton, Captain 147
Downton, Captain Nicholas 141, 142, 143, 144, 145
Drake, Sir Barnard 61
Drake, Sir Francis 20, 21, 49, 51, 52, 60, 63, 78, 79, 90, 93, 97, 130
Dublin 55, 65, 123, 215
Dudley, John, Duke of Northumberland 163
Dudley, Sir Robert 157
Dunkirk 98, 198
Dutch 12, 15, 41, 48, 67, 82, 90, 115, 117-121, 127-130, 137-138, 179, 184, 197
    See also: Holland/Netherlands

E

East Countries, the 66, 99
East India Company 47, 60
East Indies 47, 51, 60, 142, 144, 149, 157
East Sussex 62, 68, 102, 185
Edinburgh 170, 200
Edwards, Francis, spy 171
Edward VI 163
Effingham, Howard of, Lord-Admiral 20, 61, 78
Elizabeth, Queen 9, 19, 20, 21, 24, 25, 26, 36, 48, 49, 50, 52, 53, 54, 55, 56, 58, 68, 70, 79, 88, 89, 94, 95, 98, 99, 101, 117, 120, 149, 156, 157, 163, 164, 170, 178, 187, 200
Endach, David, Burgess of Aberdeen, Scotland 199
English Channel 9, 11, 24, 171, 192, 198, 211, 212
English Royal Navy 19, 25, 26
Exeter 52, 54
explorations 47, 60, 66, 160, 187

F

Falmouth 62, 79, 91, 117, 119, 124, 127, 213
Fargue, Giullemettes de la 126
Fennar, Captain Edward 97
Feversham 24, 62
fire 10, 11, 51, 65, 123, 143, 144, 145, 148, 151, 211
fish 47, 53, 54, 57, 60, 63, 68, 79, 96, 103, 107, 108, 112
Flamborough Head 163
Flanders/Flemish 12, 69, 115, 120, 183, 184, 196, 198, 200, 202
Flower, Master John 67
Flushing 57, 99, 105, 119, 197, 215
Fordred, William 24, 61
Foster, Edward 65
Foxcraft, Samuel 22
fragrances

ambergri 150
civet 150
frankincense 150
musk 150
France/French 10, 13, 36, 49-58, 60,
　　63, 64, 66-70, 88, 91-97, 101,
　　104, 105, 106, 109, 110, 112,
　　118, 125, 162, 163, 164, 170,
　　171, 179, 185, 195, 202, 203
　　211, 213
François II, Dauphin and later King
　　of France 170
French Guinea 171
Frobisher, Sir Martin 51, 57, 70, 79,
　　100, 108, 113
Froume, Captain John 94
fruit 115
Fuentes, Don Rodrigo de 158
furniture 49, 52, 60, 66, 70, 77, 91,
　　92, 103, 105, 107, 109, 112,
　　113, 115, 117, 119, 121, 122,
　　123, 124, 125, 126, 127, 128,
　　129, 130, 179, 184, 201, 202,
　　215

G

Galicia 126, 142
Galiot 12
galleon(s) 11, 12, 13, 21, 23, 49, 117,
　　123, 153
galleys 12, 17, 20, 58, 66
Galway 111
Gatenbury, Captain John 24, 63
German/Germany 114, 115, 117,
　　120, 121, 122, 123, 124, 126,
　　127, 128, 130, 185, 186, 197,
　　212
Gerrard, Sir Thomas 120
Ghana 171
Gibraltar 52, 98, 192, 193, 196
Gilbert, Sir Humphrey 160
Gilbert, Sir John 122, 127
ginger 110, 117, 118, 150, 192, 213
Glemham, Captain Edward 51, 124

Goa 149, 157
gold 9, 10, 91, 100, 123, 150, 157,
　　158, 159, 171, 194
Goodwin Sands 61, 90, 187, 212,
　　214
Gorge, Captain Nicholas 22, 97
Gower, Walter, Captain 20, 78
grain 55, 65, 121
　corn 36, 58, 66, 93, 99, 105, 106, 111,
　　121, 122, 125, 128, 129, 130
　oats 116, 127
　rye 121, 125
　wheat 36, 46, 47, 52, 55, 57, 61,
　　65, 67, 91, 102, 116, 119, 121,
　　170, 171, 193, 212
Granville, Sir Richard, Admiral
　　151–155
Greece 193
Greenland 47, 60, 96
Greenwell, Lancelott, pirate 52
Gresham, Thomas 178
Grete, Captain Albert 114
Grey, Lady Jane 163
Grise, Gilbert 62
Guatemala 147
Guernsey 91
Guinea 171
gunners 9, 14, 17, 18, 19, 26, 36, 48,
　　49, 50, 53, 54, 56, 57, 58, 62,
　　64, 65, 66, 68, 71, 77, 87, 89,
　　90, 92, 94, 95, 96, 97, 98, 99,
　　100, 101, 102
gunpowder 93

H

hackbutters 36, 54, 62, 65, 68, 92, 99
Hage (Hague) 89, 101
Hall, John 51
Hall, William 52
Hamburg 17, 49, 55, 102, 115, 116,
　　122, 126, 214
Hamilton, Frank. *See* Sturgis, Frank
Hampshire 68, 198

Harborough 98
Harvey, William 48
Harwich 24, 27, 67, 147, 212
Hawkins, Captain William 21, 63
Hawkins, Sir John 20, 50, 78, 94,
    101, 108, 112, 113, 121, 122,
    127, 147, 148, 149
Heard, Oliver 53
Helford Haven 126
hides 47, 104, 121, 150, 213
high court of the admiralty 212
Holiday, William, pirate 213
Holland 36, 46, 47, 57-59,, 65, 67,
    68, 70, 78, 79, 93, 97-99, 101,
    108,111, 112, 114, 116, 121,
    127, 128, 213
Honduras 147
horses 10, 53, 170
hose/stockings 58, 97, 101
Houghton, Peter 51, 124, 210
Howard, Lord Thomas 126, 130,
    151, 152
Howard, Lord Thomas, Captain 156
hoy(s) 12, 17, 184
hulk(s) 12, 117

I

Iceland 96
Ile du Levant 96
India 47, 60, 145, 149, 150
Ireland 12, 36, 48, 49, 50, 53, 56,
    57, 58, 60, 61, 64, 65, 66, 67,
    70, 78, 90, 91, 93, 94, 95, 96,
    97, 98, 99, 100, 101, 109, 110,
    111, 114, 115, 116, 119, 121,
    122, 123, 127, 129, 184, 199,
    202, 212, 213, 215
Isle of Gurnsey 46, 67
Isle of Scilly 115
Isle of Wight 106, 118, 193
Italian/Italy 12, 52, 107, 118, 119,
    123, 128, 194, 214
ivory 150

J

Jansen, Captain Mathew 128
jewels 62, 123, 149, 157, 159, 194
Johnston, Lawrence 179

K

Kent 53, 66, 113, 201

L

La Rochelle 211
Lawson, William 50
Leighton, Sir Thomas 67, 107
Leveson, Sir Richard 49, 50, 79, 89,
    101
Lewis, Captain Edward 105
Lincoln, Anthony 184
liquor 47
Lisbon 55, 57, 115, 146, 149
London 10, 13, 22, 35, 46, 51, 53, 55,
    5-62, 66-69, 87-93, 99, 100,
    102-106, 115, 116, 119, 121,
    128, 129, 142, 145-147, 150-
    153, 157, 159, 162, 179, 186,
    187, 192, 193, 196, 198, 200,
    201, 211, 212
Low Countries (see Holland) 36, 57,
    59, 65, 67, 68, 70, 78, 79, 99,
    108, 111, 112, 114, 127
Lubeck 114, 115, 126

M

Mallibre, Captain Jehan 105
man of war 13
Marchaunt, Captain John 21, 66,
    124
Martins, John 124
Mary I 12, 14, 16, 17, 18, 19, 20, 26,
    36, 54, 62, 65, 110, 111, 124,
    163, 164, 170, 171, 178, 179,
    200
Mary Queen of Scots 171
master ship builder 53
masts 10, 11, 12, 13, 64, 113, 118,

119, 124, 127, 146
medicinal drugs 150
  Benjamin 144, 150
  camphor 150
Mendoza, Don Fernando de 149
Mercado, Christoval de 159
Mercury, Duke of (Philippe-Em-
    manuel de Lorraine, Duc de
    Mercoeur) 36, 60
Middleborough 47, 61, 122, 214
Millard, Captain 65
Monson, Sir William 45, 49, 89, 97
Moors 149, 158, 194
Morgan, Captain William 116, 127
Morocco 192, 193, 195, 196
Morries, James 51
Mowter, John 66
Mozambique 144, 145
  Sofala 144, 149
munitions 52, 60, 69, 94, 100, 102, 105,
    107, 114, 115, 116, 121, 125,
    126, 127, 184, 185, 202, 215
Musgrave, Captain Alexander 78

N

Narrow Seas 48, 63, 64, 69, 88, 94
Newcastle 52, 53, 68, 99, 107, 125,
    184, 185
Newfoundland 52, 54, 60, 63, 66,
    107, 112, 117, 160, 162
Newhaven 53, 55, 89, 96, 101, 108,
    109, 171, 201
Newport 109
Newport, Captain Christopher 147,
    148
Newton, Captain Richard 53
Noailles, François de, Ambassador 163
Norfolk 55, 66, 106, 197, 203, 211
North Sea 93, 164, 197, 203, 211,
    212, 214
Northumberland 120, 200
North West, the 57, 92, 97
Norton, Captain 147
Norway 105, 162, 179

Nova Hispania 147
Nutshaw, William 36

O

oil (cooking oil) 56, 105, 108, 109,
    112, 113, 121
oils 69, 99, 110, 117, 192, 212, 213
olives 99
Orange, Prince of 115
ordnance 10, 11, 12, 13, 16, 27, 36,
    52, 54, 62, 63, 79, 89, 92, 96,
    100, 103, 107, 110, 112, 113,
    116, 119, 120, 125, 126, 128,
    130, 143, 145, 146, 148, 149,
    170, 171, 184, 185, 202
ore 53, 57, 70, 79, 126
Orkney 66
Osborn, Alderman 67

P

Palmer, Sir Henry, Admiral 20, 56,
    89, 101
Pawlet, Sir Hugh 65
pearls 194, 213
Pereira, Nuno Velio, former Gov of
    Mozambique 144
Perrotte, Sir John 94
Petite, Captain John 52
Philip II, King of Spain 10, 122, 125
Philippines 147
picard 12
pink 12
pinnace 13, 16, 46, 65, 120, 122, 142
piracy/pirates 9, 10, 48, 51, 52, 53,
    55, 56, 58, 66, 67, 69, 77, 90,
    97, 98, 105, 107, 108, 109,
    110, 111, 112, 113, 114, 116,
    119, 120, 121, 126, 127, 128,
    201, 214
pitch 201
Pitt, Captain Christopher 23, 63
Plymouth 21, 47, 50, 55, 59, 64, 93,
    98, 100, 105, 107, 108, 109,
    111, 112, 114, 115, 116, 117,

118, 119, 120, 121, 124, 125, 126, 128, 129, 142, 192, 213

Poland 57, 88, 91, 99, 116, 211

Pomerania 116, 211

porcelain 150

Portsmouth 49, 54, 55, 56, 69, 95, 96, 103, 105, 112, 115, 117, 122, 129, 130, 145, 193

Portugal 11, 36, 46, 51, 55, 61, 63, 79, 90, 91, 93, 102, 106, 107, 112, 115, 117, 118, 121, 122, 123, 125, 128, 129, 142, 143, 144, 148, 149, 157, 171, 185, 192, 194

powder 10, 62, 63, 68, 69, 94, 100, 102, 145, 170, 184, 185

prisoners 55, 183, 195, 196, 202

Privy Council 36, 50, 59, 69, 78, 103, 110, 117, 122, 124, 126, 179, 183, 184, 186, 192, 197, 198, 199, 202, 210, 212, 213, 214, 215

Protestants 163, 164, 170

Prussia 93, 116, 119, 128

Puerto Rico 157, 158

Pullison, Captain Alderman 64

Q

quicksilver 147

R

Raiman, Captain George 97

raisins 120, 122

Raleigh, Sir Walter 62, 91, 96, 102, 106, 125, 147, 148, 152, 154

Randolph, Hugh 92

refit 64, 151

rigging 49, 64, 113, 116, 119, 120

Roan, Edward (pirate) 67

Rosendale, Captain Cornelius 120

Rostock 114, 127

Rotterdam 95

Rye 24, 62, 65, 68, 102, 106, 183, 185

S

Sackford, Henry 47, 115

sails and rigging 11, 12, 47, 61, 64, 90, 107, 113, 115, 120, 126, 146, 153, 179, 185, 201, 215

Saint John de Luz 162

salt 47, 49, 56, 58, 67, 92, 106, 107, 108, 111, 112, 113, 116, 118

Sambitores, John Baptista de 63

Sandwich 24, 70, 113

Schult, Master Urin 115

Scotland/Scottish 10, 12, 66, 69, 77, 95, 106, 116, 119, 120, 124, 125, 126, 163, 164, 170, 171, 185, 199, 200, 203

Seville 152, 156

Seymour, Captain Henry 20, 89

Sherley, Sir Thomas, sheriff of Sussex 201

Sherwood, William 99

ship of the line 13

ships of war 9, 11, 146, 163, 178

ships (types of)

carrack 11, 50, 59, 142, 143, 144, 145, 148, 149, 150, 171

galleon(s) 11, 12, 13, 21, 23, 49, 117, 123, 153

galleys 12, 17, 20, 58, 66

hoy(s) 12, 17, 184

hulk(s) 12, 117

pinnace 13, 16, 46, 65, 120, 122, 142

shoes and boots 49, 58, 97, 101

silver 10, 123, 147, 157, 159

Smith, Robert, pirate 109

Sneyd, George Ramon. *See* Ray, James Earl

Southampton 49, 50, 53, 58, 61, 97, 105

South Sea 46

South Wales 185, 186, 198

spices 99, 115, 150, 187

cinnamon 3, 133, 150
cloves 3, 76, 133, 150
fennel seed 123
ginger 3, 76, 110, 117, 118133, 150, 192, 213
nutmeg 76., 150
pepper 110, 124, 125, 150
Staper, Richard 193
Stapler, Richard 67
St. Jean de Lux 96
St. Lucar 94, 146, 215
St. Mallows 60, 89, 101
St. Malo 64, 106, 111
stockings/hose 49, 97
Straits of Magellan 46
Strange, Patrick 47
Suffolk 55, 66, 186
sugar 49, 53, 56, 59, 67, 70, 88, 94, 112, 116, 117, 122, 125, 127, 192, 213
Sussex 117, 187, 201, 212
Sweden 117, 127, 128

T

tackle 52, 66, 70, 77, 103, 105, 107, 109, 112, 113, 115, 117, 120, 121, 122, 123, 124, 125, 126, 127, 129, 130, 184, 185, 198, 201
tallow 69
Tesson, Captain Pierre 109
textile supplies 105, 109, 118, 198
Thames River 51, 52, 57, 58, 63, 68, 79, 91, 101, 111, 147, 164, 186, 187, 201, 211
Thornton, Captain George 64
timber 53, 70, 143, 198, 201
Tokins, Captain William 63, 112
tonnage 13, 79, 149
Torres, Don Rodrigo de 158
Tucker, Thomas, shipmaster 23
Tyrone, Earl of 99

V

Vavasour, Sir Thomas 151, 156
Venables, Captain Thomas, pirate 69
Venice 47, 51, 115, 118, 124, 125, 130
Villaunce, John 52

W

Wales 54, 61, 94, 116, 127, 202, 211, 215
Walwin, Captain John 92
Watson, Captain George 62
wax 61, 90, 123, 129
Webb, Captain Nicholas 96
Webb, Captain Thomas 120
West Africa 171
West Indies 147, 157
West, Master Thomas 50
Weymouth 23, 52, 69, 103, 105, 125, 160
Weymouth, George 47, 60
Whidden, Captain Jacob 114
Whiddon, Captain Jacob 154
Whitbrook, Captain Thomas 97
White, Captain Thomas 146
Willard, John. *See* Ray, James Earl; *See* Ray, James Earl
Williams, Hazel. *See* Fazzino, Hazel; *See* Fazzino, Hazel
Williams, Sir John, Captain 78
wine 36, 56, 57, 61, 69, 91, 94, 104, 105, 106, 108, 109, 110, 111, 112, 115, 116, 117, 120, 122, 123, 126, 129, 142, 147, 170, 171, 185, 192, 201, 211, 212, 213
Wiottie, David 77
wood 47, 67, 115, 116, 119, 128
  cypress 150
  ebony 150
Wood, Captain Benjamin 157
Woodhouse, Captain Thomas 92
Woolrich 65

Wynter, Admiral Sir William 163, 164

Y

Yarmouth 24, 96, 197
Young, Captain John 21, 23, 24, 69

Z

Zealand 47, 65, 93, 98, 105, 115, 117, 178
Zeeland 94, 117, 192, 213, 215

Printed in the United States
by Baker & Taylor Publisher Services